THE WORKING OF STOCK EXCHANGES IN INDIA

THE WORKING OF STOCK EXCHANGES IN INDIA

Third Edition

H.R. Machiraju
PH.D. (INDIANA, U.S.A.)
Financial Economist

PUBLISHING FOR ONE WORLD

NEW AGE INTERNATIONAL (P) LIMITED, PUBLISHERS

New Delhi • Bangalore • Chennai • Cochin • Guwahati • Hyderabad
Jalandhar • Kolkata • Lucknow • Mumbai • Ranchi
Visit us at www.newagepublishers.com

Published by New Age International (P) Ltd., Publishers
First Edition: 1995
Third Edition: 2009

Branches:

- 36, Malikarjuna Temple Street, Opp. ICWA, Basavanagudi, **Bangalore**. ✆ (080) 26677815
- 26, Damodaran Street, T. Nagar, **Chennai**. ✆ (044) 24353401
- Hemsen Complex, Mohd. Shah Road, Paltan Bazar, Near Starline Hotel, **Guwahati**. ✆ (0361) 2543669
- No. 105, 1st Floor, Madhiray Kaveri Tower, 3-2-19, Azam Jahi Road, Nimboliadda, **Hyderabad**. ✆ (040) 24652456
- RDB Chambers (Formerly Lotus Cinema) 106A, Ist Floor, S.N. Banerjee Road, **Kolkata**. ✆ (033) 22275247
- 18, Madan Mohan Malviya Marg, **Lucknow**. ✆ (0522) 2209578
- 142C, Victor House, Ground Floor, N.M. Joshi Marg, Lower Parel, **Mumbai**. ✆ (022) 24927869
- 22, Golden House, Daryaganj, **New Delhi**. ✆ (011) 23262368, 23262370

ISBN : 978-81-224-2383-9

Rs. 200.00

C-08-06-2666

Printed in India at Nisha Enterprises, Delhi
Typeset In-house

PUBLISHING FOR ONE WORLD

NEW AGE INTERNATIONAL (P) LIMITED, PUBLISHERS
4835/24, Ansari Road, Daryaganj, New Delhi - 110002
Visit us at **www.newagepublishers.com**

Dedicated to

The lotus feet of
Bhagwan
Shri Satya Sai Baba

PREFACE TO THE THIRD EDITION

The book has been thoroughly revised and updated to cover the developments since the publication of second edition.

Preface to the Second Edition

Since the publication of the book in February 1995, several changes have taken place in the area of secondary market. First, the relative importance of exchanges has changed. Bombay is no longer the premier exchange. Now National Stock Exchange occupies the dominant position. Chapter III takes into account this development while presenting the major stock exchanges in India. Secondly, SEBI has initiated several measures to control volatility, enhance liquidity and ensure transparency in dealings. A new modified carry forward system (MCFS) consequent to the recommendations of J.R.Varma Committee (1997) has been introduced. It should lead to a strong and vibrant *badla* market, generating liquidity, reducing volatility and providing a medium for hedging. These developments are covered in Chapter VII. SEBI has also implemented uniform settlement and screen based on-line trading which have been covered in the relevant places in the book. The setting up of depositories to facilitate quick and easy settlement has been covered in the new Chapter VIII.

Chapter X relating to stock exchanges abroad has been considerably revised taking into account the current relative importance of markets in the developed and emerging markets. Now markets in seven developed and six emerging countries in Asia, Africa and Latin America have been presented. The new edition covers also in Chapter XI the enforcement of insider regulations to protect the integrity of the market in HLL case and inclusion of negotiated deals under trading.

The introduction of stock index futures recommended by the Committee on Derivatives (1998) has been covered in Chapter XIII. The discussion of options in the earlier edition has been retained in view of the importance of the subject. Other chapters in the book have also been revised taking into account new developments and data have been updated.

In view of the contemplated proposal to replace the existing securities contracts legislation with a consolidated securities law, the Appendices at the end of the book have been dropped.

H.R. Machiraju

PREFACE TO THE FIRST EDITION

This book is the second of the capital market twins. The first, Merchant Banking, dealt with the primary market; and the second, the present book deals with the secondary market. Both markets have registered enormous growth and show maturity and sophistication. The working of the secondary market, especially in 1991-92 and 1992-93 has shown first, regulation of markets or self regulation by stock exchanges would work only if funds seeking investment in stock exchanges flow through regular channels and are accounted, (the scam occurred among others because large inflow of funds was not accounted for the purpose of regulation); secondly, supervision by SEBI would be effective if monitoring systems are in place in respect of each subject or activity being supervised, such as stock brokers and sub-brokers operations, regulation of trade by stock exchanges, acquisition and take over activities and insider trading, (the last two activities are not monitored, and finally, enunciation of capital market policy and its integration with economic policy.

Self regulation by stock exchanges would be effective if first, they constitute themselves into a proper regulatory body by eliminating the domination of member brokers. If members dominate the governing body, it would become a case of executive and judicial functions being combined into one. This has been partly set right by reducing the number of stock broker members to about half. Secondly, fool proof systems should be set up to capture all transactions of brokers into a central database maintained as and when they occur by the exchange. If enforceability of the contract is linked to such integration of records through electronic systems, an accurate and truthful picture would emerge. Further, self regulation (as well as supervision) does not provide for the monitoring of market makers. It is desirable to set up such a system on the lines that exists on New York Stock Exchange in respect of specialists. The book presents the details.

In regard to SEBI, its function in relation to capital market should be one of supervision. Selective enquiries, inspections of brokers and stock exchanges on the basis of monitoring systems would be more effective than undertaking them on a routine basis. In regard to acquisitions and takeovers as well as insider trading, monitoring systems have to be set-up. The book elaborates the monitoring systems in vogue especially in regard to insider trading. Insider regulations have also to specify the civil and criminal penalties to have the desired deterrent effect on the rampant practice. The integrity of the market has to be protected. Finally, in regard to market making, monitoring systems have to be set up not only at the exchange level but also at the SEBI level.

The capital market policy as far as the secondary market is concerned should have the objective of the promotion of a stable market reflecting the growth of the economy and the fundamentals of the company, whose shares are traded on the exchanges. Indian stock markets do not seem to reflect them. Once the flows into the market are properly regulated and accounted as outlined, the stock markets would reflect fundamentals. To achieve this objective not only demand for securities should be influenced but also their supply has to be augmented especially in view of the kind of excess demand situation that exists in the Indian stock markets. Actually, little attention has been paid to this aspect. Traditionally, in developed markets, the growth in securities market resulting from the financing of corporate sector, public utilities and government sector was adequate by and large to meet the requirements of investors. There the stock exchanges have never been used to attract and mobilise foreign savings. The practice has originated in the past decade in the emerging markets. India's ability to attract foreign savings through foreign institutional investors depends upon the inherent strength of corporate sector and their price earning ratios which are influenced partly by the availability of good scrips. To improve the qualitative adequacy and quantitative sufficiency of corporate securities, it is essential to integrate capital market policy with economic policy. The book presents methods of augmenting supply of securities through securitisation of the equity of public sector units (with the condition that the proceeds would be used to retire internal public debt held outside RBI), portfolios of development finance institutions and development of debenture market; and to strengthen the bottom line of the corporate sector, grant of incentives or concessions in taxation on a selective basis for renewal of technology which would reduce costs and improve productivity rendering the units internationally competitive.

Finally, equity cult seems to be well established. The lure of capital gains has been drawing in an ever widening circle of investors into the market. While the investor should be protected through greater transparency and disclosure of information by companies issuing securities, it has to be noted that investment in shares carries risk which can only be spread and managed. An uninformed investor should be alerted that he could get badly hurt by losing his saving while playing the market. There is however, need to ensure that the companies whose shares are traded on the exchanges disclose periodically the results of their operations, through balance sheets that reveal. The present provisions entrusting stock exchanges to monitor their compliance has not proved effective. The requirement of registration with SEBI of all issues above a specified limit (apart from clearing of issues) on the lines of U.S. SEC requirements discussed in the book and insistence of submission of periodical returns (quarterly, half-yearly or annual) of financial results to SEBI would discipline companies to make adequate disclosures.

There is a disturbing trend that regulation and supervision should eliminate risk. Such a bureaucratic approach would stifle market activity. Further, investor protection (as well as the belief of general investing class) seems to be based on the premise of homogeneity of shares, which they are not. Securities would be comparable to a certain extent if we ensure that companies before being listed have a good track record in the sense that they have been in operation for two or three years, made profits and have good balance sheets. The biblical adage that thou shalt reap as thou shalt sow would be an appropriate motto for investors.

Finally, the book examines the *badla* system and introduction of options. It is found that badla system provides a useful mechanism for transfer of market position, stock lending and borrowing/lending in money market and any proposal for its abolition has to make provision for them. Options are found to be viable, constitute a good hedge instrument and reduce volatility of the underlying share. Their introduction has no bearing on *badla* system.

H.R. Machiraju

CONTENTS

1

STOCK EXCHANGES IN INDIA

INTRODUCTION

The financial market consists of the money market and the capital market. The capital market discharges the important function of transfer of savings, especially of the household sector to companies, governments and public sector bodies.

Primary Market

Households which are in financial surplus, exchange their savings for shares, debentures and securities of the financial deficit sectors such as the companies and governments. It is the primary market. The market consists of investors or buyers, sellers, dealers and brokers and does not reflect a physical location. The participants are regulated by formal rules for originating financial securities. The primary market in which public issue of securities are made through prospectus is a retail market and is reached through direct mailing. In the primary market, new issues of equity and debt are arranged in the form of a new flotation, either publicly or privately or in the form of a rights offer, to existing shareholders. Companies raise new cash in exchange for financial claims. The financial claims may take the form of shares or debentures. Public sector companies too issue securities. The transactions in the primary market result in capital formation.

Stock Market

Capital market apart from the primary market also includes markets where securities which have been issued in the past are traded. These secondary markets are called stock markets or stock exchanges. The stock markets predominantly deal in stock or equity shares. They enable owners of shares to sell their holdings readily ensuring liquidity. The secondary market enables investors to continuously rearrange their assets if they so desire by divesting themselves of such assets while others can use their surplus funds to acquire them. Any trade of share subsequent to its primary offering is called a secondary transaction. The initial buyer in the primary market may re-offer the securities to any interested buyer at whatever price is mutually satisfactory. The stock exchanges provide a market where such mutually satisfactory prices may be determined. They offer opportunities primarily for trading risk and boost liquidity.

The presence of an active secondary market actually promotes the growth of the primary market and capital formation because investors in the primary market are assured that a continuous market exists and should occasion arise they can liquidate their investment in the stock exchange. The participants in the secondary market are linked by formal trading rules and communication networks for trading in securities.

Symbiotic Relationship between Primary and Secondary Markets

The primary and secondary markets have a symbiotic relationship which is confirmed by Granger's casuality test.[1] While the primary market creates long term securities, the secondary market provides liquidity through marketability of those instruments. Fresh capital issues are influenced by the level and trend in stock prices at the time of issue. On the other hand, a buoyant stock market induces the investing public to invest larger amount of funds in forthcoming new issues. Actually, new issue activity in the primary market adds depth to the secondary market by enlarging the supply of instruments for trading and investment in the secondary market. Stock prices in turn are influenced by the large size and bunching of new issues.

The two way relationship between the two segments of the capital market was examined by Granger's casualty test by Reserve Bank of India on the basis of monthly data on new capital issues and BSE Sensitive Index from April 1986 to March 1996. Relevant F statistics show a two way causality.

Growth and Organisation of Stock Exchanges

The stock exchange in Bombay formed in 1875 is 132 years old. The Calcutta and Madras Stock exchanges were formed in 1908 and

1. RBI, *Annual Report;* 1995-96, p. 57.

Table 1.1: Organization of Recognized Stock Exchanges in India (1992)

S. No.	Name of Stock Exchanges	Year of Establishment	Type of Association	Original Date	Recognition Period	Permanent Date	Entrance Fee/Par Value of Share Rs.	Membership Security Deposit Rs.	Annual Subscription Rs.	No. of Members
1.	Bombay	1875	Voluntary non-profit-making association of persons	31.8.1987	Permanent	—	—	200000	5000	673
2.	Calcutta	1908 (Incorporated in 1923)	Public Ltd. Company	10.10.1957	Permanent	14.4.1980	5000	200000	3000	980
3.	Madras	1908 (Recognized on 29.4.57)	Public Ltd. Company	15.10.1957	Permanent	15.10.1992	25000	50000	2000	182
4.	Ahmedabad	1984	Voluntary non-profit making association of persons	16.10.1957	Permanent	16.9.1982	—	75000	2000	323
5.	Delhi	1947	Public Ltd. Company	9.12.1957	Permanent	9.12.1982	4000	25000	2000	373
6.	Hyderabad	1943	Company Limited by Guarantee	29.9.1958	Permanent	29.9.1983	25000	50000	2000	305
7.	MP (Indore)	1930	Voluntary non-profit-making association of persons	4.12.1958	Permanent	24.12.1988	5000	25000	2000	179
8.	Bangalore	1957	Incorporated as a Private. Ltd. Co. & Converted into a Public Ltd. Co. on 3.4.1962	16.2.1963	Permanent	16.2.1983	1000	50000	2000	242
9.	Cochin	1978	Public Ltd. Company	10.5.1979	2006	—	5000	100000	2040	468
10.	UP (Kanpur)	1982	Public Ltd. Company	3.6.1982	2006	—	101000	10000	2000	514
11.	Pune	1982	Company Ltd. by Guarantee	2.9.1982	2006	—	2500	20000*	2000	197
12.	Ludhiana	1983	Public Ltd. Company	29.4.1983	2006	—	10000	150000	2000	297
13.	Guwahati	1984	Public Ltd. Company	1.5.1984	2006	—	5000	50000	2000	172
14.	ISESC	1998	Public Ltd. Company	June 1988	2006	—	—	—	—	7,000

Contd...

Chapter–1

S. No.	Name of Stock Exchanges	Year of Establishment	Type of Association	Original Date	Recognition Period	Permanent Date	Entrance Fee/Par Value of Share Rs.	Membership Security Deposit Rs.	Annual Subscription Rs.	No. of Members
15.	Kanara** (Mangalore)	1985	Public Ltd. Company	9.9.1985	5 years @	—	250	50000	1000	105
16.	Magadh	1986	Company Ltd. by Guarantee	11.12.1986	2006	—	5000	50000	3000	195
17.	Jaipur	1983-84	Public Ltd. Company	9.11.1989	2009	—	2500	50000	2000	532
18.	Bhubaneswar	1989	Company Ltd. by Guarantee	5.6.1989	2006	—	—	50000	2000	229
19.	Saurashtra Kutch	1989	Company Ltd. by Guarantee	10.7.1989	2006	—	10000	50000	2000	437
20.	OTC Exchange	1989	Public Ltd. Company	Aug. 1989	2006	—	N.A.	N.A.	N.A.	867
21.	Vadodara	1990	N.A.	5.11.1990	2007	—	25000	50000	N.A.	318
22.	Coimbatore	1991	N.A.	18.9.1991	2006	—	N.A.	N.A.	N.A.	177
23.	NSE	1992	N.A.	18.9.1991	2008	—	N.A.	N.A	N.A.	975

** Renewal of recognition was refused (order 31-8-04). The matter is before Securities Appellate Tribunal.

@ Renewed after every 5 year till grant of permanent recognition.

* Cash deposit as security and Rs. 50,000 bank guarantee or share of the market value of Rs. 75 of reputed companies.

N.A. (Not available).

Source: Bombay Stock Exchange, *The Stock Market in India*, Bombay, 1992 and SEBI, Annual Report, 2005-06.

Delhi in 1947. Table 1.1 presents the organisation of stock exchanges in India. There are twenty three stock exchanges in the country. The organisation of stock exchanges varies. Some are public limited companies (12), while others are limited by guarantees (5), or as voluntary non-profit making organisations (3). The Securities Exchange Board of India SEBI ensures broad uniformity in structure while granting recognition. (SEBI) decided in December 1996 that recognition to new stock exchanges, if considered necessary in public interest and that of trade could be allowed only on 'On Line Screen Based Trading' and establishment of clearing house within six months from the date of recognition.

Only eight exchanges have got permanent recognition. Others (12) have to renew it every year until permanent recognition is granted. NSE has got renewal for five years up to 2008. Each member of the stock exchange has to pay an entrance fee or acquire specified number of shares. The value ranges from Rs.250/- in the case of Canara (Mangalore) Stock Exchange to Rs.1,01,000 in the case of U.P. (Kanpur) Exchange. Security deposit to be made by members ranges from Rs.10,000 in the case of U.P. (Kanpur) exchange to Rs.2,00,000 in the case of Bombay. The annual subscription by members varies from Rs.1,000 in the case of Canara (Mangalore) exchange to Rs.5,000 in the case of Bombay exchange. Finally, the number of members is maximum at Calcutta with 650 whereas the Canara exchange has the smallest, 74.

Management of Stock Exchange

The stock exchange is managed by a Governing Body which consists of a President, a Vice-President, Executive Director, elected Directors, public representatives and nominees of the Government. The governing body is responsible for policy formulation and for ensuring smooth functioning of the exchange. The executive functions are discharged by the Executive Director or Secretary.

Regulation of Stock Exchanges

The legislative jurisdiction over stock exchanges is vested in the Union Government by the Constitution of India. The Union Government enacted the Securities Contracts (Regulations) Act in 1956 (SCR Act) for the regulation of stock exchanges and contracts in securities traded on the stock exchanges. The SCR Act and the Securities Contracts (Regulation) Rules (1957) constitute the legal framework for the regulation of stock exchanges and protection of the interests of investors.

The Securities Contracts Regulation Act, 1956 provides *inter alia* for recognition of stock exchanges and regulation of their functioning, licensing dealers, recognition of contracts, controlling speculation, restricting rights of equitable holders of shares and empowering government to compel any public limited company to get its shares listed.

Under the Securities Contracts Regulation Act, Government has promulgated the Securities Contracts (Rules, 1957) for carrying into effect the objects of legislation. The rules are statutory and constitute a code of standardised regulations applicable to all recognised exchanges.

The Securities and Exchange Board of India Act, 1992 provides for the establishment of the Securities and Exchange Board of India (SEBI) to protect the interest of investors in securities and to promote the development of and to regulate the securities market.

Each exchange has bye-laws and regulations, which are more or less uniform in all exchanges, for regulation and control of transactions in the exchange.

Definition of Stock Exchange

Under the SCR Act, an exchange is defined as any body of individuals, whether incorporated or not, constituted for the purpose of assisting, regulating or controlling the business of buying, selling or dealing in securities. The SCR Act stipulates that a stock exchange must be recognised by the Government of India. The twenty three exchanges that are operating in the country are recognised by the Government.

There are other statutes applicable to stock exchanges, The Companies Act 1956, Income Tax Act, 1961 and Foreign Exchange Management Act.

Until 1988, the exchanges were more or less self regulatory with a broad overall supervision by the Ministry of Finance in the Government of India. The High Powered Committee on Stock Exchange Reforms in its Report in 1985 highlighted that some of the exchanges were not discharging their self regulatory role well. As a result, malpractices had crept into trading and they were affecting the interests of the investors adversely. Consequent to the Report, Government of India issued several guidelines to stock exchanges. In 1988, the Securities and Exchange Board of India (SEBI) was constituted to ensure that stock exchanges discharge their self regulatory role well. To prevent malpractices in trading in shares and to protect the rights of investors, SEBI has assumed the monitoring function envisaged for it and requires the brokers to be registered and the stock exchanges to report on their activities.

Table 1.2: Growth Pattern of Listed Stock in Selected Years

% Increase in 1995

As on 31st March	*1946*	*1961*	*1971*	*1975*	*1980*	*1993*	*1994*	*1995*	*Over 1946*	*Over 1961*	*Over 1971*	*Over 1975*	*Over 1980*	*Over 1993*
1. No. of Stock Exchanges	7	7	8	8	9	21	22	22	214	214	175	175	144	5
2. No. of Listed Companies	1,125	1,203	1,599	1,852	2,265	6,925	7,811	9,077	707	655	468	390	301	31
3. No. of Stock Issues of Unlisted Companies	1,506	2,111	2,883	3,320	3,697	11,310	12,026	14,185	842	572	392	339	284	25
4. Capital of Listed Companies (Cr. Rs.)	270	753	1,812	2,614	3,973	56,533	1,52,322	1,74,819	64,648	23,116	9,548	6,588	4,300	209
5. Market Value of Capital of Listed Companies (Cr. Rs.)	971	1,292	2,675	3,273	6,750	2,52,845	5,41,050	6,39,575	65,768	49,403	23,809	19,144	9,375	153
6. Capital per Listed Company (Lakh Rs.)	24	63	113	141	175	816	1,950	1,925	7,921	2,956	1,604	1,265	1,000	136
7. Market Value of Capital per Listed Company (Lakh Rs.)	86	107	167	177	298	3,651	6,926	7,046	8,093	6,485	4,119	3,881	2,264	93

Source: Bombay Stock Exchange, *The Stock Exchange Official Directory,* Supplement, 4-8-1997.

Growth Pattern of Listed Stock (1946-95)

Table 1.2 presents the growth pattern of listed stock in all stock exchanges in select years between 1946 and 1995. In the period 1946-1995 the number of stock exchanges has gone up from 7 to 22 (204 per cent); number of listed companies from 1125 to 9077 (707 per cent); the stock issues of listed companies from 1506 to 14,105 (842 per cent); the capital of listed companies from Rs.270 crores to Rs.1,74,819 (64,648 per cent); market value of listed companies from Rs.971 crores to Rs.6,39,575 crores (65,768 per cent); capital per listed company from Rs.24 lakhs to Rs.1925 lakhs (7,921 per cent); and market value of capital per listed company Rs.86 lakhs to Rs.7046 lakhs.

Three features may be specially noted about the growth pattern of listed stock. First the number of companies at 7811 is the largest listed on stock exchanges in any one country and top 200 companies account for 80 per cent of the market capitalisation. Secondly the growth of capital of listed companies and capital per listed company. The average capitalisation per company has increased by a phenomenal 7,921 per cent. Finally market value has also shown a similar trend. Average market value of a company has gone up by 8093 per cent. The turning point for all these developments was 1961.

Indian Stock Exchanges Services Corporation (ISESC)

Indian Stock Exchanges Services Corporation is promoted by second rung stock exchanges of the country and is floated as a company under Section 35 of Companies Act. There are 14 members including Bangalore, Bhubaneswar, Cochin, Coimbatore, Guwahati, Hyderabad, Jaipur, Ludhiana, Madhya Pradesh, Mangalore, Patna, Saurashtra, Kanpur and Vadodara stock exchanges. ISESC would provide trading, clearing and settlement services to traders.

ISESC is mainly promoted for inter connectivity purposes. An ISESC member can choose between BOLT and ISESC. At the same time, the investors and brokers of any member stock exchange of ISESC will also have a choice of trading on the premier stock exchange. ISESC is likely to emerge as a third force after NSE and BOLT. ISESC is expected to provide a wider choice to small local and regional level companies. Such companies do not attract attention of brokers and investors of other than their local stock exchanges.

Over one lakh subbrokers besides 7,000 brokers are expected to join ISESC. ISESC became functional by June 1998.

For the investors ISESC will provide a wider choice in terms of good companies listed with different stock exchanges.

Impact of Stock Exchanges on Economic Growth[2]

Stock markets impact on economic growth by the creation of liquidity. The study by Levine found that stock market development explains future economic growth. Liquid equity markets render investment less risky and more attractive by allowing savers to acquire an asset and sell it quickly and cheaply if they need access to their savings or alter their portfolios. At the same time companies can raise equity and enjoy a permanent access. Liquid markets improve the allocation of capital and enhance the prospects for long term growth. Liquidity provided by stock markets renders investment less risky and more profitable. In the words of Levine, "investors will come if they can leave."

The three measures of market liquidity which boost economic growth are; (1) total value of shares traded on a country's stock exchanges as a proportion of GDP; (2) the value of traded shares as a percentage of total market capitalisation; and (3) value traded ratio divided by stock price volatality.

While the first measure does not directly measure the costs of buying and selling stocks at posted prices, the average over a long period is likely to vary with the ease of trading. Countries with liquid markets tend to grow faster than countries with illiquid markets. In the empirical study by Levine, India is rated liquid in terms of initial value traded ratio (initial liquidity is measured by the ratio in 1976 of the value of shares listed to GDP). Secondly, the turnover ratio indicates potential for economic growth. The more liquid, the markets are the faster they are likely to grow. India was found to be very liquid in the study. Thirdly, trading to volatility ratio shows that markets that are liquid can handle heavy trading without large price swings. Countries with higher trading to volatality ratios are likely to grow faster.

Market Capitalisation and GNP

The growth in the listed companies' paid-up capital and market value of shares is also reflected in the rising proportion of market value of listed equity in Gross National Product (GNP) from 8.6 per cent in 1986-87 to 56.4 per cent in 1991-92, 75.8 per cent at end March 1995 and 92.2% in 2003-04 (Table 1.3). While stock market size in terms of market

2. Ross, Levine, "Stock Market: A Spur to Economic Growth", *Finance & Development*, March 1996.

capitalisation divided by GNP measures stock market development, it is not a good predictor of growth. It is not the size that matters but the ease with which the shares can be traded.

Table 1.3: Market Value of Equity (All Stock Exchanges) and Gross National Product (1986-87 – 2003-04).

(Rs. Crores)

Year	*Gross National Product (Current Prices)*	*Market Value of Listed Equity*	*Col. 3 as % of Col. 2*
1	*2*	*3*	*4*
1986-87	2,58,225	22,159	8.6
1987-88	2,92,232	26,511	9.0
1988-89	3,48,210	38,133	10.9
1989-90	4,02,931	55,409	13.8
1990-91	4,70,269	82,810	17.6
1991-92	5,42,691	3,05,987	56.4
1992-93	6,18,969	2,52,485	40.8
1993-94	7,19,548	5,41,050	75.1
1994-95	8,43,294	6,39,575	75.8
1995-96	10,89,800	5,72,257	52.5
1996-97	12,72,200	4,88,332	38.3
1997-98	14,13,200	4,89,816	41.7
1998-99	15,98,127	5,74,064	35.9
1999-2000	17,61,838	10,22,299	58.0
2000-01	19,02,999	63,06,98	33.1
2001-02	20,81,474	12,49,085	60.0
2002-03	22,54,888	11,09,331	49.2
2003-04	25,19,785	23,22,183	92.2

Source: Government of India, *Economic Survey* 1996-97, 1998-99, 2003-04 and 2004-05.

Trends in Savings of Household Sector

Households constitute the primary source for capital formation in the country. Of the savings ratio (the ratio of gross domestic savings to gross domestic product) of 28.1 per cent in 2003-04, households accounted for 86.5 per cent; and household sector ratio was 24.3 per cent. However, in financial analysis, net savings ratio and investment in net financial assets are considered.

Net savings ratio during the period 1986-87 – 2003-04 has registered a substantial increase from 11.8 per cent of net domestic product to 28.0 per cent in 2002-03 (Table 1.4). Net financial assets of households as a per cent of net domestic product had gone up from 8.8 per cent of net

Table 1.4: Net Domestic Savings and Savings of the Household Sector in Financial Assets (1980-81, 1986-87 to 1996-97 and 1997-98 to 2002-03 (New Series))

Year	*Net Domestic Savings*	*Net Domestic Saving as Per cent of NDP*	*Net Financial Assets of Households*	*Net Financial Assets of % of NDP*	*Investment in Shares and Debentures*	*Investment in Shares and Debentures as % of Net Financial Assets*	*Investment in Units of UTI and Mutual Funds*	*Investment Units of UTI and Mutual Funds as % of Financial Assets*
1980-81	16355	13.2	8609	7.0	412	4.8	31	0.3
1986-87	30989	11.8	23016	8.8	1255	5.4	943	4.0
1987-88	39169	12.8	26075	8.7	708	2.7	1196	4.6
1988-89	50837	14.5	28475	8.1	818	2.9	1427	5.0
1989-90	64722	15.8	41943	10.3	2823	5.2	2147	3.9
1990-91	71527	14.9	45103	9.4	4117	7.1	3300	5.7
1991-92	85408	15.6	58408	10.7	4252	5.8	8000	11.0
1992-93	99441	10.4	65700	10.4	8212	12.4	5612	8.5
1993-94	124381	17.1	95020	13.2	10067	10.5	4705	5.0
1994-95	149772	17.6	108088	12.7	11611	8.2	3908	2.8
1995-96	173743	17.6	92799	8.4	5880	5.9	262	0.2
1996-97	208011	18.1	138021	12.0	6696	0.5	3376	0.3
1997-98	200181	20.0	171740	17.2	4464	2.5	595	0.3
1998-99	206593	19.5	207103	19.5	5105	2.5	1887	0.9
1999-2000	286322	25.2	236351	20.8	16308	6.9	1811	0.8
2000-01	298091	25.2	248774	21.0	11148	4.9	–934	–0.4
2001-02	317431	25.6	289953	23.3	9634	3.3	–1856	–0.6
2002-03	362654	28.0	336609	25.9	7122	2.1	–1617	–0.5

Source: Reserve Bank of India, *Report on Currency & Finance* – 1987-88, 1988-89 and 1991-92, 1995-96 and 1997-98, Vol. II, *Annual Report* 1991 and Hand Book of Statistics 2003-04.

domestic product in 1986-87 to 13.2 per cent in 1993-94 and then registered a substantial decline to 8.4 per cent in 1995-96 on account of the collapse of the primary market in the second half of 1994-95; and have registered a continuous improvement since to 25.9% in 2002-03. Households' investment in shares increased from 5.4 per cent of net financial assets in 1986-87 to 12.4 per cent in 1992-93 on account of potential for large gains from the free pricing of capital issues. Thereafter, it registered a continuous decline and reached 0.5 per cent in 1996-97 on account of the collapse of the primary market in 1994-95. They have improved to 6.9% in 1999-00 and thereafter declined to 2.1% in 2002-03. There has, however, been a substantial increase in investment in units of UTI and mutual funds in the period, from 4 per cent in 1986-87 to 11 per cent in 1991-92. Since then there has been a steady decline until they reached 0.3 per cent in 1996-97 on account of large redemption by UTI. After 2000-01 there were large outflows.

New Issue Market

In the new issue market, equities show a steady upward trend from Rs.1,007.9 crores in 1986-87 to Rs.17,453.9 crores in 1994-95 and registered a sharp decline to Rs.6,152.4 crores in 1996-97 and further to Rs.1,162.4 crores in 1997-98 on account of the collapse of the primary market. Equity market has become moribund since and the amount raised was Rs.1,958.7 crores in 2003-04. There was a remarkable pickup in 2004. Public issuance of equity at Rs.33,475 crores in 2004 (calendar year) was the highest ever level in India's history over two times higher than the previous peak of 1995. The mean IPO size rose from Rs.31 crores in 2001 to Rs.870 crores in 2004 (see Table 1.5). There have, however, been wide fluctuations in debentures mainly on account of offer of mega issues in some years; and preference shares have more or less lost significance. The total capital issued of Rs.2,564.9 crores in 1986-87 rose to Rs.6,475.1 crores in 1989-90 (of which debentures accounted for Rs.5,246.4 crores) declined in 1991-92 to Rs.5,750.8 crores and spurted to Rs.26,456.2 crores in 1994-95. Debentures have also registered decline after 1994-95 and in 1996-97 non convertible debentures came into prominence because of private placement and the amount raised in bonds became prominent since 1999-2000 and they account for entire debt of Rs.1,250.9 crores raised in 2003-04.

EQUITY CULT

If we consider a longer period, we find that the participation of households in the new issue market and stock market has led to a sizable

Table 1.5: Capital Issued by Non Government Public Limited Companies (1986-87 – 2004-05)

(Rs. Crores)

Year	Equity	Pref.	Debentures			Total
			Conv.	Non	Total	
1986-87	1007.9	0.7	—	—	1556.3	2564.9
1987-88	1102.8	6.9	—	—	664.2	1773.9
1988-89	1007.0	3.3	—	—	2124.9	3135.9
1989-90	1218.8	7.9	4762.2	484.2	5246.4	6473.1
1990-91	1247.5	13.3	2288.7	652.3	2941.0	4201.8
1991-92	1729.5	1.5	3489.2	530.6	4019.8	5750.8
1992-93	9981.0	0.5	7864.9	1979.2	9844.1	19825.6
1993-94	10113.2	63.4	8106.9	1218.0	9324.9	19501.5
1994-95	17453.9	131.3	7643.0	1228.0	8871.0	26456.2
1995-96	12052.1	150.1	3438.4	531.7	3970.1	16172.3
1996-97	6152.1	71.9	527.4	3705.8	4233.2	10457.5
1997-98	1162.4	4.3	1471.6	500.0	1971.6	3138.8
1998-99	2562.7	59.7	190.7	2200.0	2390.7	5013.1
1999-2000	2752.5	0	50.8	—	2400.8	5153.3
2000-01	2607.6	142.2	36.2	54.0	3068.3	5818.1
2001-02	860.4	0	518.0	255.9	4832.0	5692.4
2002-03	460.2	0	217.5	—	1417.5	1877.7
2003-04	1958.7	0	—	—	1250.9	3209.6
2004-05	34475.0	0	N.A.	N.A.	2383.0	35859.0

Source: Reserve Bank of India, *Report on Currency and Finance* 1988-89, Bulletin October 1992 (Supplement), Annual Report, 1992-93; 1994-95, 1996-97, 1998-99 and Hand Book of Statistics 2003-04.

increase in the number of individual share owners from about 24 lakhs in 1980 to 90 lakhs in 1990.[3]

Data relating to ownership pattern are available only for 1978, when individuals held 37.3 percent of shares in listed companies;[4] and it is of interest to note that individuals occupied a similar position in the U.K. and Japan.

It was only in the United States that they accounted for 52.7 per cent (1975). It is also observed that while the share of the individuals declined, the share of institutions had increased not only in India but

3. Gupta, L.C., *Indian Shareowners*, Society for Capital Market Research and Development, New Delhi, 1991, p. 15.
4. Individual ownership is placed at 45.9 per cent in 1989 in Dr. V.A. Avadhani, "Ownership and Distribution Pattern of Shareholding Companies" and 42.32 per cent in 1986 by IDBI as quoted by Dr. Avadhani.

also in the UK and Japan. Direct subscription and investment in shares through purchases in the stock exchanges is being replaced by indirect purchases through mutual funds.

While individual investors participated widely in the primary market for new issues and secondary market in the stock exchanges directly, a portion of their savings went into mutual funds. Mutual funds along with the support of their principals in some cases, especially those set up by banks, became large participators in the stock markets. Mutual funds have grown both in size and importance. They play a pivotal role in mobilising savings of the households by providing them the benefits of expert portfolio management aimed at both minimising risks by spreading them across a large number of securities and realising a fair return on investment. Unit Trust of India, set up in 1964 is the leading institution in mutual funds and its total investible funds amounted to Rs.61,109.7 crores as at the end of June 1998. In 1993 mutual funds in the private sector are allowed to be set up. Mutual Funds are governed by SEBI (Mutual Funds) Regulations, 1993. By end of March 2004, there were 34 mutual funds. Apart from UTI there are 10 public sector mutual funds and 24 private sector mutual funds which together offered 84 schemes. The total funds mobilised by mutual fund industry were Rs.64,849.5 crores at end of June 1999. They rose steadily since the assets under the management of mutual funds stood at Rs. 5,49,936 crores at the end of 2007.

Secondary Market for Debt

In the secondary market for debt, Government of India (GOI) securities account for the major part of activity. In terms of market size of GOI bonds, the gross issuance of GOI dated securities in 2006 amounted to Rs. 147.000 crore. By end of year 2006, market capitalisation of GOI securities was Rs. 11,31,558 crore.

The corporate debt market in India is at a nascent stage of development. Banks and financial institutions would not be able to meet the financing needs of a growing corporate sector. A developed debt market would supplement the resources raised through equity and provide a healthy debt equity mix to sustain growth on along term basis. The Union Budget for 2005-06 announced the setting up of an Expert Committee on corporate bonds and securitization to look into the legal, regulatory and mortgage design issues in the corporate bond market. The Expert Committee in its report submitted in 2005 made wide ranging recommendations for the development of the corporate debt market. They are:

- The stamp duty on partly secured and unsecured debentures should be made uniform across all the States and should be linked to the tenor of the securities, with an overall cap.
- The tax deduction at source (TDS) rules for corporate bonds should be similar to those applicable to Government securities
- The time and cost of public issuance and the disclosure and listing requirements for private placements should be reduced and made simpler.
- Banks should be allowed to issue bonds of maturities of over 5 years for ALM purpose in addition to floating bonds against lending to the infrastructure sector as at present.
- A suitable market making scheme for corporate bonds should be evolved, including permission to undertake repos in corporate bonds.
- For already listed entities, disclosure requirements should be substantially abridged. They may be required to make only some incremental disclosures every time they approach the market with a fresh issue either to the public or through private placement, but should include rating rationale on their disclosure document.
- For unlisted companies, the disclosure requirements should be stringent including rating.
- The role of debenture trustees should be strengthened and also provide for more accountability on their part.
- Investor base may be broadened by enhancing the scope of investment by banks, FLLs, provident/pension/gratuity funds and insurance companies in corporate bonds. Rating should form the basis of such investments rather than the category of issuers. Retail investors should also be encouraged to participate in the corporate bond market through mutual funds.
- To enhance liquidity, consolidation of the issuance process may be streamlined to create large floating stocks.
- A centralised database of all bonds issued by corporates may be created immediately.
- Steps should be taken to immediately establish a system to capture all information related to trading in corporate bonds as accurately and close to execution as possible, and disseminate it to the entire market.

- The clearing and settlement of trades in this market must follow the IOSCO standards and the global best practices by way of well established clearing and settlement procedures through recognised clearing and settlement agencies.
- Efforts should be made to develop screen based, online, order matching trading platforms for corporate bonds.
- The current shut period in corporate bonds is very high and needs to be reduced and aligned to that for Government securities.
- The standardised practice of 30/360 day count convention, followed for dated Government securities, may be made mandatory for all new issues of corporate bonds.
- Repos in corporate bonds may be allowed.
- Steps may be taken to introduce the revised and approved exchanged traded interest rate derivative products.
- The minimum market lot criteria of Rs. 10 lakh for trading in corporate bonds at the stock exchanges should be reduced to Rs. 1 lakh.
- Central Government should consider notifying PTCs and other securities issued by securitised SPVs/ Trust as 'securities' under SC(R)A to facilitate their listing on the stock exchanges.
- Steps should be taken to introduce credit enhancement for corporate bonds.
- Special debt fund may be created, particularly for the infrastructure sector.
- Government should consider establishing an appropriate institutional process to evolve a consensus across States on the affordable rates and levels of stamp duty in debt assignment, PTCs and Security Receipts.
- The taxation issues relating to corporate debts should be rationalised.
- Fiscal concession may be given for municipal bonds and bonds issued by SPVs for infrastructure development.

The market capitalisation of corporate bonds was Rs. 68,074 crores at the end of December 2007.

References

Bombay Stock Exchange, *Annual Reports*, 1987 - 1991-92. *The Stock Market Today*, 1992; *The Stock Market in India*, 1995 and Directory Supplement 4-9-1997.

Government of India, *Economic Survey*, 1990-91. Government of India, *Report of the Powered Committee on Stock Exchange Reforms*, 1985.

Gupta, L.C., Indian Share Owners, Society for Capital Market Research and Development, 1991.

Levine, Ross, "Stock Markets: A Spur to Economic Growth", *Finance and Development*, March 1996.

Reserve Bank of India, Bulletin, October 1992 (Supplement); *Annual Report*, 1994-95, 1996-97 and 1998-99. *Report on Currency and Finance*, 1988-89,1989-90,1990-91 and 1991-92, 1994-95, 1995-96, 1996-97 and 1997-98 and *Hand Book of Statistics*, 2003-04.

SEBI, *Annual Reports*.

Government of India, *Economic Survey*, 2007-08.

2

FUNCTIONS OF A STOCK EXCHANGE

INTRODUCTION

The stock exchanges provide an organized market-place for the investors to buy and sell securities freely. The market for these securities is an almost perfectly competitive one because a large number of sellers and buyers participate. The shares listed, however, are not really homogeneous like a commodity in a perfectly competitive market. They vary broadly in terms of credit rating and often involve carrying costs.

In the stock exchange, there is active bidding and a two way auction trading takes place. The bargains that are struck are the fairest price determined by the basic laws of supply and demand. The stock exchanges provide an auction market in which members of the stock exchange participate to ensure continuity of price and liquidity to investors.

The efficient functioning of the stock exchange creates a climate conducive for an active and growing primary market for new issues. An active and healthy secondary market in existing securities leads to a better psychology of expectations. Considerable broadening of investment enquiries renders the task of raising resources by entrepreneurs easier. Good performance and outlook for equities in the stock exchanges imparts buoyancy to the new issue market.

Functions of Secondary Markets

The three important functions of secondary markets are: price discovery process which results from the interactions of buyers and sellers in the market when they trade assets; provision of liquidity by providing a mechanism for an investor to sell financial assets; and finally low cost of transactions and information.

Continuous Market

The basic function of a stock market is the creation of a continuous market where securities are bought and sold in volume with little variation in current market price as trades succeed one another. A continuous market provides liquidity through sale or purchase of securities, quickly and easily, at a price that varies little from the previous selling price. The indicators of a continuous market are,

- frequency of sales,
- narrow spread between bids and offers,
- prompt execution of orders, and
- minimum price changes between transactions as they occur[5].

Frequency of Sales

The primary criterion for a good market is whether investor can sell their portfolio holdings quickly with minimal price fluctuation at the time of sale. Liquidity occupies a central place in evaluating the efficiency of an exchange.

The characteristics of a liquid market are depth, breadth and resiliency. A market has depth if buy and sell orders are forthcoming around the price at which the share is transacting. A market that lacks depth is shallow. Further, the orders forthcoming should be in adequate volume which gives breadth to the market. If adequate volume needed to provide liquidity is not there, the markets are called thin markets. The response of orders to price changes renders the market resilient[6].

Impact Cost: Liquidity Measure

The cost of doing transactions on the market referred as impact cost also measures the liquidity. A liquid market is a friction market. High liquidity corresponds to low market cost. During the period 2001-2004, NSE impact cost for doing trades to buy or sell Rs.5 million of Nifty has dropped from 0.27% to 0.09%. The improvement in market liquidity is attributable to the shift to rolling settlement and adoption of derivative trading. The impact cost of Nifty Junior has also gone down from 0.62%

5. Teweles, Rechard H., Bradley, Edward S. and Teweles, Ted M., *The Stock Market*, 6th Edition, John Wiley & Sons Inc., New York, 1992.
6. Francis, J.C., *Investments: Analysis and Management*, Fifth Edition, McGraw Hill International Edition.

to 0.31%. Nifty Junior also benefited indirectly from access to index derivatives trading.

Empirical Measurement of Liquidity

Empirically, liquidity is measured by the number of days a company's share is traded out of the number of days in the year during which market is open. Normally a share is considered actively traded and liquid if it is traded on 50 per cent of the days when the market is open. Liquidity of the market is also measured by the variation of price from one trade to another. If the difference between lowest asked (or offered) price and the highest bid price is wide the market is said to lack depth and is considered shallow. Actually, the bid-asked spread is an inverse measure of liquidity[7]. For example, in the United States variation of one-eighth point in price from the immediate preceding trade is considered liquid. In our own country, the minimum tick starts from Re. 0.25.

Fair Price Determination

The prices in the stock market are determined by the interplay of forces of supply and demand. In the stock exchange, there is active bidding and a two way auction trading takes place. The result is as near a market for free competition as can be found anywhere. The bargains that are struck are the fairest price determined by the basic laws of supply and demand.

The functioning of the market has been subject at times to manipulation. Bull runs, to push up prices to create an artificial value, have been witnessed on a large scale in 1991-92. On the other hand, prices in the market were pushed down by bear raiders without regard to fundamental values. Manipulation cannot, of course, occur if the exchanges are alert. In the long run interests of the securities market, no scope should be given for operators to indulge in practices of price manipulation.

The performance of the functions of the stock exchange is also subject to hinderance by speculation which drives up prices above investment worth at times and below it at other times. For considerable stretches of time the stock market prices in the past were dormant, especially before 1987. And since 1988-89, they have been above investment worth.

7. Tinic S., "The Economics of Liquidity Services", *Quarterly Journal of Economics*, 1992.

In 1991 some shares are 50-70 times their earnings. There is no obvious relationship between book value, par value and market value for many shares. The price rise especially in 1990-91 and 1991-92 was an account of surge in demand for shares occasioned by massive flow of funds into the stock markets from individual investors (some of whom disinvested their investment in contract business, transport and other retail trades) and mutual funds without any corresponding increase in the supply of scrips. The massive inflow of funds into the stock market was no doubt motivated by the prospect of capital gains. But there were not enough shares to absorb the demand. It was typically a situation of too much money chasing too few scrips. Normally, one would leave the situation to forces of the market, what buyer and seller are willing to bid and offer. But in our country, we would like to make shares attractive for investment by foreign institutional investors who evaluate our market in relation to other emerging markets. Even now (May 1998) price earning ratios have moved to a range considered high. In this context stabilization of stock market prices around a reasonable level of mid teens would be desirable.

Aid to Financing Industries

Listed companies find it easy to sell further issues of their shares in the primary market. An active market in the shares of the company and good market price of the share reflecting the past performance and future prospects renders the task of raising funds through further issues easier. Rights themselves have an immediate and wide market in the stock exchanges, unless the price including premium does not reflect a fair value. By creating a continuous market for the rights, stock exchanges enable a company to market further issues successfully.

Liquidity plays a major role in improving allocation of capital and enhances prospects for long term economic growth. Companies enjoy permanent access to capital raised through equity issues. Stock market liquidity results in an increase in investment by making it less risky and more profitable. Liquid markets improve the allocation of capital and long term growth by facilitating longer term and more profitable investment.

Other Functions

Other functions performed by stock exchanges are that the market prices established in trading are useful for tax purposes. The stipulation on disclosures and transparency ensure availability of information on the listed companies particularly in regard to financial condition and protects investors' interests by eliminating dishonest and irregular practices in the brokerage trade.

Efficient Transformation into Real Capital

The ability of the financial intermediaries to ensure the most efficient transformation of mobilized funds into real capital has not however, received the attention it deserves. Institutional mechanisms to ensure end use of funds have not been efficient in their functioning, leaving investors unprotected. Efficient financial intermediation involves reduction of the transaction cost of transferring funds from original source to financial investors. The total cost of intermediation is influenced by financial layering which makes the individual institution's costs additive in the total cost of intermediating between saver and ultimate borrowers. The aggregate cost of financial intermediation from the original saver to ultimate investor is much higher in developing countries than in developed countries.

Financial services contributed 6 per cent of GNP (1995) as compared to 3.7 per cent before liberalization in late eighties. Theories of endogenous growth have established linkages between financial intermediation and economic growth.

Market Efficiency

An efficient capital market is one where prices fully and instantaneously reflect all available relevant information. The two characteristics of efficient markets are external efficiency and internal efficiency. A market has external efficiency when buyers and sellers will trade securities at prices reflecting a fair or equilibrium price.

The expected return has to be commensurate with the security's risk. Internal efficiency characterizes a market if transaction costs (commission, clearing fees and bid-ask spread) and taxes are low enough so as not to distort the impact that new information provides about the value of the financial asset. Market efficiency ensures that investors as well as the economy benefit when capital is exchanged.

Perfect Capital Market

On the other hand, a perfect capital market which is only a concept constitutes a benchmark for evaluating the operation of capital market which has no taxes, transaction costs, regulations, assets are perfectly divisible, existence of a number of buyers and sellers and free access to information. A perfect capital market is externally efficient because the prices of assets are equal to risk adjusted rates of return for all participants. It is internally efficient because transaction costs are zero and there are no taxes. The real world, however, is characterized by imperfections. But markets can be efficient if costs of imperfections are small. Asset prices can still convey information about company. The cost should be enough to provide a fair rate of return to ensure internal efficiency of the market. Flow of low cost information to a sufficient number of market participants leads to determination of prices reflecting the economic value of the asset. Trading on the basis of insider information is prohibited because the information is not available to all market participants. External efficiency is facilitated by liquid markets. The characteristics of a liquid market as we have noted above are depth, breadth and resiliency.

Working of the Stock Exchanges (Patel Committee)

It has been observed by several Committees in the past that our stock exchanges do not assure liquidity and the investor can liquidate his shares only at a loss and after considerable delay. The High Powered Committee on Stock Exchange Reforms (Patel Committee) in 1984 pointed out that lack of liquidity in a number of securities listed on the stock exchange as a major problem confronting the investors.

The Committee observed that: A recent analysis of the frequency of transactions in equity shares on major stock exchanges reveals that out of 3401 companies listed on the stock exchanges in 'A' and 'B' group of shares,

(i) shares of 959 companies were traded once a year,
(ii) shares of 954 companies were traded once a month,
(iii) shares of 396 companies were traded once a fortnight;
(iv) shares of 538 companies were traded once a week; and
(v) shares of 207 companies were traded daily.[8]

(See Table 2.1).

The Committee further observed that: "It may be coincidental that equity shares of about 200 companies figure in "specified lists" where settlement trading takes place."[9] In regard to non-specified

8. Final Report of the High Powered Committee on Stock Exchange Reforms, 1985, p. 17.
9. *Ibid*, p.17.

Table 2.1: Frequency of Transactions in Equity Shares (1984)

S. No.	Frequency of transactions	Group	No. of companies Bombay	Delhi	Madras	Calcutta	Total
1.	Daily	A	40	4	2	12	58
		B	69	10	6	64	149
2.	Frequently	A	26	3	15	13	57
		B	89	28	11	162	290
3.	Once in a week	A	—	6	10	3	19
4.	Once in a fortnight	A	—	—	2	—	2
		B	142	40	38	174	394
5.	Once a month	—	318	176	148	312	954
6.	Once in a year	—	300	262	165	232	959
Total listed companies		—	1151	617	415	1218	3404

Source: Final Report of the High Powered Committee on Stock Exchange Reforms, 1985, p. 246.

shares on Bombay Stock Exchange, the Committee remarked that during June to August 1984 nearly 50 per cent of the scrips were not traded at all, while 30 per cent of the scrips were traded only on 50 per cent of the trading days (Table 2.2).

Table 2.2: Activity in 'B' Group Securities (1984) Frequency Distribution of Securities According to % Days Traded

% of Days Traded	No. of Securities	% to Total
91-100	33	1.72
81-90	206	10.71
71-80	76	3.95
61-70	52	2.71
51-60	62	3.22
41-50	55	2.86
31-40	45	2.34
21-30	78	4.06
11-20	86	4.47
1-10	301	15.65
Not Traded	929	48.31
Total No. of Securities	1923	100.00

Based on activity in June, July and August, 1984.

Source: Final Report of the High Powered Committee on Stock Exchange Reforms. 1985, p. 246.

Pherwani Study Group 1991

The High Powered Study Group on Establishment of New Stock Exchanges (the Pherwani Study Group) 1991 in its Report projected lack of liquidity as a major structural deficiency of the existing stock exchanges. The Committee observed that: "As a principal objective, therefore, Exchanges must provide both the environment and infrastructure to ensure that there is adequate liquidity in the market. On the supply side this implies that exchanges must be able to attract a sufficiently large number of companies for listing as well as provision of adequate number of trading hours. On the demand side, its members must be of sufficient financial soundness to perform market-making function, with adequate infrastructure for efficient inter-market operation, effective trading and settlement system etc."[10] The Committee also referred to the liquidity problem at smaller exchanges (outside Bombay, New Delhi, Calcutta, Madras and Ahmedabad) in terms of depth and breadth. The Expert Study on Trading in Shares by Dr. L.C. Gupta (1991) claimed that lack of liquidity in thinly traded shares, especially of small and medium companies, is on account of the neglect on the part of the stock exchanges.

Analysis of Trading in Shares

Data relating to trading in 1988-89 and 1989-90 of shares listed on Bombay Stock Exchange are presented in Table 2.3. The data show that actively traded shares constituted 36.5 percent of the listed companies in 1988-89; and rose to 69.3 percent in 1990-91. A rising market apparently fosters active trading of shares of an ever widening circle of listed scrips.

Trading frequency of listed stocks in 2003-04 at BSE and NSE are presented in Table 2.4. A comparison of Table 2.3 and 2.4 shows that number of companies traded on BSE on 91-100 days and above has gone up from 20% in 1988-89 to 47.2% in 1990-91 to 77.5% in 2003-04; and on NSE it was 93.1% in 2003-04. In 2004-05, trading frequency of stocks at BSE was 3049 and NSE 956; and at BSE 86% of stocks were traded for more than 100 days and 92% at NSE. The liquidity of shares has certainly gone up in the 15 years period. Another interesting development that percentage of companies traded on 30 days or less has come down. The period witnessed the entry of foreign institutional investors and formation of several mutual funds in the public and private sectors which had an enormous impact on trading frequency of listed companies.

---

10. Report of the High Powered Study Group on Establishment of New Stock Exchanges, 1991, p. 60.

Table 2.3: Frequency Distribution of BSE Listed Companies by Number of Days (%) Traded in 1988-89 (215 days) and 1990-91 (186 days)

Percent of Total Days	*No. of Listed Companies 1988-89*	*Percent to Total*	*No. of Listed Companies 1990-91*	*Percent to Total*
91–100	456	20.0	795	47.2
81–90	152	6.7	185	11.1
71–80	94	4.1	83	4.9
61–70	57	2.5	63	3.7
51–60	72	3.2	40	2.4
41–50	66	2.9	46	2.7
31–40	51	2.2	38	2.3
21–30	79	3.5	40	2.4
11–20	93	4.1	66	3.9
1–10	1155	50.8	329	19.5
Total Traded	—	—	1685	100.00
Total traded as % of listed Cos.	—	—	1685	68.2
Not Traded	—	—	786	31.8
Total	2275	100.00	2471	100.0

Source: Bombay Stock Exchange

Table 2.4: Trading Frequency of Listed Stocks

Trading Frequency (Range of Days)	*2003-04*			
	BSE		*NSE*	
	No. of Companies Traded	*Percent to Total*	*No. of Companies Traded*	*Percent to Total*
Above 100	1960	75.10	741	92.20
91–100	65	2.50	7	0.90
81–90	54	2.10	8	1.00
71–80	49	1.90	3	0.40
61–70	46	1.80	2	0.20
51–60	58	2.20	11	1.40
41–50	61	2.30	8	1.00
31–40	56	2.10	2	0.20
21–30	52	2.00	7	0.90
11–20	63	2.40	8	1.00
1–10	146	5.60	7	0.90
Total	2610	100.00	804	100.0

Source: SEBI *Annual Report*, 2003-04.

Chapter–2

Thin Trading

The phenomenon of scrips having few and intermittent bids or offers is referred to as thin trading[11]. Thin trading fails to assure liquidity and has undesirable consequences all-around: for the investor inability to convert his investment into cash at an economical cost; for the companies, non-availability of market valuation would render raising of additional funds for expansion or diversification difficult and distorts financial planning; and for the stock exchanges, the image is damaged because it reflects adversely on their efficiency.

It should be noted, however, that trading is a function of demand and supply. In discussions on the problem of thin trading, there is an implicit assumption that all securities are alike and are more or less like a homogeneous commodity as assumed in the theoretical model of perfect competition. Securities would be comparable to a certain extent if we ensure that companies before being listed have a good track record in the sense that they have been in operation for two or three years, made profits and have good balance sheets. That is how things are in stock markets abroad, but in our country companies get listed before operations start.[12] The situation is a little better now since the financial institutions lend first and let the units raise equity just before start up. Earlier, they wanted to postpone lending and so let the units raise equity first. But even after successful operation for a year or two or much later, a unit can go bust. Abroad, one can close shop with the help of bankruptcy laws. In our country, exit does not exist and a social stigma is attached to bankruptcy. The financial institutions also penalize the entrepreneur if his venture fails by refusing a second chance. The provisions we have for winding up under the company law are so time consuming that several non operational companies are shown under listed companies.

Returning to the question of trading, stock exchange offers a market place to conduct auction of securities to its members. It cannot by itself create demand or supply for scrips. A large number of scrips listed are just bad eggs and no amount of improvement of facilities would bring

---

11. Friend, Irwin & others, *The Over the Counter Securities Market*, McGraw Hill Company, 1958.
12. This has since been set right in 1996 by restricting access to capital market to companies with dividend payment for three years or appraisal of their projects by financial institution or commericial bank and such appraising entity participates in funding the project.

in buyers. In the case of good scrips, the situation is different. They are in short supply because they are good and the owners, be they owners of the company or institutions, do not want to part with them. Sometimes, the owners may be motivated to keep out outsiders since they like to preserve it as a closely-held company. We cannot compel them to sell their holding. Perhaps we may be able to do that with public financial institutions, but with the entry of private sector mutual funds that would be difficult. It is as good as asking them to forego profit. One has to accept the laws of demand and supply and unless a buyer voluntarily comes forward, there is a no way to sell a share. The situation does not alter even if we adopt the system of market-makers. It works abroad because, as we mentioned above, basically an equity share represents interest in an operational company with profit-making opportunities. In our country, the cost of acquiring a long position which is difficult to liquidate is heavy. Jobbers are also unwilling to take a position in thinly traded shares because of inadequate availability of credit and its high cost.

Results of Empirical Analysis

An empirical investigation by the author has revealed that thin trading is not as pervasive as it is claimed (being confined to 10 per cent of the live manufacturing companies) and the explanation for thin trading should be sought in narrow capital base, small pubic holding of shares, small number of shareholders, poor record of profits and dividend payments[13].

The benefits of a continuous market are that it creates marketable liquid investments and facilitates collateral lending. Listed shares are good collateral for secured loans although the margin is as high as 50 per cent (used to be 75 per cent before 1993).

---

13. Machiraju, H.R., *Problem of Liquidity of Thinly Traded Shares*, The Stock Exchange, Bombay, 1993.

References

Avadhani, V.A., *"Ownership and Distribution Pattern of Shareholdings of Companies."*

Eiteman, Wilford J.E. and others, *The Stock Market*, Fourth edition, McGraw Hill Co., New York, 1964.

Francis, J.C., *Investment Analysis and Management*, Fifth Edition, McGraw Hill International Edition.

Friend, Irwin and others, *The Over the Counter Securities Market*, Securities Research Unit, Wharton School, University of Pennsylvania, McGraw Hill Co., 1958.

Government of India, *Report of the High Powered Study Group on Establishment of New Stock Exchange*, 1991.

Government of India, *Report of the High Powered Committee on Stock Exchange Reform*, 1985.

Gupta, L.C., *Expert Study on Trading in Shares*, Society for Capital Market Research & Development, New Delhi 1991.

Gupta L.C., *Indian Share Owners*, Society for Capital Market Research & Development, New Delhi, 1991.

Levine, Ross, "Stock Markets: A Spur to Economic Growth", *Finance and Development*, March 1996.

Machiraju, H.R., *Problem of Liquidity of Thinly Traded Shares*, The Stock Exchange, Bombay, 1993.

Teweles, Richard J., Bradley, Edward S., Teweles Ted M., *The Stock Market*, 6th edition, John Wiley & Sons Inc., New York, 1992.

Tinic S., *The Economics of Liquidity Services*, Quarterly Journal of Economics, Feb. 1972.

3

MAJOR STOCK EXCHANGES IN INDIA

INTRODUCTION

The total equity market capitalization of the 23 stock exchanges amounted to Rs.13.77 trillion ($310 billion) 2004. The equity market capitalization worked out to 49% of GDP. By turnover and market share, the two exchanges, the National Stock Exchange, the Bombay Stock Exchange, together account for 98.9 per cent of the market for stock trading. The remaining 21 stock exchanges are fighting for 1.1% per cent of the total market. Although OTCEI has a very small capitalization and turnover concept is quite significant. It has all that NSE has as far as trading and settlement practices are concerned but it is ahead of its time.

Turnover and Market Share of Stock Exchanges

Table 3.1 presents the turnover and market share of 23 stock exchanges. The turnover on all the 23 stock exchanges amounted to Rs.16,20,498 crores in 2003-04 (as compared to Rs.9,68,909 crores in 2002-03). The turnover in 2003-04 was 11.77 per cent of market capitalization; while the turnover was 133.6% in 2002-03. Of the turnover in 2003-04 NSE accounted for 67.9 per cent and BSE 31.0 per cent together accounting for a market share of 98.9 per cent of the total turnover on all exchanges.

As the share of many exchanges declined, they joined together to set up the indian Stock Exchange services corporation (ISESC) to pool their markets together. Table 3.1 shows that their turnover was 0.05 crore in 2003-04.

The small exchanges floated subsidiaries, which became brokers of the big exchanges and their brokers became sub-brokers of the subsidiaries. The subsidiaries of all small exchanges taken together accounted for only 3.47% of total turnover in 2003-04.

NATIONAL STOCK EXCHANGE

The NSE was incorporated in November 1992 with an equity capital of Rs.25 crores. The International Securities Consultancy (ISC) of Hongkong has helped in setting up NSE. ISC has prepared the detailed business plan and installation of hardware and software systems. The promotors for NSE were financial institutions, insurance companies, banks and SBI Capital Market Ltd., Infrastructure Leasing and Financial Services Ltd. and Stock Holding Corporation Ltd. It has been set up to strengthen the move towards professionalisation of the capital market as well as provide nation-wide securities trading facilities to investors. NSE transcends geographical barriers and overcomes fragmentation by providing screen based system instead of a trading ring. It has resulted in greater order depth and liquidity and in the process reduced the transaction costs.

Objectives of NSE

The objectives of NSE are to provide a nation-wide trading facility for equities, debt instruments and hybrids; to ensure equal access to investors all over the country through an appropriate communication network; to provide a fair, efficient and transparent securities market to investors using electronic trading systems; to enable shorter settlement cycles and book entry settlement systems, and to attain current international standards of securities market.

Two additional market segments exclusively for institutions, the institutional lot segment and trade for trade segment are set up to encourage an institutional market where large volume trades take place for settlement in jumbo lots.

Order Driven System

NSE has an order driven system and allows members to undertaken jobbing in securities of their choice. Several members undertake jobbing because of ease of entry and exit and narrow margins resulting in improvement of liquidity and reduction of transaction costs.

Mark-to-Market

NSE is the first exchange in the country to introduce mark to market system of margin which reduces the risk of default by members. NSE calculates the market margin as the cumulative loss in excess of 50 per cent of the initial security deposit kept with the exchange by way of cash deposit, bank guarantee or approved securities. At present the initial security deposit kept with the exchange by way of cash deposit, bank guarantee or approved securities with the exchange by corporate trading members is Rs.45 lakhs in cash and by the individual/partnership trading members is Rs.30 lakhs in cash.

As trading volumes for members have begun to increase substantially, members have been advised to bring in the remaining security deposit of Rs.25 lakhs (corporate members) and Rs.17.5 lakhs (individual/partnership members). Members will be required to bring

Table 3.1: Turnover and Market Share of Stock Exchanges (2002-03 and 2003-04)

Rs. Crores

Stock Exchange	2002-03	2003-04	Market Share %	
			2002–03	2003–04
Ahmedabad	15,458.6	4,544.4	1.6	0.5
BSE	3,14,073.2	5,02,618.4	32.4	31.0
Bangalore	0.0	0.05	0.0	0.0
Bhubaneswar	0.0	0.0	0.0	0.0
Calcutta	6,539.9	1,927.5	0.6	0.1
Cochin	0.0	0.0	0.0	0.0
Coimbatore	0.0	0.0	0.0	0.0
Delhi	11.1	3.4	0.0	0.0
Guwahati	0.05	0.0	0.0	0.0
Hyderabad	4.6	1.9	0.0	0.0
ICSE	64.8	0.05	0.0	0.0
Jaipur	0.0	0.0	0.0	0.0
Ludhiana	0.0	0.0	0.0	0.0
Madras	0.0	100.8	0.0	0.0
Magadh	0.5	0.07	0.0	0.0
Mangalore	0.0	0.0	0.0	0.0
MPSE	0.0	0.0	0.0	0.0
NSE	6,17,988.6	10,99,533.9	63.8	67.9
OTCEI	0.1	15.7	0.0	0.0
Pune	1.8	0.0	0.0	0.0
SKSE	0.0	0.0	0.0	0.0
UPSE	14,763.4	11,751.0	1.5	0.7
Vadodara	2.5	0.14	0.0	0.0
Total	**9,68,909.15**	**16,20,497.31**	**100.0**	**100.0**

Source: SEBI, *Annual Report*, 2003-04.
NA : Not applicable

Chapter–3

in additional funds whenever the cumulative losses marked to market at the end of the day exceeds Rs.35 lakhs for corporate trading members and Rs.24 lakhs for the individual trading members, provided the remaining deposit in excess of the initial Rs.45 lakhs and Rs.30 lakhs respectively, has been brought in.

Trading members will be required to make up the shortfall in the mark to market margin, rounded off to the next higher multiple of Rs.5 lakhs, to the exchange within two working days. The day's closing price or the last available price will be considered as the valuation price for calculating the mark to market loss.

Any shortfall in payment of mark to market margin will be treated as a serious violation of the exchange regulation and will attract penal charges to the extent of 0.15% of the shortfall amount per day for the period of shortfall. Any member found to be habitually having a shortfall on this account will invite serious action including suspension from trading.

Price-Bands

Under the new system (10.9.97), the price-bands are based on the liquidity of company's shares and not on volatility alone as the potential for price manipulation is more in the case of illiquid securities. The criteria for determining the measure of liquidity of a security are; frequency of trading, average daily volume of trading, average daily value of trading and average daily number of trades.

NSE has now decided that 100 companies comprising the NSE-50 index and the NSE-50 mid-cap securities will be placed on the daily price-band of 10 per cent and a weekly price band of 25 per cent.

Securities with reasonable liquidity, numbering 491, have been put on 7 per cent daily and 20 per cent weekly price-band. The balance 908 securities have been put in the price band of 5 per cent daily and 15 per cent weekly. The securities with a price of less than Rs.10 will remain in the price band of 15 per cent daily and 30 per cent weekly. The price-band system earlier was based on the observed volatility of securities during the last 150 trading days. As per this system, volatile securities are placed in the 5 per cent, 7 per cent and 10 per cent daily price-bands for which the weekly price-bands were 15 per cent, 20 per cent and 25 per cent respectively. The change in the price-bands became effective from September 10, 1997.

Minimum Paid-up Capital

The exchange has also modified two of its listing clauses. In September, 1997 the minimum paid-up capital requirement for initial public offering has been increased from Rs.10 crores to Rs.20 crores.

With regard to companies whose shares are already listed on another exchange, there will now be a requirement of a minimum market capitalization of Rs.20 crores for companies with a paid up capital of at least Rs.10 crores or a market capitalization of Rs.40 crores for companies with a paid up capital of less than Rs.10 crores.

Companies which have not paid dividend in at least two of the last three years will now be required to have a net worth of at least Rs.50 crores for seeking listing on NSE.

OPTIONS AND FUTURES

Options and futures trading restricted to corporate members with a net worth of Rs.5 crores for membership has been launched in May 1996.

TRADING ON NSE

The National Stock Exchange of India started its operations in debt market segment (WDM) from June 30, 1994 and in capital segment (CM) on November 3, 1994. It has expanded its trade operations to more than 100 cities in India. At the end of 1996 there were 899 trading members of whom 495 are from places outside Mumbai. The NSE has adopted fully automated screen based trading system which allows trading members to trade from their offices through a communications network. Price, time and volume conditions are quite flexible. Securities such as government bonds, Treasury bills, PSU bonds, CPs, floating rate bonds and Unit 64 of UTI are traded on the exchange. In the capital market segment trading in equities and retail trade in convertible/non-convertible debentures and hybrids are covered.

Wholesale Debt Market

Two distinctive segments representing Wholesale Debt Market (WDM) and Capital Market started operations in 1994-95 providing secondary market trading facilities. WDM is a facility for institutions and bodies corporate to enter into high value transactions in instruments such as government securities, Treasury Bills, PSU bonds, Unit 64 of UTI, CPs and CDs. The segment is characterized by few large investors

Table 3.2: National Stock Exchange – Wholesale Debt Market

(Amount in Rupees Crores)

Security	1996 – 97			1995 – 96			1994 – 95 @		
	No. of Issues	Market Capitalization	Turnover	No. of Issues	Market Capitalization	Turnover	No. of Issues	Market Capitalization	Turnover
1	2	3	4	5	6	7	8	9	10
1. Bank Bonds	7	1,784 (0.5)	16.11 (0.1)	—	—	—	—	—	—
2. Certificate of Deposit	15	189 (0.1)	487.02 (1.6)	3	52 (–)	136.75 (1.4)	1	115 (0.1)	104.50 (2.5)
3. Commercial Paper	1	45 (–)	128.00 (0.4)	2	10 (–)	539.00 (5.6)	6	51 (–)	187.50 (4.5)
4. Corporates	86	6,070 (1.8)	478.64 (1.5)	26	3,251 (1.4)	54.87 (0.6)	12	2,277 (1.3)	5.29 (0.1)
5. Government Securities (including Treasury Bills)	147	2,21,526 (67.3)	27,053.44 (86.6)	132	1,69,391 (73.4)	7,552.22 (78.6)	116	1,38,750 (78.9)	2,947.12 (71.2)
6. State Government Loans	109	20,656 (6.3)	298.81 (0.9)	72	15,815 (6.9)	175.54 (1.8)	38	7,832 (4.5)	79.30 (1.9)
7. PSU Bonds	202	37,936 (11.5)	1,968.53 (6.3)	168	32,079 (13.9)	996.03 (10.4)	150	19,907 (11.3)	757.55 (18.3)
8. Institutional Bonds	89	20,956 (6.4)	799.95 (2.6)	53	10,140 (4.4)	153.44 (1.6)	20	6,896 (3.9)	66.18 (1.6)
9. Unit Trust of India	1	20,000 (6.1)	0.03 (–)	—	—	—	—	—	—
Total (1 to 9)	657	3,29,172	31,230.53	456	2,30,738	9,607.85	352	1,75,828	4,147.44

@ During June 30, 1994 to March 31, 1995, — Not applicable (–) Negligible

Note: 1. The number of issues and market capitalization pertain to end of the respective financial year.

2. Figures in brackets indicate percentage to total.

Source: Reserve Bank of India, *Annual Report*, 1996-97.

and a high average trade value. The principal participants are banks, corporates and mutual funds. There are two types of entities on WDM, Trading Members and participants. Trading members are the recognized members of NSE. They can either trade on their own account or on behalf of their clients, including participants.

Participants are the organizations directly responsible for the settlement of trades. They include trading members. In 1996, there were 62 participants including 24 foreign and private banks, 25 PS banks, 6 financial institutions and corporates and mutual funds. In WDM segment of the exchange more than nine categories of instruments are allowed for trading. In 1998-99, 1071 securities (listed and permitted) were traded. Volume in 1998-99 was Rs. 1,05,469 crores. The volume of corporate debentures traded was Rs. 878 crores in 1998-99. For generating liquidity in the debt market, RBI allowed repo transactions from June 24, 1995 in all Treasury Bills and five dated securities. Market preference was for shorter maturity (upto 3 years). In the WDM 657 issues were traded in 1996-97 and the turnover was Rs.31,230 crores (see Table 3.2). Table 3.2 reveals that government securities (including treasury bills) at Rs.2,21,526 crores account for 67.3 per cent of market capitalization.

As on March 31, 2006, 3174 securities were available for trading and their total market capital is at on was Rs 15, 67, 57 crores.

Capital Market Segment

The capital market segment of NSE commenced operations on November 3, 1994 to provide trading facilities for institutions and retail investors. The exchange has allowed 1482 securities for trading of medium and large companies with nation-wide investor base. By virtue of nation-wide equal access such securities can be traded any where in the country at the same price.

The NSE through its nation-wide network (with connectivity to over 100 cities) has acquired in 1996-97 the status of a premier stock exchange in the country. The turnover on the capital segment in 1998-99 at 4,14,474 crores was 30% more than that on BSE.

At the end of March 1999, 64.5 scrips were listed on NSE with a market capitalisation of Rs.3,35,209 crores. Further 609 scrips were permitted for trading with a market capitalisation of Rs.1,55,967 crores. (See Table 3.3)

Table 3.3: National Stock Exchange (Capital Market-Segment) Indicators for 1994-95 – 1998-99

Rs. Crores

Indicators	*1994-95 (November 94 to March 95)*	*1995-96*	*1996-97*	*1997-98*	*1998-99*
1. Turnover	1805	67,287	2,94,504	3,70,193	4,14,474
2. Number of Companies	678	1,268	1,482	1,357	1,254
a. Permitted Companies	543	846	932	745	609
b. Listed Companies	135	422	550	612	645
3. Market Capitalization	3,63,350	4,01,458	4,19,367	4,87,503	4,91,176
a. Of Listed Companies	73,223	2,17,721	2,52,894	3,08,520	3,35,209
b. Of Permitted Companies	2,90,127	1,83,737	1,66,473	1,72,983	1,55,967

Source : Reserve Bank of India, *Report on Currency and Finance*, 1996-97, Vol I, VI-51 and Annual Report, 1998-99.

Electronic Trade Monitoring System (1.9.1997)

The stock-watch system is a computer system designed and programmed to monitor market activity and identify aberrations from historical patterns.

The algorithm for the NSE system is somewhat similar to the one prevalent at NASDAQ in the United States. Since the trading system at NASDAQ and NSE are totally different the algorithm of NASDAQ has been adopted to NSE's trading conditions.

The system will enable NSE to electronically monitor the trading patterns which would lead to a more effective surveillance. Currently, NSE officials have to manually screen the trading patterns to ascertain any strange price fluctuations. The electronic trading system will automatically kick off alerts. It will make the task of surveillance easier and more effective. There is a great need to enhance information flow and this will go hand in hand with better monitoring of trading patterns to reduce cases of price manipulation. SEBI will define what kind of information stock exchanges need to perform their enforcement job more effectively.

This will include setting up of an issuer data base as it is felt that in several cases it is the issuer who is responsible for price manipulations and not necessarily the brokers.

Counter Guarantees

NSE's Clearing Corporation stands guarantee to all trades done in the cash market on the exchange. The counter guarantee of the Clearing Corporation ensures that no default, either of payment or delivery takes place for trades done on NSE. A settlement guarantee fund has been set up in June 1996 with a corpus of Rs.300 crores. The clearing and settlement operations of the exchange are managed by its wholly owned subsidiary the National Securities Clearing Corporation Limited (NSCCL) which began operations in April 1996.

BOMBAY STOCK EXCHANGE

Turnover and Deliveries

Data relating to turnover and deliveries, both in terms of the number of shares and their value, for Bombay Stock Exchange which accounted for 19 percent of the activity of all stock exchanges in India are presented in Table 3.3.

BSE had a turnover of Rs.5,18,717 crores and a market capitalization of Rs.16,98,428 crores in 2004-05. Rolling settlement cycle for all scrips and screen based trading facility have been adopted. A trade guarantee fund (TGF) to protect the interests of investors is set up. TGF provides many-times-over cover to value at risk at any point of time.

LISTING REQUIREMENT

Listing on a stock exchange can shift business risk from a single family to thousands of investors worldwide. The Securities Contracts (Regulation) Act stipulates compulsory listing of companies. As per the Securities Contracts (Regulation) Rules, 1957 guidelines issued under Securities and Exchange Rules, Bye-laws and Regulations, a company must comply with the following in order to get its shares listed on any recognized stock exchange. The exchange has freedom to charge listing fees. Basic listing requirements are as follows:

(i) The memorandum and Articles of Association must not contain any provisions that restrict free transfer of shares.

(ii) The company must offer for public subscription at least 25 per cent of its issued capital.

(iii) The minimum issued capital of the company should be at least Rs.10 crores in the case of BSE and Rs. 5 crores in others.

(iv) Applications should be invited in denominations of market units of trading.

(v) Previous track record of dividend payment for three years is necessary.

Listing Agreement and Corporate Governance

SEBI amended clause 49 of the Listing Agreement to bring about improvements in corporate governance practices.

- All compensation paid to nonexecutive directors to be fixed by board of directors and approved by shareholders.
- Code of conduct for board members and senior management should be laid down by company boards.
- Audit committee should review financial statement and draft audit report with company management.
- Chief executive and Chief finance officer should certify the balance sheet, profit and loss account and cash flow statements in the Directors' Report.

Central Listing Authority (CLA)

To facilitate the emergence of a uniform national market and bring uniformity in the due diligence process in scrutinising applications, the listing requirements and their implementations has been standardized across all exchanges by setting up a Central Listing Authority on August 21, 2003.

The Central Listing Authority was notified on August 21, 2003. To ensure a uniform national market, the listing requirements and the implementation of the same across all exchanges a single listing authority was set up by SEBI.

Demutualization of BSE

Historically stock exchanges were set up the world over as nonprofit organizations owned by their member brokers. BSE is no exception. However, on several occasions in the past conflict of interest has arisen at BSE because members of the exchange who own the exchange enjoy trading rights.

Further, the broker managed stock exchanges are relatively slow and reluctant to respond to changes. This has proved at times detrimental to the interests of other stakeholders. In recent years, there has been a move towards corporate service provider model. Demutualization involving separation of trading rights from ownership and management control has been followed in the case of NSE and OTCEI. The Union

Budget for 2002-03 emphasized the need to separate trading, ownership and management in stock exchanges. A group constituted by SEBI (Chairman Justice M.H. Kania) recommended that the three stakeholders, shareholders, brokers and the investing public should be equally represented on the governing board of a demutualised stock exchange, with a ceiling of 5% of voting rights which can be exercised by a single entity or groups of related entities irrespective of the size of ownership of the shares held. The Chairman of the board should not be an active broker. The Group recommended that the trading card system should be replaced by the deposit system wherein the money deposited by a member to obtain trading rights only be considered as deposit with the stock exchange for trading purposes. The Group suggested a onetime exemption from taxes for the newly demutualised stock exchanges.

According to the gazette notification issued on May 20, 2005, BSE from being an association of persons with no profit objective, is required to acquire a corporate form of organization. On August 21, 2005 SEBI notified corporation and demutualization schemes for ten more exchanges including Calcutta and Delhi stock exchanges. The notification gives details of the plan to transform the exchanges comprehensively. The role of brokers will be constrained. Trading members cannot have voting rights in excess of 5%. The number of brokers on the governing board will not exceed a quarter of the total strength. SEBI will have overriding powers to appoint directors. The chief executive is expected to be a stock market professional and will be an ex-officio director. The stock exchange's clearing house will be handed over to an independent clearing corporation with the approval of SEBI. The exchange will be known as Bombay Stock Exchange Ltd.

The Government of India has envisaged a comprehensive plan to make all stock exchanges function as corporate entities. The new entities after converting themselves into demutualized entities will issue share capital to the public. All the stock exchanges in the country will be corporatised and demutualized. At the end of 2007 there were 18 corporatised and demutualised stock exchanges in the country.

The division of ownership between members and outsiders can lead to a balanced approach, remove conflicts of interest and create greater management accountability, transparency and market discipline. There is an urgent need to invest in technology upgradation to face the competition from newly created technology-oriented market entities.

Many stock exchanges abroad such as Frankfurt, Stockholm, Amsterdam and Australiad demutalized and have become publicly listed companies. New York stock exchange has announced plans to shift to a corporate form. It is transforming itself through a reverse merger with a much smaller electronic exchange called Archipelago.

Demutualization has raised the issue of compatability of the demutualized structure with the role of stock markets as self regulators and support of funding for regulation. They may also be reluctant to bring enforcement actions against holders of trading rights if they are also major stakeholders. To resolve the problem, it is suggested that after demutualization, the stock exchange should merely be a transaction clearing entity and not a self regulatory organization. It should not have special powers over other companies whose shares are also listed and traded. Divesting demutualized exchanges (companies) of listing powers is suggested as a matter of fair play. Stock exchanges were exempted form payment of capital gains tax on corporatization.

OVER THE COUNTER EXCHANGE OF INDIA

Introduction

The Over the Counter Exchange of India (OTCEI) was incorporated under Section 25 of the Companies Act in October 1990 and started functioning from September 1992. OTCEI has been set up to meet a long felt need for a second tier market where companies with small paid-up capital and with less onerous conditions could have the advantage of listing. With this end in view, OTC Exchange of India was promoted by all India financial institutions, merchant banks, and subsidiaries of public sector banks and established as a recognized stock exchange under Section 4 of the Securities Contracts (Regulation) Act. Companies listed on the OTC Exchange enjoy the same status as companies listed on any other stock exchange in the country as regards taxes and interest on borrowings. In October 1992, a computerized trading system called Automated Securities Trading Over the Counter System (ASTOCS) was installed.

OTC Exchange is now nation-wide and operates from more than 400 cities in India through the nation-wide information dissemination network, Intext. Any city in India can receive the scrip prices of OTCEI Intext. Scrip prices are generated by OTCEI's central computer in Bombay and then broadcast on Intext.

OTC Market in USA

OTCEI with ASTOCS is modelled on National Association of Securities Dealers Automated Quotation System (NASDAQ) in the United States of America. In the USA all off exchange trading was referred to as the Over the Counter (OTC) market. It emerged originally as a way of buying and selling shares of companies that were unlisted and therefore did not have a quotation on one of the stock exchanges. OTC market before the introduction of NASDAQ System in 1971 consisted of traders at different firms connected with telephones. They were located in hundreds of different cities and towns all over the United States. Traders were dealers who made markets in various shares. They made a two sided market by quoting a price they would pay a prospective seller or a price they would charge a prospective buyer. Trading is executed on a dealer basis as opposed to the broker basis used by stock exchanges. Dealers who were market makers did not deal with public but with traders at other market making firms or with order desks of retail oriented brokers buying on behalf of their customers. The market was largely retail.

OTC market is a negotiated market in contrast to a stock exchange which is an auction market. In the exchange market exemplified by NYSE, there is a single designated market maker (the specialist) and an auction system based on current high bid low offer. On the other hand OTC market has no restrictions limiting the number of market makers in a given company's share. With the introduction of computerized trading system in 1971, a quick scan of an electronic screen reveals the best market for an order. NASDAQ is a system of computers and special electronic terminals that provide instantaneous bid and asked quotation in over the counter securities. Traders can gauge the market at a glance and investors can be certain that they are getting the best price.

NASDAQ provides three service levels. Level 1 service is the one that retail brokers and their customers may view on the terminal located at broker's desk which displays the high current bid and the low current offer. Levels 2 and 3 display firm quotations of all registered NASDAQ market makers. Market makers have to subscribe to Level 3 which has the connection that allows the subscriber to change his display of quotation as the market changes. It permits the dealer to enter or change the quotation displayed on the system.

The typical bid offer spread on shares traded on NASDAQ is very narrow ensuring the execution of order at the last sale price or at a minimum price variation away from that sale. OTC market is well regulated by SEC, transparent and liquid. For small companies the system of competing market makers provides deeper liquidity than is true for floor exchanges.

The OTC in USA is thus builtup from below. There are 7,000 member firms that operate over 20,000 branch offices and employ 5,00,000 registered representatives who sell securities in OTC market. Whereas in India, we have created a OTC market without dealers and securities to trade in.

Objectives of OTCEI

OTCEI has been setup to help small investors who face the problem of access, liquidity, delays in payment and delivery and uncertainty about prices at which shares are bought and sold; and companies who face the problems of prohibitive issue costs and restricted access to the market.

Members and Licensed Dealers

The market constituents are companies, investors, members and licensed dealers.

Members

Members are expected to come from the ranks of financial institutions, banks, mutual funds, venture capital funds and large financial companies having a minimum net worth of Rs. 2.5 crores since appraisal capability and resources are required. The functions of members are:

(a) appraise and evaluate proposals,
(b) value the scrip,
(c) sponsor the scrip to other market participants,
(d) hold the scrip till project completion,
(e) arrange for an additional market maker, and
(f) offer.

Dealers

The dealers would be a corporate body, partnership firms and individuals having a net worth of Rs. 5 lakhs. In the case of individuals, proof of having tangible liquid assets of Rs. 5 lakhs, 2 independent references and a reference from the bank regarding the financial standing has to be furnished. The individual should atleast be a graduate.

Dealers are expected to have adequate financial strength to be able to carry on the trading and market making functions. The net business exposure on OTCEI will be limited as a percentage of the networth which is committed to OTC Exchange operation. The exact percentage will be determined by OTC Committee from time to time.

Dealers should possess adequate organizational infrastructure to carry on the functions of investment, trading and market making and OTC counter management.

Dealers should possess adequate office space to carry on the activities mentioned above.

Dealers should have adequate knowledge of trading, stock valuation, share transfer rules and laws relating to the above. OTC Committee may in consultation with Government of India, lay down the exact mode of testing the knowledge as above mentioned.

Dealers are selected after an interview by the OTC Committee. Both in the case of members and dealers, the OTC Committee will prescribe the nature and extent of electronic equipment including computers, which will be needed to be installed at the members/dealers work place. Members/dealers should be agreeable to fund the investment in such equipment.

Members and dealers will observe high standards of fair-play in all their dealings on OTC Exchange of India.

Members and licensed dealers will both make market in scrips listed on OTC exchange, i.e., they will trade/deal in all scrips. Market making consists of quoting two way prices at which the member/licensed dealer is willing to buy or sell a standard lot which will be continuously quoted.

Members on being appointed by the company act as sponsors to listing of new scrips.

Sponsorship includes the following functions:

(a) appraise the project of a company,

(b) value the scrips to be listed on OTC exchange,

(c) sponsor the scrip to other members and licensed dealers and place the entire scrip with them,

(d) make market for three years from the date scrips are offered for public trading compulsorily, and

(e) arrange for one more member, licensed dealer to make market for the scrip for at least one year.

Voluntary market making could be for limited periods of three months.

Fees

For Members: one time non-refundable admission fee is Rs. 10 lakhs (Rs. 5 lakhs and Rs. 5 lakhs after one year). The annual subscription fee is Rs. 1 lakh. Shareholders are exempted from payment of admission fee as well as annual subscription.

For Dealers: one time non-refundable admission fee is Rs. 2 lakhs. The annual subscription is Rs. 5,000/-.

OTCEI may collect security deposit of an amount and for a period as may be considered necessary depending upon the extent of business experience on the OTC Exchange.

OTCEI reserves the right to recover fees/charges for other services if any, and/or revise the above fee structure from time to time.

Listing on the OTC Exchange

SEBI guidelines (1992) on public issues envisage listing of securities on any stock exchange or OTCEI.

Listing on OTCEI may be sought by companies with equity capital of less than Rs.10 crores, closely hold companies wanting to attain listed company status and companies assisted by venture capitalists.

Listing Requirements of OTCEI

1. The minimum issued share capital of a company must be Rs. 30 lakhs.
2. For companies with an issued share capital of more than Rs.30 lakhs but less than Rs.300 lakhs, the minimum public offer should be 25 per cent of the issued capital or Rs.20 lakhs worth of shares (face value) whichever is higher.
3. Companies with an issued equity capital of more than Rs.300 lakhs seeking listing on the OTC will have to comply with the listing requirements and guidelines as are applicable to such companies for enlistment on other recognized stock exchanges. In November, 1996 SEBI has removed the upper limit of Rs.25 crores and allowed all companies irrespective of size to list on OTCEI. The number of companies listed

were 146 at end of March 1998. The turnover of the exchange during 1997-98 was Rs.283 crores.

Guidelines for Issue of Shares

1. Public issue without sponsor taking any shares should conform to normal guidelines for disclosure and investor protection.
2. In case the sponsor has taken up the shares they may be offered to public at a later date at a price decided by sponsor in accordance with regulations. The sponsor should act as market maker for three years and find additional market maker. The sponsor has to give two way quotes based on minimum or maximum trading prices.

Revised Guidelines for Bought-out-Deals (BODs) (22.1.1996)

1. The offer of BODs should be made only to OTCEI members and dealers. If participation is not forthcoming, they can be offered to others.
2. The members and Dealers should take up a minimum of 10 per cent of BODs.
3. The offer for sale should ensure a minimum 25 per cent of the post issue paid-up capital to the public.

OTCEI commenced its operations in 1992 and has opened 20 representative offices in all major cities of the country. The OTCEI entered into Memorandum of understanding with the National Association of Securities Dealers Automated Quotation (NASDAQ) in February 1994 for enhanced cooperation with the two exchanges in the area of market technology, regulations and business development. OTCEI would support NASDAQ in their effort to encourage international listing of Indian issues while NASDAQ will support OTCEI in its efforts to establish a market of international standards in India.

Trading

Permitted securities category for trading was initiated in 1994-95. After obtaining SEBI's approval for listing, finance, investment, leasing, and hire purchase companies OTCEI issued guidelines for listing of such companies on April 7, 1995. OTCEI invited applications for dealership in 54 cities in 19 states. The number of companies went up to 146 as of end March 1997. About 82 equities and 24 debentures under the permitted securities category are listed.

OTCEI will trade in, besides equity shares, preference shares, CPs, convertible and non-convertible debentures, bonds, warrants and exim scrips. Since November, 1996 SEBI has allowed even unlisted companies to trade on OTCEI.

Methods of Offer

Companies can go public on the OTC Exchange by two methods as shown in the Chart 3.1.

Chart 3.1
METHODS OF OFFER

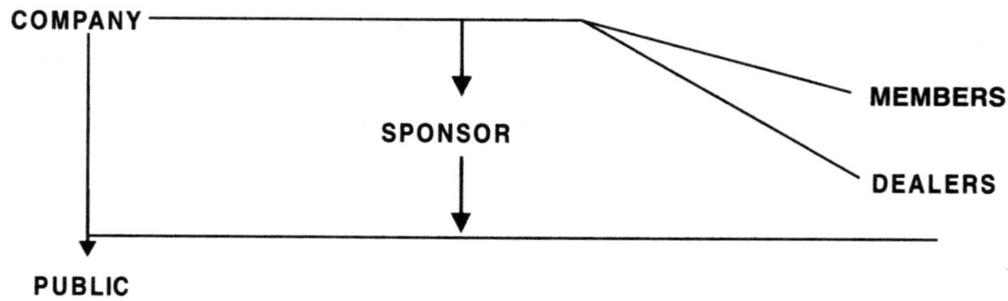

(A) Primary issues: As in new issues, companies directly offer their shares to the public. The sponsor for these shares mainly carries out the function of issue management, and acts as the sole underwriter. He may sub-write his liability with a syndicate of members and dealers.

(B) Secondary issue: Companies may offload the shares, to be offered to the public, to the sponsor at an earlier date. The sponsor may hold these shares till ready for public participation.

Companies would benefit by availability of capital at an earlier date for their projects. The sponsor also acts as a manager at the time of public issue. All costs involved in the issue can be negotiated by companies with members of the OTC Exchange, at the time of appointment of sponsors.

LISTING PROCEDURE

The listing procedure is presented in Chart 3.2.

All quotes and transactions are recorded in the central OTC computer, which can be accessed by any dealer's computer, through telephone lines with modems. The PTI OTC Scan at each dealer's counter will continuously display the best buy and sell quotes offered by market makers, as also all market related information.

Chart 3.2
LISTING PROCEDURE OF OTCEI

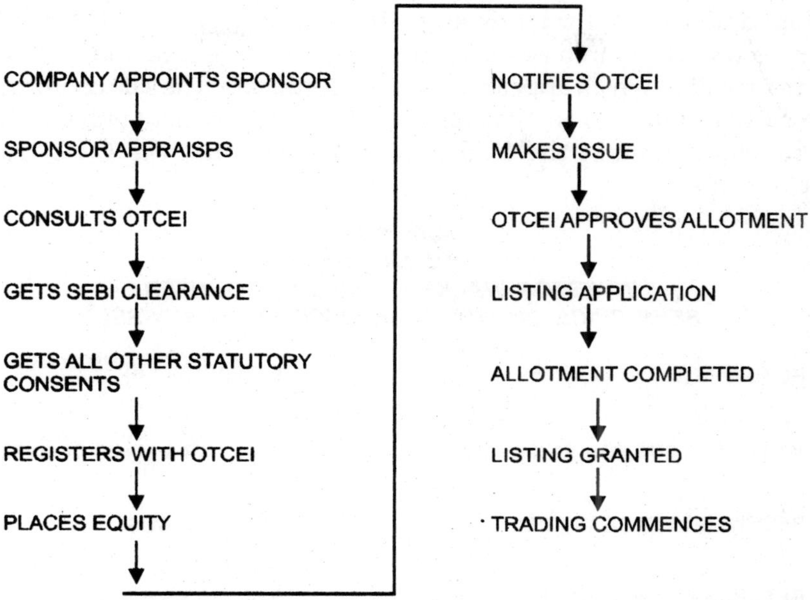

The OTCEI introduced trading in PSU bonds and launched a new segment, the listed mutual fund segment.

The OTC trading system is presented in Chart 3.3.

Chart 3.3
OTC MARKET IN OPERATION

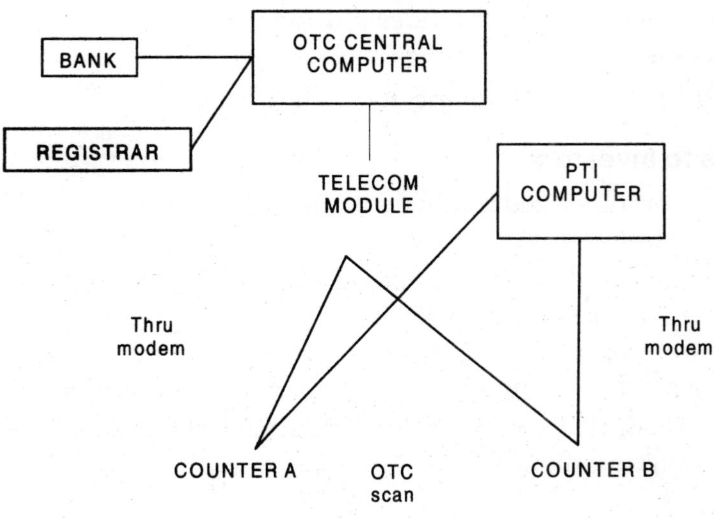

Trading Mechanism

The two trading documents on the OTC Exchange are the counter receipt and sale confirmation slip. The counter receipt (CR) is issued to an investor who purchases a scrip. The CR is tradeable and contains all the information which appears on a share certificate. The sale conformation slip (SCS) is issued to an investor selling a scrip. Payment will be made to an investor against the SCS. Chart 3.4 presents the OTC trading mechanism.

Chart 3.4
OTC TRADING
INVESTOR WALKS UP TO OTC COUNTER
SEES PRICE ON OTC SCAN DECIDES TO BUY/SELL

BUYING	SELLING
↓	↓
MAKES CHEQUE FOR PAYMENT	GIVES CR & TD TO COUNTER
↓	↓
RECEIVES TEMPORARY CR	RECEIVES SCS
↓	↓
RETURNS WHEN CHEQUE CLEARED	RETURNS WHEN CR & TD
↓	↓
COLLECTS FINAL CR	CLEARED, COLLECTS FINAL CHEQUE

Settlement

In November 1996 as an experiment, the settlement period was revised from T plus 3 days to T plus 5 days because of inadequacies in the banking system which render it difficult to adhere to the norm on all India basis.

Chart III: 4 presents buying and selling activities.

Benefits to Investors

(i) Computerized trading with immediate confirmation of transaction facilitates quick payment and delivery of scrips.

(ii) Registrars for companies on the OTC Exchange are allowed to transfer up to 0.5% of a company's equity without referring to the company. This means that share transfers could be done quickly for the smaller investors.

(iii) The OTC Exchange being a computer network linked through telecommunications, the investor may find an OTC dealer's counter in his neighbourhood, making the capital market more accessible,

(iv) Display of prices and market information at every dealer's premises allows the investor to make a good investment decision.

(v) Sponsorship of every scrip on the OTC Exchange enhances quality of investments,

(vi) The market making mechanism on the OTC Exchange allows for easier access to and guaranteed exit from the market.

Dave Committee Report

The Dave Committee (April 17, 1996) on OTCEI has recommended relaxation of the maximum size of the issues that may be listed on OTCEI, relaxation in listing criterion and a shift from a rolling (T+3) settlement to five day account period settlement being followed by other exchanges. The recommendations for making OTCEI more effective and viable have been accepted by SEBI.

Financial Performance of Exchanges

Profits or revenue of stock exchanges depend *not only on the volume* of turnover but on its composition. Trading in derivatives and government securities which are growing contribute less to revenue. The profits of all exchanges in 2002-03 amounted to Rs.68.7 crores representing a return of 2.52% on assets of Rs.2,730.24 crores. Exchanges actually earn substantial amount of non business income from listing, interest and rent. Listing contributed Rs.33 crores in 2002-03. The income from interest and dividend has been increasing on account of collection of custodial deposits for risk management. For the small exchanges non business income contributes a major portion; business income contributed 10% of total income (against 43% for big exchanges). The small exchanges may witness further erosion of income from all sources for several reasons. Listing may not be sought by companies making IPOs and delisting will be resorted by companies with poor trading reducing custodial deposits and interest income. The loss is likely to erode assets and represents market failure. If economic agents do not receive or fail to receive the signals from the economic environment and respond appropriately, the market has failed to arrive at desirable outcome in resource use.

References

Bombay Stock Exchange *Annual Report,* 1987, 1988-89, 1989-90, 1990-91, 1991-92 and 1996-97.

Friend, Irwin and others, *The Over the Counter Securities Market,* Securities Research

Unit, Wharton School, University of Pennsylvania, McGraw Hill Co., 1958.

Loll, Leo ML, and Buckley, Julian G., *The Over the Counter Securities Market,* Third Edition, Prentice Hall Inc., Englewood Cliffs, New Jersey, 1973.

OTCEI, *Opening up the Market of the Future,* Brochure published by OTCEI.

Reserve Bank of India, *Annual Report* 1996-97, *Report On Currency and Finance,* 1994-95, 1995-96 and 1996-97, Vol.1.

Ravimohan, R., *OTC Exchange of India: A Brief Outline,* 1992.

SEBI, 2002, *Report on the Group on Corporation and Demutualisation of Stock Exchanges.*

Sahoo, M.S. and Rath, Prabhask K, "Who Moved My Cheese", *Executive Chartered Secretary,* November 2004.

Teweles, Richard J., Bradley, Edwards, and Teweles Ted M., *The Stock Market,* 6th Edition, John Wiley & Sons Inc., New York, 1992.

4

REGULATIONS RELATING TO STOCK EXCHANGES

RECOGNITION OF STOCK EXCHANGES

The Securities Contracts Regulation Act 1956 provides *inter alia* for recognition of stock exchanges and regulation of their functioning, licensing dealers, recognition of contracts, controlling speculation, restricting rights of equitable holders of shares and empowering government to compel any public limited company to get its shares listed.

Under the Securities Contracts Regulation Act, Government has promulgated the Securities Contracts (Rules) 1957 for carrying into effect the objects of legislation. The rules are statutory and constitute a code of standardized regulations applicable to all recognized exchanges.

The Securities and Exchange Board of India Act, 1992 provides for establishment of Securities and Exchange Board of India (SEBI) to protect the interest of investors in securities and to promote the development of and to regulate the securities market.

SC(R)A permits the functioning of only those stock exchanges which have been recognized by the Union Government to function in any notified state or area. The Act vests the Government with wide powers of supervision and control. Recognition is accorded only if the government is satisfied that the rules and bye-laws of the stock exchange conform to the conditions prescribed for ensuring fair dealings and protection of investors. Further, government has to be satisfied that such recognition is in the interests of the public and trade.

SEBI decided on December 10, 1996 that recognition to new stock exchanges, if considered necessary in public interest and of trade could be allowed subject to trading only on On Line Screen Based Trading and establishment of a clearing house within 6 months.

Control over Stock Exchanges

The rules and bye-laws of the stock exchange have to be approved by the government. In the interest of ensuring uniformity, government insists that the exchange seeking recognition should conform to the model rules and bye-laws.

The rules of the recognized stock exchange relating to constitution of the exchange, constitution and composition of the general body, the powers of management of the governing body, the admission of members, the qualification for members, the expulsion, suspension and readmission of members, the registration of partnership and the appointment of authorized representatives and clerks must be duly approved by Government. Change in rules can be affected only with the consent of the Government.

The regulation and control of contracts in securities and for every aspect of trading activities of members has to be sanctioned by Government and changes have to be approved by Government.

Finally, the Government on its own *(suo moto)* can make or amend any rules or bye-laws of a recognized stock exchange, if it is in the interests of trade and public.

The SC(R)A confers on the government drastic powers to make inquiries into the affairs of a recognized stock exchange and its members, to supersede the governing body and take over the properties of a recognized stock exchange, to suspend its business and withdraw recognition in the interest of trade and public. Where there are no stock exchanges, SC(R)A empowers the government to license dealers in securities and prescribe the conditions subject to which they deal in securities.

SEBI has enhanced the powers of Executive Director on the lines of BSE to improve efficiency and effectively regulate the market.

Under the SC(R)A, only contracts entered into through, with or between members of recognized stock exchanges are legal. The Act also empowers the government to control speculation, to declare sale or purchase of specified securities in any notified area or state except to the extent and in the manner prescribed. Forward trading in shares was declared illegal in 1969; and options and futures in securities have since been provided.

The Act also imposes restrictions on the right of equitable shareholders to recover dividends from registered shareholders and confers powers on government to compel any public limited company to get its shares listed on a recognized stock exchange.

Securities Contracts (Regulation) Rules, 1957

To carry into effect the objects of SC(R) Act the Securities Contracts (Regulation) Rules (SC(R) Rules) were promulgated. The rules provide *inter alia* for the procedure to be followed for recognition of stock exchanges, submission of periodical returns and annual returns by recognized stock exchanges, inquiry into the affairs of recognized stock exchanges and their members and requirements for listing of securities.

Procedure for Recognition of Stock Exchange

An application under Section 3 of the SC(R) Act has to be made for recognition of the stock exchange with a fee of Rs. 500/-. The application should be accompanied by four copies of rules (including the Memorandum and Articles of association where the applicant stock exchange is an incorporated body) and bye-laws. The government may make enquiries and require further information to be furnished relating the application. Recognition may be for one year or permanent. The recognition is subject to stock exchange complying with the conditions imposed under SC(R) Act and rules from times to time. Application for renewal should be made 3 months before expiry along with a fee of Rs. 200/-.

Books of Account and Other Documents to be Maintained by Stock Exchanges

Every stock exchange should maintain and preserve the following books of account and documents for a period of five years.

1. Minute books of the meetings of
   (a) members,
   (b) governing body,
   (c) any standing committee of the governing body or general body of members;
2. Register of members;
3. Register of authorized clerks;
4. Register of authorized remisiers or authorized assistants;
5. Record of security deposits;

6. Margin deposits books;
7. Ledgers;
8. Journals;
9. Cash book; and
10. Bank pass books.

Submission of Annual Returns

1. Every recognized stock exchange has to furnish Central Government/SEBI annually with a report about its activities during the preceding year which shall *inter alia* contain detailed information about the following matters:
   (a) Changes in rules and bye-laws if any;
   (b) Change in the composition of governing body;
   (c) Any new committee set up and changes in the composition of existing one;
   (d) Admissions, readmissions, deaths or resignation of members;
   (e) Disciplinary action against members;
   (f) Nature and number of disputes for arbitration between members and non-members;
   (g) Defaults;
   (h) Action taken to combat any emergency in trade;
   (i) Securities listed and delisted; and
   (j) Securities brought or removed from the forward list.
2. Furnish audited balance sheet and profit and loss account for the preceding year.

Submission of Periodical Returns

Periodical returns have to be submitted by the stock exchanges to Central Government/SEBI relating to

(i) the official rates for the securities listed thereon;
(ii) the number of shares delivered through the clearing house;
(iii) the making up prices;
(iv) the clearing house programmes;
(v) the number of securities listed and delisted during the previous three months;
(vi) the number of securities brought on or removed from the forward list during the previous three months; and
(vii) any other matter as may be specified by Central Government/SEBI.

Inquiry into the Affairs of Stock Exchanges or Members

The Central Government/SEBI can appoint two or more persons to enquire into the affairs of the governing body of a recognized stock exchange or member. A statement of issues to be inquired is to be handed over by the inquiring authority and reasonable opportunity is given to governing body/member to state their case. The inquiring body has to submit its report to Central Government/SEBI.

Surveillance at Stock Exchanges

An effective monitoring and surveillance mechanism is an important element contributing to the efficiency and integrity of stock exchanges. The automation process initiated at the BSE , NSE, OTCEI and other exchanges has made it possible to put such monitoring mechanism in place. The reach of the capital market is also increasing significantly through the same process of automation. SEBI allowed expansion of the trading terminals of screen based trading systems of stock exchanges to cities having no stock exchange. Expansion to cities with stock exchanges has also been permitted, subject to an understanding with the local exchange allowing the installation of outside terminals within its jurisdiction. The participating exchange would keep its membership open to the brokers of the other local exchanges. It will ensure an adequate arrangement for resolving investor grievances for timely settlement of arbitration of cases arising out of trades executed on the extended terminals. The expansion of Bombay On Line Trading (BOLT) system of the stock exchange, Mumbai to the trading systems of these exchanges will be subject to general conditions. These include ensuring adequate monitoring and surveillance mechanism, stipulation of usual margins, capital adequacy, intra-day trading limits fixed for the broker stock exchange and the introduction of trade guarantees. The expansion of trading networks will lead to healthy competition between various stock exchanges and increase their efficiency.

SEBI has directed all stock exchanges to set up clearing houses or clearing corporations and to provide trade guarantees. This would reduce counterparty risks and enable investors trading through the exchanges to take advantage of settlement of transactions through a depository. Uniform norms and procedures for timely resolution of bad deliveries have been prescribed and are soon expected to become operational with the setting up of Bad Delivery Cells in the exchanges. The National Securities Clearing Limited(NSCCL) is entrusted with the task of guaranteeing settlement of trades in the capital market segment of the NSE. It has made considerable progress in enhancing clearing facilities in other regions by establishing regional clearing facilities. The setting up of Delhi Regional Clearing House and other regional clearing facilities of the NSCCL, will enable the regional relocation of the settlement facilities. This will increase the efficiency of the system and lead to timely settlement of transactions on the NSE.

Stock Watch System

To detect abuses such as market manipulation and insider trading SEBI has proposed a stock watch system similar to those operational on New York Stock Exchange and other developed markets. The system helps in identifying abnormal stock price behaviour as well as member-broker trading pattern. The Stock Watch System would be designed for surveillance of market activity by the utilization of computers programmed to identify aberrations from historical patterns that are identified and followed upon by specially trained analysts and investigations. The system thus enables identification of cases for further investigation.

The main objectives of the Stock Watch System, according to SEBI, are:

- provision of on-line and historical data;
- generation of alerts and freezes for unusual trading activity based on definable parameters;
- dynamic updation of information security-wise and brokerwise;
- graphical representation of data for analysts; and
- provision of various mathematical and statistical tools for analysts.

SEBI has classified the components of a Stock Watch System into three specific segments – alert segment, data analysis segment and report generation segment. According to SEBI the parameters for the generation of alerts should be defined by the exchange on a periodic basis. The alert segment is further classified into three main segments such as scrip alert, member broker alert and trade alert. According to SEBI, scrip alerts would be based on pre-set parameters such as high/low difference for a day or for consecutive days, open/close difference – the absolute value of one day's closing price minus the next day's opening price – close/close difference for a day or consecutive days or for any two days, and trade prices having seen a major difference in various market segments.

Trade alerts: Member-broker alerts were proposed to be raised based on parameters such as the day's activity of a member, change in the turnover of a member-broker between two days or periods and the difference in pay – in amounts between two settlement periods.

The parameters suggested by SEBI for trade alert include traded volume for a particular member being greater than a certain percentage of the total volume traded for the scrip and the traded price being greater than a certain percentage of the last trade price.

According to SEBI once an alert is generated, the system must be capable of generating a complete audit trail for all kinds deals (negotiated/ normal/institutional/trade for trade/spot) deals done by the brokers. The system must also be able to identify those member-brokers whose activity was responsible for the unusual activity in the stock for further inspection.

SEBI has also proposed ways to overcome false alerts. According to it, over and above the trading data, the exchange must be able to retrieve pertinent security-specific corporate action for the relevant period. This way, false alerts generated by, say, declaration of good results etc., can be ignored.

The data analysis segment would be complementary to the alert segment, wherein analytical information and graphs would be generated for scrips/members where unusual activity was observed.

The report generation segment would provide a report on an online basis with two kinds of reports. While the routine reports cover daily and settlement-wise reports, the special reports would be prepared on a case-to-case basis as an when required.

With a view to checking abnormal price variations of traded scrips on different stock exchanges, SEBI has directed all the exchanges to also maintain a weekly cap of 25 per cent in the band for scrips that are traded above par. Stating that the weekly band need not be applied on scrips traded below par, the regulatory body said that exchanges are free to fix daily price-bands at their own discretions.

5

REGULATIONS RELATING TO STOCK BROKERS

REGULATION BY SEBI OF STOCK BROKERS

Stock broking activity is regulated by the Securities and Exchange Board of India under the powers delegated to it under the Securities Contracts (Regulation) Act, 1956 and Government of India Stock-brokers and Sub-brokers Rules, 1992. Stock brokers could be individuals, partnerships or corporates. In the old exchanges, most of the brokers are proprietary in nature where as in the new exchanges they are corporate members.

Table 5.1 presents distribution of stock brokers registered with SEBI as on March 31, 2004 on the 23 exchanges. They numbered 9368, and of the total number corporate members constituted 40.43 per cent. Corporate membership rather than individual or proprietor form was highest of the total number of members at 88.97 per cent on NSE and 77.75 per cent at OTCEI. Mumbai lagged behind at 71.17 per cent. The Calcutta stock exchange has the highest number of brokers (980). NSE with 970 brokers ranks second in terms of number of brokers followed by OTCEI and BSE.

Powers of SEBI

The Securities and Exchange Board of India Act, 1992 setting up the Securities and Exchange Board of India (SEBI) has come into force from January 30, 1992. Under the provisions of the Act, it shall be the duty of SEBI to protect the interest of investors in securities and promote, development and regulate the securities market. To carry out its objectives SEBI has been vested with the following powers:

(a) regulating the business in stock exchanges and any other securities markets;

(b) registering and regulating the working of stock brokers, sub-brokers, share transfer agent; bankers to an issue, merchant bankers, underwriters, portfolio managers, investment advisors and such other intermediaries who may be associated with securities markets in any manner.

(c) registering and regulating the working of collective investment schemes, including mutual funds;

(d) promoting and regulating self-regulatory organizations;

(e) prohibiting fraudulent and unfair trade practices relating to securities markets;

Table 5.1: Distribution of Stock Brokers (2003-04)

Stock Exchange	*2003-04*		
	Total Brokers	*Corporate Brokers*	*Corporate Brokers as a Percentage of Total Brokers*
Ahmedabad	323	152	47.06
Bangalore	242	116	47.93
BSE	673	479	71.17
Bhubaneshwar	229	18	7.86
Calcutta	980	200	20.41
Cochin	468	82	17.52
Coimbatore	177	61	34.46
Delhi	373	215	57.64
Guwahati	172	5	2.91
Hyderabad	305	119	39.02
Inter-connected Stock Exchange	633	248	39.18
Jaipur	532	19	3.57
Ludhiana	297	85	28.62
Madhya Pradesh	179	35	19.55
Madras	182	70	38.46
Magadh	195	22	11.28
Mangalore	105	10	9.52
NSE	970	863	88.97
OTCEI	867	675	77.85
Pune	197	59	29.95
Saurashtra Kutch	437	86	19.68
UPSE	514	104	20.23
Vadodara	318	64	20.13
Total	9,368	3,787	40.43

Source: SEBI, *Annual Report*, 2003-04.

(f) promoting investors' education and training of intermediaries in securities markets;

(g) prohibiting insider trading in securities;

(h) regulating substantial acquisition of shares and takeover of companies;

(i) calling for information from, undertaking inspection, conducting inquiries and audits of the stock exchanges and intermediaries and self regulatory organizations in the securities markets;

(j) performing such functions and exercising such powers under the Securities Contracts (Regulation) Act, 1956 as may be delegated to it by the Central Government[14];

(k) levying fees or other charges for carrying out its work;

(l) conducting research for the above purposes; and

(m) performing such other functions as may be prescribed.

Powers Delegated to SEBI under SC(R) Act

Under the SEBI Act some of the powers exercised by Central Government under SC(R) Act 1956 have now been vested with SEBI. They relate to

(a) powers to call for periodical returns or direct enquiries to be made from any recognized stock exchange;

(b) grant approval to any recognized stock exchange to make bye-laws for the regulation and control of contracts;

(c) powers to make or amend bye-laws of recognized stock exchanges;

(d) licensing of dealers in securities in certain areas;

(e) powers to compel listing of securities by public companies;

(f) granting approval to amendments to the rules of a recognized stock exchange;

(g) powers to ask every recognized stock exchange to furnish to SEBI a copy of the annual report containing particulars as may be prescribed;

(h) powers to direct recognized stock exchanges to make rules;

(i) powers to supersede the governing body of a recognized stock exchange;

14. After the repeal of Capital Issues (Control) Act 1947 on 29.5.1992, SEBI has been given the necessary powers so far exercised by Controller of Capital Issues.

(j) powers to suspend business of any recognized stock exchange; and

(k) powers to prohibit contracts in certain cases.

Government of India: Stock Brokers and Sub-brokers Rules 1992

Under the SEBI Act, the Central Government issued a notification on August 20, 1992 laying down rules relating to stock brokers and sub-brokers.

Definition of Stock Broker

The rules define a stock broker as a member of stock exchange; and sub-broker as any person who acts on behalf of a stock broker as an agent or otherwise for assisting the investors in buying, selling or dealing in securities through such brokers.

Conditions for Grant of Certificate to Stock Broker

The rules stipulate that registration with SEBI is necessary for acting as broker or sub-broker. The conditions for grant of a certificate of registration to act as stock broker are,

(a) he holds the membership of a stock exchange;

(b) he shall abide by the rules, regulations and bye-laws of the stock exchange of which he is a member;

(c) in case of any change in the status and constitution, the broker shall obtain prior permission of SEBI to continue trading in securities;

(d) he shall pay the amount of fees for registration; and

(e) he shall take adequate steps for redressal of grievance of the investors within one month of the date of receipt of complaint and keep SEBI informed about the number, nature and other particulars of the complaints received from such investors.

Conditions for Grant of Certificate to Sub-broker

The conditions for grant of a certificate to sub-broker are,

(a) he is authorized in writing by a stock broker being a member of a stock exchange for affiliating himself in buying, selling or dealing in securities;

(b) he shall pay the fees;

(c) he shall take adequate steps for redressal of grievances of the investors within one month of the date of their receipt of the complaint and keep SEBI informed about the number, nature and other particulars of the complaints received; and

(d) in case of any change in the status and constitution, the sub-broker shall obtain prior permission of SEBI to trade in securities.

SEBI: Stock Brokers and Sub-brokers Regulations, 1992

The stock brokers and sub-brokers regulations were issued by SEBI through a notification on October 23, 1992 with the prior approval of the Central Government.

The regulations specify the procedure for registration of stock broker and sub-broker.

Registration of Stock Broker

The application for grant of a certificate has to be made in Form A through the stock exchange of which he is a member. The application must be forwarded by the exchange within 30 days to SEBI. SEBI may require the applicant to furnish further information or clarification regarding the dealings in securities and matters connected. SEBI may also require personal representation.

While considering the application, SEBI takes into account all matters relating to buying, selling or dealing in securities. It also considers whether the stock broker is eligible to be admitted as a member of a stock exchange, has the necessary infrastructure like adequate office space, equipment and manpower to effectively discharge his activities, past experience in securities business and is subjected to any disciplinary proceedings under the rules, regulations and bye-laws of stock exchange with respect to his business as a stock broker involving himself or any of his partners, directors or employees. On being granted a certificate in Form D, the stock broker has to abide by the code of conduct. The code of conduct lays down general rules, duty to investors and towards dealings with other stock brokers.

General Rules

A stock broker is expected to maintain high standards of integrity, promptitude and fairness in the conduct of his business. He is expected to exercise due skill, care, diligence and comply with statutory requirements and not to indulge in manipulation and malpractices.

Duty to the Investor

A stock broker shall execute orders at best available market price and not refuse to deal with small investors. He should promptly inform his client about the execution or non-execution of an order and make payment for sale and delivery of securities purchased. A contract note should be issued promptly. He is expected to maintain confidentiality about his client's investments. Stock brokers should not encourage sales or purchases of securities or furnish quotations, information and advice to earn brokerage and commission. Stock brokers are not expected to deal with clients who are in default with other stock brokers. Stock brokers should also disclose to clients whether he is acting as a principal or broker and avoid conflict of interest. Investment advice should not be given unless suitable on the basis of information given by the client about his financial situation, security holdings and investment objectives. Stock brokers should render fair, prompt and competent services to their clients. Every broker should disclose to his client whether he does client based business or proprietary trading as well.

Towards other Stock Brokers

A stock broker should cooperate with other brokers in comparing unmatched transactions, replacing documents declared bad delivery, protection of client's interests, and settlement of transactions. A stock broker should not advertise his business and induce through unfair means clients from other brokers. Finally, a stock broker shall not neglect or fail or refuse to submit required returns to SEBI and stock exchange and not make false or misleading statements in any such returns.

Registration Fees

Every stock broker shall pay registration fees of Rs. 5,000/- for each financial year where the annual turnover does not exceed Rs. 1 crore; where the turnover exceeds Rs. 1 crore during any financial year, Rs. 5,000 plus 1/100 of one percent of turnover in excess of Rs. 1 crore for each financial year. After expiry of five years from the date of initial registration, he shall pay a sum of Rs. 5,000/- for a block of five years commencing from sixth financial year after the grant of initial registration to keep his registration in future.

General Obligations and Responsibilities

1. Every stockbroker should keep and maintain the following books of accounts, records and documents;
   (a) register of transactions (sauda Book);
   (b) clients ledger;
   (c) general ledger;
   (d) journals;

(e) cash book;

(f) bank pass book;

(g) documents register of shares and securities received and delivered;

(h) members contract books showing details of all contracts entered into by him with other members of the same exchange or counterfoils or duplicates of memos of confirmation issued to such other member;

(i) counterfoils or duplicates of contract notes issued to clients;

(j) written consent of clients in respect of contracts entered into as principals;

(k) margin deposit book;

(l) register of accounts of sub-brokers; and

(m) an agreement with a sub-broker specifying the scope of authority and responsibilities of stockbroker and each sub-broker.

2. The stockbroker should inform SEBI the place where the books of accounts, records and documents are maintained and kept.
3. Stockbroker should furnish SEBI after close of each accounting period copy of the audited balance sheet and profit and loss account.

The books of account, records and documents should be preserved for a period of five years.

Inspection of Accounts, Records and Documents by SEBI

Inspection of accounts, records and documents may be undertaken by SEBI to ensure that they are maintained in the manner required and provisions of SEBI Act, rules regulations and SC(R) Act and the rules made thereunder are complied with, investigate into the complaints received from investor, other stockbrokers, sub-brokers or any person bearing on the activities of the stockbroker and investigate *suo-moto* in the interest of securities business or investor's interest into the affairs of the stockbrokers. SEBI can also appoint a qualified auditor to investigate into the books of account or affairs of the stockbroker.

The inspection may be undertaken after giving reasonable notice or without notice if investor's or public interest require. The stockbroker has to cooperate by producing all records and giving access to the premises. SEBI communicates the findings of inspection and gives the stockbroker an opportunity of being heard before action is taken.

Default

A stockbroker who fails to comply with any conditions of registration, contravenes any of the provisions of the SEBI Act, rules or regulations, contravenes the provisions of the SC(R) Act or the rules made thereunder, contravenes the rules, regulations of the stock exchange is liable to suspension of registration after an enquiry for a specified period or cancellation of registration.

The penalty of suspension may be imposed if a stockbroker violates the provisions of SEBI, rules and regulations, does not follow the code of conduct, fails to furnish information relating to his transactions in securities as required by SEBI, furnishes wrong or false information, does not submit periodical returns as required by SEBI, does not cooperate in an enquiry conducted by SEBI, fails to resolve the complaints of investors or fails to give satisfactory reply to SEBI in this behalf, indulges in manipulating or price rigging or cornering activities in the market, guilty of misconduct or improper business like or unprofessional conduct, deterioration in financial position which is not in the interest of investors or other stockbrokers, failure to pay fees, violation of conditions of registration and suspension of membership by the stock exchange.

Penalty of cancellation of registration is imposed if the stockbrokers violate regulations relating to insider trading or takeover, is guilty of fraud or convicted of a criminal offence and membership by the stock exchange is cancelled.

Suspension or cancellation order is issued only after enquiry with due notice. The stockbroker is given a reasonable opportunity to be heard. An appeal may be preferred to Central Government against the orders of SEBI.

Registration of Sub-Brokers

There were 12,817 sub-brokers registered in the 23 stock exchanges. Table 5.2 presents their distribution. The oldest exchange BSE has the largest number (51.5%) followed by NSE (36.8%). Between them they share almost nine-tenth of the sub-brokers. Some exchanges have no sub-brokers. Among the structural changes that have taken place in the capital market, the sub-broking community seems to be on the wane. An application in Form B for registration to SEBI should be accompanied by a recommendation letter from a stockbroker with whom he is affiliated along with two references including one from the banker should be submitted to the stock exchange of which the stock-broker with whom he is to be affiliated is a member. The stock exchange has to verify the information and certify that the applicant is eligible for registration. The stock exchange should forward the application within 30 days in the case of an individual. The applicant should be 21 years of age, should not be convicted of fraud or dishonesty and should have passed 12th standard or equivalent examination.

Table 5.2: Registered Sub-Brokers (2003-04)

Stock Exchange	***Sub-Brokers During the Year 2003-04***	
	No.	***Percentage to Total***
Ahmedabad	124	0.97
Bangalore	156	1.22
BSE	6,600	51.50
Bhubaneshwar	17	0.13
Calcutta	92	0.72
Cochin	42	0.33
Coimbatore	24	0.19
Delhi	363	2.83
Guwahati	4	0.03
Hyderabad	199	1.55
Inter-Connected Stock Exchange	3	0.02
Jaipur	34	0.27
Ludhiana	38	0.30
Madhya Pradesh	115	0.90
Madras	3	0.02
Magadh	1	0.01
Mangalore	5	0.04
NSE	4,717	36.81
OTCEI	25	0.20
Pune	161	1.26
Saurashtra Kutch	0	0.00
UPSE	19	0.15
Vadodara	73	0.57
Total	12,817	100.0

Source: SEBI, *Annual Report*, 2003-04.

If SEBI is satisfied that the sub-broker is eligible for registration a certificate in Form E is made and the stock exchange is informed.

Fees

The sub-broker has to pay a fee of Rs. 1000/- for each financial year for an initial period of five years. After the expiry of five years, the sub-broker should pay a fee of Rs. 500/- for each financial year as long as the certificate remains in force.

The sub-broker should abide by the code of conduct. He should maintain high standards of integrity, promptitude and fairness in the conduct of investment business and act with due skill, care and diligence.

Duty to the Investor

In regard to the investor, the sub-broker should execute orders at best market price and promptly finalize the transactions. Purchase or sale notes for all transactions entered into by him with his clients should be issued promptly. Scripwise split purchase or sale notes and similarly bills and receipts showing brokerage separately have to be issued. He can split contract notes issued by affiliated brokers clientwise and scripwise into different denominations. A sub-broker should not match purchase and sale orders of his clients. They should be routed through the member broker with whom the sub-broker is affiliated.

He should not commit breach of trust by disclosing confidential information about his clients. He should not encourage sales or purchases to earn brokerage and commission. A sub-broker is expected not to deal with defaulting clients. He should disclose to clients that he is acting as an agent and avoid conflict of interest. Investment advice should not be given unless suitable on the basis of information given by the client about his financial situation, security holdings and investment objectives. Sub-brokers should render fair, prompt and competent services to his client.

Towards Stock Brokers

A sub-broker should cooperate with his broker in comparing unmatched transactions, replacing documents declared as bad delivery, protection of clients interests and settlement of his transactions with his broker. A legal agreement specifying the rights and obligations of the sub-broker and principal broker should be executed. A sub-broker should not advertise his business and induce through unfair means clients from other brokers. Finally, a sub-broker shall not neglect or fail or refuse to submit returns to SEBI or the stock exchange and not make false or misleading statements in any such returns.

References

Bombay Stock Exchange; *Rules, Bye-laws and Regulations,* 1957.

Bombay Stock Exchange; "Listing Guidelines"-*Bombay Stock Exchange Directory.*

Government of India, *Securities Contracts (Regulation) Act,* 1956.

Government of India, *Securities Contracts (Regulation) Rules,* 1957.

Securities and Exchange Board of India, *The Stock Broker and Sub-broker Regulations,* 1992.

6

TRADING IN STOCK EXCHANGES

AUCTION MARKETS VS. BROKER-DEALER MARKETS

Trading in stock exchanges takes place either on the basis of the auction system on a trading floor which is order driven or customer driven or a broker-dealer market which is quote driven or dealer driven. Every one of the world's stock markets uses one of two trading systems or a hybrid of both. In an order driven system, customers buy and sell orders reach a central point where they are matched. In a quote driven system dealers compete to give customers the best price. Electronic trading simply carries out the same functions automatically. In order driven markets, it matches buyer and seller and in quote driven ones it finds for the customer the best price available. An example of an auction market which is order driven is New York Stock Exchange (NYSE); and of a broker dealer market which is quote driven or dealer driven is the over the counter market served by a computerized network called National Association of Security Dealers Automated Quotation System (NASDAQ). We have auction markets in general which are order driven at the stock exchanges except Bombay. Bombay has a hybrid market, auction market but quote driven. National Stock Exchange is an order driven market with fully automated screen based trading system.

Specialist's Role in Auction Markets

In the auction market, there is a single designated market maker (the specialist) and an auction system based on a current high bid-low offer. Those not meeting either of those prices may not participate in the auction. The auction system allows the buyer and seller to find a mutually agreeable price with no intervention of broker-dealers.

The buy and sell orders are automatically matched with specialists filling in the gap when an imbalance occurs. The specialist system emerged precisely because in a continuous auction market where brokers trade with each other, there is no guarantee of a simultaneous coincidence of buyer and seller. Specialists ensure greater liquidity because they are obliged to stand in the market at all times. The auction market is more transparent and when combined with monopoly specialists who provide liquidity for the shares, is more efficient.

Auction plus specialist market offers most protection to investors especially retail ones. In 90 per cent of the trades in NYSE buyers meet sellers directly and negotiate the best price.

Market Maker's Role in Broker-Dealer Market

On the other hand, broker dealer market such as the over the counter market is a negotiated market. Dealers who regularly buy and sell a particular security are said to make a market in that security much like the specialists on NYSE. There are no restrictions limiting the number of market makers in a given share. Competing market makers are obliged to quote prices through the system. Market makers offering the best price are assigned orders on a rotating basis. Prices are arrived at by dealers negotiating with other dealers in order to arrive at the best prices. Dealers make two sides (bid-offer) market by quoting a price they would pay a prospective seller (bid) or a price they would charge a prospective buyer (an offer or asking price). Competitively negotiated bid and asked prices are thus determined by 500 OTC market makers. Market makers for most of the active shares transmit their quotations electronically so that they would be visible to all other market participants. A quick scan of an electronic screen instantly reveals the best market for an order. Competitively negotiated bid and asked prices are thus determined by about 500 market makers.

The auction market and the broker dealer market depend for their effective functioning on specialists and market makers, respectively.

Specialists on NYSE

New York Stock Exchange has about 90 specialist firms who are members of the exchange and act as brokers or dealers in shares[15].

15. Since membership is restricted to individuals, the specialist firms are required to have one general partner (in case of firm or partnership) or voting stock holder (in the case of a corporation). Large specialist units have 15 to 30 members.

The specialists on the floor of exchange are members of one of the specialist firms. Specialists have a dual function representing customers buy and sell orders and trading on behalf of their own account. They buy and sell shares of one or more companies and help in maintaining a free and continuous market in the shares of companies in which they act as specialists. The specialists are expected to maintain a fair and orderly market for shares in which they act as specialists. In their capacity as brokers they execute orders for other brokers on a commission. In their capacity as dealers they act for their own accounts, profits and risks. As dealers they buy from the public when it offers shares for sale but other public bids for purchase are not available, and sells to the public when it bids but other public offers to sell are not available at or near the price of last transaction. The customers of the specialists are other members of the exchange, as specialists they do not transact business directly with the public.

Specialists are required to make a continuous market in shares assigned to them. They are expected to provide two sided market, by quoting a bid indicating the price at which they will purchase shares from a seller and an offer or asking price and a price at which they will sell shares to a buyer. Specialists act as brokers when they accept orders for execution from other members of the exchange. They provide a conduit of information electronically quoting and recording current bid and asked prices for the shares of companies assigned to them. This disseminates information about prices and supply and demand position for any share listed on NYSE. Most orders left with specialists are either limit or stop orders which are too far from the current market level. Specialists act as dealers when they buy or sell shares for their own account. Dealer function is played when necessary to maintain market. Specialists have to carry 4000 shares of each company.

Broker-Dealer Markets: Market Makers

To make a market means that the dealer creates and maintains a market in a security. A dealer is said to maintain a market in a security when he is known to be willing at all times to buy or sell that security, usually for his own account and risk at the prices he quotes in amounts at least equivalent to the security's trading unit. The dealer's quotations consist of his bid and asked or offer prices. The price a dealer will pay for a given security is called his bid. The price at which a dealer will sell a given security is called his asked price or offer. The difference between bid and asked prices in any quotation is the spread.

Quotes are displayed on NASDAQ terminals by market makers who are obliged to offer a continuous two-way market in all securities in which they are registered. They are also obliged to execute trades at their displayed price and size. There are on average 11 market makers for each listed security although for the most active shares this figure can be as high as 40 and low as two for the lesser traded issues. NASDAQ has 500 market makers. Transactions are reported within 90 seconds of execution.

A dealer may take a position in a security by buying for inventory (long position) or by selling securities that he has not yet purchased. A quotation at all time must include both sides of the market even though one side may be nonexistent.

Broker-Dealer

Broker-Dealer registered with SEC may buy and sell securities for his own account or risk, or as agent purchase and sell securities for the account and risk of other. Broker and agent mean the same. A broker-dealer can handle purchase orders

1. If he makes a market in a particular share a customer wants to buy, he can sell it out of his inventory.
2. When he gets the order, for a share in which he does not make a market he can act as agent and buy it from some other dealer who makes market in it or some one who owns the securities.
3. He can buy it for his own account and resell it.

Advantages of Broker-Dealer Markets (NASDAQ)

1. Bid and asked quotations are instantly provided to all market makers in a particular share as well as representative bid and asked quotations on 3000 different shares on NASDAQ.
2. Investors can be assured of the best execution of their order. They can be sure that the traders have checked all market makers in the share.
3. Traders can gauge market quickly.
4. Competition is stimulated.
5. Issuing companies stay on and do not move to floor stock exchanges as soon as they qualify.
6. Information to public on volume, indexes of OTC shares and individual trades is available.

Hybrid Market: Bombay Stock Exchange

Bombay stock market is a hybrid. It has an auction type of trading with bids and offers being made by open outcry and a quote driven system is prevalent. BSE was influenced by the pattern set by London Stock Exchange, which had an auction type of market with jobbers giving two way quotes. A jobber had no duty in London Stock Exchange to maintain an orderly and continuous market like the specialist at NYSE. Jobbers were acting on their own behalf and never as agents. Their income was derived from spread between bid and offer prices or by assuming a position in a particular share. As a result, large price discontinuities were common. Later in 1987 after the Big Bang London adopted the NASDAQ system and jobbers went out of the picture. Bombay Stock Exchange has an informal system of jobbers. SEBI has stipulated in 1993 that market makers should be appointed initially in scrips which are not included in the BSE, National Index. In London computerization and screen based trading had rendered jobbers redundant. But even in a screen based trading, market makers are required as NASDAQ has. London had to adopt a system of market makers for the thinly traded shares while retaining screen based system for actively traded shares.

Market Makers in Order Driven Markets in India

The exchanges in the rest of the country are mainly order driven markets with the buyers and sellers transacting directly with each other. Although this has the advantage of giving the investors a better price, growth of the markets has been hampered by a relatively high degree of volatility and illiquidity. SEBI has proposed a system of market makers on the exchanges at Bombay, Calcutta, Delhi and Madras in April 1993 on the recommendations of the exchange. Any member of the those stock exchanges can with prior approval of SEBI can become a market maker. He is approved by SEBI on the recommendation of the exchange after taking into account financial strength, volume of business done in the scrips he chooses to become market maker, his total turnover for the corresponding period, turnover as a jobber if he is operating as jobber in any of the scrips, defaults by the member, timely payment of margins, disciplinary action and pending arbitration. The list of scrips for which he chooses to act as market maker has to be furnished and approved by SEBI.

Each market maker approved by SEBI should make a market for a minimum of five companies shares. The shares should not be included in

BSE National Index. Market makers are required to acquire atleast 30,000 shares. Two market makers in each stock exchange would be approved. The jobbers working at present in different scrips could continue to do so.

Under the scheme, the market maker would be required to give a continuous two way quote along with the depth (number of tradable lots) for the scrips in which he is authorised to operate as a market maker. He cannot vary his quote unless he concludes at least one transaction at that quote during the day. The spreads would be determined by the market. Separate trading counters will be provided to market makers on the floor of exchange.

If the market maker acts as a broker as well, he will have to maintain separate books of accounts for market making and broking which have to be reported daily to the exchange in a segregated manner.

The market maker has been exempted from the margin requirements for trading in the scrips in which he is making the market. Credit for market makers approved by SEBI will be provided by commercial banks against the collateral of securities (other than the scrips in which market making operations are undertaken). RBI has issued a detailed set of guidelines on August 5, 1993 authorizing the banks to prescribe normal prudential margins based on their commercial judgement.

Impact of Advances in Communications Technology

The exchange traded markets such as stock and futures exchanges are shedding their trading floors. The open outcry trading method of futures exchanges is threatened by computer. Computers save costs and electronic exchanges are between two and ten times cheaper than their open outcry rivals. Open outcry exchanges suit some products like spread trade better[16]. Spread traders need to make sure that they are not net buyers or sellers but are merely taking a bet on the spread between the prices of different contracts. Spread trades involving half a dozen or more contracts at exactly the same time can best be done in trading pits. The advantage cannot however be sustained since computers are getting better at mimicking the flexibility of pit trading. Further electronic exchanges have their computers network which allows the exchange to reach new trading members who are beyond the grasp of open outcry exchanges.

The online trading of National Stock Exchange and BSE have the advantage of reaching remote trading members.

---

16. Spread trade in short term interest rate futures consists of selling a three month interest rate future of delivery in June and buying equal amount of September contract.

New modular systems like the one at London's futures electronic exchange, [London International Financial Futures and Options Exchange (LIFFE)] permits exchange members to plug their own trading systems into LIFFE or use a third party's system such as Reuters or Internet to route orders.

Trading of Government Securities

Trading in government securities on nation-wide anonymous, order driven and screen based trading system of the stock exchanges, was launched. India is the first jurisdiction, which allows government securities to trade through screen based, automated, anonymous, price time priority system on the stock exchanges. World over the market is limited to select players and is solely a negotiated/telephone market. All government securities, as notified by RBI from time to time, would be traded along with the equity segment of the eligible exchanges where the minimum order size of 10 units of rupees one hundred each and multiplies there of and the traded price would be inclusive of interest.

Internet Trading

Internet trading is now (1998) offered by more than 70 on-line brokerages in America. The number of Americans investing by using the internet are about 5 million. On-line trades number 26 million and accounted for forty per cent of all retail trades. Internet trading is quite cheap offering \$20 trades compared with \$60 plus charged by traditional brokerages. The Internet brokers are trying to augment their income by offering investors research and financial services such as bill payments by setting MP websites, as "Destination E Trade." The internet could force margins down across all brokerage business especially the full service brokerage.

SEBI has allowed the Internet to be used as an order routing system (ORS) through registered stockbrokers on behalf of clients for execution of trades. ORS would be compatible with existing screen based electronic trading capabilities. By March 2000 Internet trading is expected to commence. BSE expects that some stockbrokers would offer net trading facilities to their clients in January 2000. The move to an electronic trading system has resulted in transparency in trades, better price discovery and lower transaction costs. The operational efficiency of the market has improved through faster execution of trades.

Margin Trading

Margin accounts or margin trading is in vogue in the U.S.A. It is trading with borrowed resources, funds or securities and is an important element in the integration of money and capital markets. Investors can open a cash account or a margin account with a member firm. In the case of cash account cash is payable for any securities purchased. In case of margin accounts investors have to furnish more information because they are applying for permission to buy securities on credit. NYSE requires a minimum initial deposit of $2000. While it is enough for Merrill Lynch, Salomon Brothers and Goldman Sachs require $ 1 million to open an account. Through margin trading a customer gains leverage by the use of borrowed funds. It arises in a market where there is insufficient flow of supply and demand forces due to lack of liquidity. Margin trading injects liquidity which adds depth to the market and facilitates price discovery. Margin accounts can also be used for short sales and naked call writing and spreads. Margin accounts are also used as a device to procure quick and easy loans when needed than for leverage. J.K. Galbraith had mentioned margin loans as a major cause for the gravity of the market downturn that brought forth the Great Depression. A low margin requirement in stock index futures was cited by Brady Commission as a reason for 1987 crash. Margin loans reduce the credit available for more legitimate uses, i.e., it affects the way credit is allocated.

When investors buy securities on margin, they buy some shares with cash and borrow from the broker to pay for additional shares, using the paid shares as collateral. The margin customer has to sign a margin agreement, pledging securities as loan collateral. To lend the clients margined securities, the brokers also ask the customers to sign a stock-consent form. Margins are regulated by Federal Reserve which stipulates 55 per cent of margin.

Member brokers are allowed to provide margin trading facility to their clients in the cash segment since April 1, 2004.

Eligibility of securities for margin trading facility is to confined those with mean impact cost of less than or equal to one and traded at least 80% of the days (+/– 5%) during the previous 18 months.

Corporate member brokers should have a net worth of at least Rs.3 crores to participate. Prior permission has to be obtained by the broker to extend the facility. Funds for the purpose may be brokers own or funds borrowed from commercial banks or replaced NBFCs. A broker can extend the facility up to 5 times his net worth. Total exposure should not exceed borrowed funds and 50% of net worth. Exposure to a single client should not exceed 10% of total exposure of broker.

Initial and maintenance margin for the client is 50% and 40% respectively which has to be paid in cash. Initial margin is based on transaction value and maintenance margin on market value on the last closing price. Margin calls are made if the client's margin trading account falls below the maintenance margin. The broker can liquidate the securities if the client does not meet his obligations. Brokers have to maintain separate client wise accounts on the basis of margin trading with depositories which may be inspected by SEBI and Stock Exchange.

To carry on margin trading and/or short sales securities lending and borrowing facility by approved intermediaries securities lending and borrowing facility is formulated. The registered intermediaries may borrow securities on behalf of the member for the propose of meeting short falls, subject to conditions such as maximum period of seven days.

SEBI modified on March 4, 2004 the margin trading and securities lending and borrowing scheme with respect to securities eligible for margin trading facility, margin requirements, no objection certificate and procedures of securities lending and borrowing.

Trading Procedures

There are several kinds of orders used in trading shares. While investors and brokers may use only a few kinds of orders familiarity with all kinds of orders is useful. Such knowledge would enable them to know their rights and liabilities and the results to expect from different orders. Sometimes individual stock exchanges may not allow certain types of order as is the case when heavy market activity precludes the use of certain types of orders. Orders may be classified according to (1) size, (2) type of transaction, (3) price limits (4) time limits and (5) special types. With a view to improve market microstructure SEBI prohibited 'All or none' or 'Minimum fill order' facility in the trading system (1999).

(1) By Size of Orders

Round lots and odd lots. A round lot is one for the limit trading or some multiple thereof and odd lot is one less than number of shares required for trading. Round lots can be of 10, 50, 100 depending on the unit of trading and odd lots can be from 1-9, 11-49 and 51-99. Odd lot trading on a per share basis runs higher than that of round lots.

(2) By Type of Transactions

Buy or sell order is placed when a rise in market price is anticipated. Such an order may represent the establishment of a new position or may cover a short position. In the first case, the customers position is said be long and in the second, the position has gone from short to flat.

Similarly sell orders may be for selling either long or short. Selling long would constitute a liquidation of a long position. Selling short is in anticipation of a price decline.

SHORT SELLING

Nature

In a market investors can assume a long position involving purchase and holding the asset or a short position in which short seller sells an asset he does not own to a second party who takes a long position in the asset. Short sales are used by speculators, risk averters, arbitragers and other professionals. Short selling has acquired notoriety in India because it is employed as a speculative device. The critics of short selling view it as a potential risk that can destabilise the market. The exponents consider short selling as a desirable feature of the securities market as it improves efficiency of the market through price discovery and enhances liquidity of the related securities. Indeed, most of the securities market regulators world-wide have recognised short selling as a legitimate investment activity and permitted short selling transactions in their respective jurisdictions with adequate safeguards to prevent any abusive/ manipulative market practices.

Definition

The Securities and Exchange Commission (SEC) of U.S.A. defines short sale as any sale of a security which the seller does not own or any sale which is consummated by the delivery of a security borrowed by or for the account of the seller. The short seller may have to borrow stock because he does not own it or he may own it but prefers to sell it short. The later transactions are called sales against the box because sellers have the securities in their safe deposit box or account and can actually deliver them at the time of sale but choose not to. SEC is of the view that although the majority of short sales are legal, abusive short sale practices are illegal. The International Organisation of Securities Commissions (IOSCO) has reviewed short selling and securities lending practices across markets and has recommended transparency of short selling, rather that prohibit it. Many emerging markets like Hong Kong, Korea, Japan, Singapore etc., have permitted short selling in their respective jurisdictions on certain designated securities subject to disclosure of such transactions and tick rules which prohibit short selling transactions during a falling market.

Short Sales for Speculation

Short selling is used to describe the practice of selling stock, delivery of which is to be effected by borrowing shares. When a share is sold short, the short seller expects the price to fall and wants to profit from that price fall. Short sales are used by bearish speculators in search of profits from price decline. Short position is also used to create another new position that is negatively correlated with the existing position in order to reduce risk in the aggregate position. The practice is of particular importance to specialists, arbitragers and other professionals. Short sales are used by speculators, risk averters and arbitragers.

There is no distinction between naked and covered sales; and naked short sales show up as settlement shortages. Naked shorting can cross the time however, if a trader does not intend to borrow shares to settle the trade.

Constraints on Short Sale

Short sales can, however, be made only on an 'up-tick' that is a trade in which the stock's price was bid up. When a cash dividend is paid on stock while on loan to short seller, the short seller must pay the dividend to the third party share owner who lent the shares. Short selling may also involve a deposit of 100 per cent of the value of borrowed shares as collateral to protect the third party who lent the shares. There could be delays until the short seller enjoys any liquidity the position may generate. Finally, the short seller can be involuntarily 'forced out' of his position any time if the third party who lent the shares demands them back.

Short Position for Hedging

Apart from the motive of speculative gain from a short term price fall, the increased use of stock index and other forms of arbitrage trading abroad had created new uses for short sale. Short sales are used as hedge against possible losses. Put and call option traders, foreign exchange dealers, futures contract traders and security investors use hedging tactics to limit their risk exposure. Hedging is undertaken when an investor both buys and sells the same or similar asset at the same time.

Francis defines hedging, "as arranging for two different positions such that the potential loss from one of the positions tends to be, more or less, offset by profits from other position. Alternatively hedging can be defined as the establishment of offsetting long and short positions in order to diminish the loss that could, result from an adverse price movement."[17]

17. Francis, John Clark, *Investment: Analysis and Management*, McGraw Hill Inc. 1991, p. 394.

A perfect hedge requires that equal rupee amount must be held in both long and short positions and the purchase for the long position must be identical to the sales price for short sale. A perfect hedged position is one when the profits and losses from short and long position sum up to zero at any value the market price may attain[18]. Perfect hedges are created by risk averters. Risk averters seek to reduce their risk and are willing to give up an opportunity to earn gains in order to limit their possible losses.

Short Position for Arbitrage

Short position or a hedge is also held to carry an arbitrage. Arbitrage is similar to hedge because the arbitrager and hedger buy and sell either the same or similar items. Arbitrage can be defined as simultaneously buying long and selling short the same (or different but related) assets in an effort to profit from unrealistic price differentials. It can take place in the same or different markets. Arbitrage is profitable when the same security is sold at different prices in different markets. They buy it in the market where its price is lowest and sell in the market where the stock's price is highest. The economic law of one price requires that any given moment in time, identical goods should sell at identical prices everywhere in the world. Transaction costs, "frictions" that slow up arbitrage however erode arbitrage profits.

The measures to contain short selling include asking short sellers to declare their position on a daily basis and authorising stock exchanges to impose margins they consider appropriate on short sales with effect from 29-11-1996. In June 1998 short sales were banned temporarily in response to market volatility. SEBI removed the restrictions on short sales with effect from July 6, 1998. It was reintroduced in March 2001. After introduction of rolling settlement in July 2001, the ban was withdrawn on short sales by retail investors.

The secondary market advisory committee which reviewed the issue recommended in 2006 that,

- Institutional investors who are currently prohibited, should be permitted to short sell;
- Institutional investors should not indulge in day-trading;
- Naked short selling should not be permitted and all investors would be required to mandatorily honour the obligation of delivering the securities at the time of settlement;

18. *Ibid*, p. 395

- The stock exchanges should frame a uniform penalty structure and take appropriate action against the brokers for failure to deliver securities at the time of settlement which would act as a sufficient deterrent against naked short selling;
- In the absence of a vibrant market for securities lending and borrowing, short selling may not work effectively. Therefore, a full fledged securities lending and borrowing scheme must be put in place to provide the necessary impetus for short selling.
- To begin with, short selling may be permitted only in those stocks in which derivative products are available.
- Institutional investors would be obligated to disclose upfront at the time of placement of order whether the transaction is a short sale and demonstrate their ability to borrow securities to the satisfaction of the broker. However, the retail investors would be permitted to make a similar disclosure before the end of the trading hours on the transaction day.
- To ensure sound audit trail, all stock brokers should be mandated to maintain sufficient documentation regarding the ability of their clients to borrow and deliver securities at the time of settlement.
- Margin on short selling transactions by the institutional investors should be similar to those executed by the retail investors.
- Lending and borrowing transactions should be executed on an automated screen based platform which enables real time matching of the demand and supply.
- Stock exchange should disseminate the information on lending and borrowing transactions to the general public.

Consequent to the recommendations SEBI issued revised guidelines on 22-03-07 permitting FIIS, mutual funds and other intitutions to short sell stocks.

Till now, institutions took positions in the futures and options (F&O) market to go short. Once the new guidelines are in place, they will be in a position to short-sell even in the spot or cash market. While this may deepen the market and improve liquidity, a lot will depend on the mechanism through which the investor going short borrows the shares to meet his commitment. Just like an investor borrows money from a bank to buy stock, he should be in a position to borrow stocks from other entities to sell in the market. Understandably, there will be costs of borrowing like margins and interest charge. The system will take off only if such lending and borrowing mechanism is easy, and the cost is affordable.

Short-selling will also enable institutions to go short on scrips that are not included in the F&O list.

Further, they will be in a position to gain from transactions like reverse arbitrage (when the spot rate is more than futures price). Currently, only the retail investor can do an intra-day short-selling in the spot market — this can be a blank short-sell where the investor sells the shares even without owning them.

However, an institution cannot sell shares unless it owns the stock. So, what it will be allowed to do is borrow the stock (from a depository), sell it in the market and buy it back before market close to return the stock to the lender. Once the borrowing mechanism is implemented, the institution can carry forward this short position as long as regulation permits. The market participants feel that this is a move in the right direction. This will enable foreign institutional investors and domestic institutions to hedge their risks. It will also help contain volatility and create a deeper market.

(3) Price Limits

(i) Market Order

Market order is to be executed at the best possible price as soon as the order reaches the trading floor of the exchange. They are executed immediately. Market orders account for half of the volume and are easily executed. The advantages of the order are speed and certainty since they are given priority in execution. Any delay may involve a change of price and would constitute missing the market.

(ii) Limit Orders

Customer sets a price in advance at which he desires to trade. The order is to be executed at the limit or better. In this type of order one can buy at less or sell at more than the market price prevailing when the order was placed. The disadvantage of the order is that it may miss the market. Price or limit orders have a definite relationship to market. Limit order to buy is at or below current market price and sell above market price.

Limit orders are most popular after market orders and account for 50 per cent of value.

(4) Time Limits

All orders are day orders unless specified. Other orders are week orders, month orders or open orders.

Open orders or GTC (Good Until Cancelled) are used when investors believe that they will get the share at a specific price they have in mind. GTC orders have to be confirmed once a month or quarter.

(5) Special Type of Orders

They are designed to either protect a customer's existing profit or limit potential losses. They are in the nature of a suspended order coming into effect if the share touches or passes by certain price. Price used on a stop order bears a relationship to the market price that is exactly opposite that or limit order. The danger of the order is that the investor runs the risk of being whip sawed, selling a security with a future of long price appreciation in a temporary decline.

The order could be used for protection for the customers existing profit on a long purchase or protection of short sellers existing profit on short sale. Preventive use would be reduction of loss on a long purchase or reduction of loss on short sale.

(i) **Stop Orders and Limit Orders:** They are placed on different sides of the market. Limit order to buy is placed below the market and reverse to sell. Limit never becomes market when the limit is reached. The stop order always does. Stop order may cause avoidable loss; it may possibly be executed at some distance away from the stop price; and stop orders if accumulated may cause a sharp break in price of an issue and exchange will suspend stop order when the traders need most protection.

Stop limit orders to sell are used by share owners. It is effective as soon as there is a sale at the stop price or lower and then it is executed if possible at the limit or higher. The orders specify the stop price and the limit price the customer is willing to buy or sell. The customer must be willing to run the risk that the share will not reach the limit price, resulting in no trade.

In a falling market, the order has more chance of execution under the stop price than at the stop price or higher.

A stop limit order to buy is the reverse of sell. It is used by short sellers. These orders in a falling market are dangerous when the objective should be to minimize losses.

(ii) **On the Opening:** On the opening, refers to first sales of the share being bought or sold and not to opening of the exchange. Purpose is tactical. If trader believes that share will move in an anticipated direction immediately after the opening and if it does not, position should not be taken.

(iii) On the Close: The order is always a market order. A seller may believe that market will close on a strong note. If anticipated rise does not materialize, the trader may sell on close rather than remain in the market. On close has to be filled within 30 seconds of closing.

(iv) Discretionary Order: In a discretionary order customer gives latitude to the broker to fill the given order. Prior written authorization has to be there.

(v) Limited Discretion: In limited discretion prior verbal authorization indicating time and price is necessary. The second form of limited discretion directs the floor broker to use his judgement on floor conditions at the time of entry. This type of order is popular with institutional trade.

(vi) Immediate or Cancel: Immediate or cancel order specifies a price and demands execution or cancellation immediately. The trade may fill as much as possible and cancel the remainder.

(vii) Fill or Kill: This type of order is filled or cancelled immediately. No partial filling of order is envisaged. SEBI has prohibited on 13.1.1999 stock exchanges from allowing the 'All or None' 'Minimum Fill Order' facility in their trading system.

(viii) All or None: In this type of order a price is specified but requires the filling of entire order.

(ix) Do Not Reduce (DNR): A limit order to buy or sell is reduced automatically when a share goes ex-dividend. But some investors do not care how it is reduced. They want the order to be filled and mark it DNR (do not reduce).

(x) Alternative: The order may be for buy one of the two specified shares at limits below current market price. Very often both can be filled. Brokers do not accept alternative order because the shares may be traded at different areas of an exchange floor. Alternative order can also take the form of OCO (order cancels order or one cancels the other). Fill one and cancel the other or sell at X (limit) or X-l stop.

(xi) Contingent Orders: The order instructs broker to do some thing only after something else has been done. The order may be for sell a share at one price and when sold, immediately to buy another.

(xii) A Switch: A switch or swap order is a variation of contingent order but specifies a price difference rather than one or more price levels. Sell one and buy another at specified price difference per share or more. Brokers are responsible for filling them properly.

(xiii) Scale: Customers who wish to buy multiple lots of shares in a market they regard as bottoming output in series of bids at specified difference.

If the price does not reach the bottom, the order would not be completely filled. The customer would, however, get the order partly filled. The order may also specify scale up from the fill.

(xiv) Stop-Loss: To help investors SEBI has directed that 'stop loss' should be provided by all the exchanges having on line trading system. It would help investors to limit their losses.

(xv) Cash: A share may be sold for cash. Such shares are delivered the same day. Cash transactions are used to adhere to deadlines for ex-dividend or ex-bonus.

(xvi) Cancel Order: There are two type of cancel orders. First straight cancel or cancel former order. Straight cancel cancels the previous orders and cancel former order also cancels previous order but is replaced by a new order with some alteration in character.

Trading in Penny Stocks

In India, stocks with a face value of Rs. 10 or less and market capitalisation of less than or equal to Rs. 200 crore, quoting at less than the face value, are generally referred to as "penny stocks" or "small cap stocks." In the recent times, SEBI has been keeping a close watch on the trading of such stocks. Following suspicion, SEBI initiated quick and rapid investigation into several such scrips and entities that were active in the trading of such scrips. In these companies, generally a common *modus operandi* was noticed. It was observed that these companies have been making a flurry of seemingly price sensitive announcements detailing proposed corporate developments, status of business, projects and status thereof, corporate actions such as dividend, bonus, stock split etc., which were not mandated under the law. It was also noticed that the promoter shareholding in several such companies decreased following such announcements. This indicates that promoters took advantage of the price rise and benefited from it. To protect the investors' interests and ensure the orderly functioning of the stock markets. SEBI passed interim *ex parte* orders, pending investigation in respect of transactions in such scrips against Minal Engineering Ltd., Interlink Financial Services Ltd., Konkan Tyres, Prime Property Development Corp. Ltd., Ind Tra Deco Ltd., Mega Corporation Ltd., Eltrol Ltd., Karuna Cables Ltd. and Millennium

Cybertech Industries Ltd. Following initiation of action by SEBI, there was a sharp decrease in the trading volume of penny stocks.

Rolling Settlement

In the dematerialized shares rolling system on T + 2, basis exists. Since July 1997 the rolling settlement has been in place at NSE on a set of demat stocks. OTCEI had abandoned it after operating it for a short while since it was found to be too rigorous. In a rolling system trades are netted on a daily basis. The actual pay-in/delivery may take place later after a specified number of days 5 days in the case of T + 2 settlement but the position cannot be carried over to the next day. Rolling settlements are quicker. Speculation is limited to a day rather than one week. The benefit of rolling settlement are:

- reduction of risk since each trading day's position would come up for settlement.
- the process of price formation in the cash market would improve considerably.
- the anomalies of the present system in which the prices in the cash and forward market are mixed up would be avoided.

The prerequisite for rolling settlement however is dematerialization. After setting up of National, Securities Depositories Limited, it has become possible to introduce (April 1, 2003) T + 2-settlement in dematerialized shares.

Compulsory rolling settlement in 10 scrips outside the ones eligible for carry forward and subject to compulsory demat was introduced by SEBI on January 10, 2000 on stock exchanges which are connected to the depositories. Intra day squaring of open positions are allowed. But the open positions at the end of the trading day can be frozen for settlement at the end of the prescribed period for rolling settlement. Irrespective of time period, T + l, T + 2 or T + 5 there would be a settlement every day which could act as a check on the influence of speculative factors on prices. Since rolling settlement involves the conversion of the market into a cash market, there is no mechanism to introduce speculators who provide the bulk of the volume.

Bargains

While there are four types of bargains, spot delivery (delivery and payment on the same day), hand delivery, special delivery and for clearing (delivery and payment through a clearing house), all trading is basically conducted as hand delivery contracts, for delivery and payment within T + 2 days or on the date stipulated which is not more than 3 days following the date of contract.

Screen Based Electronic Trading

The open outcry trading system has been replaced by on line screen based electronic trading in all the 23 stock exchanges trading terminals exist.

Straight Through Processing (STP)

The capture and processing of transactions at one pass, first deal to final settlement, is called STP. It will obviate the need for manual entry and reentry of data of trade particulars which is time consuming and prone to errors. STP requires messaging standards by market participants, electronization of contract notes and connectivity among the market participants. SEBI introduced STP with effect from December 2, 2002 on a voluntary basis. To make the trading system efficient and less time consuming it was made compulsory for all institutional trades from April 1, 2004.

References

Bombay Stock Exchange, *Technology Perspective*, Bombay, 1991.

Loll, Leo Mand Buckley, Julian G., *The Over the Counter Securities Market*, Third Edition, Prentice Hall Inc. Englewood Cliffs, N.J. 1973.

Mayya M.R., "Indian Stock Markets", *Handbook of Articles from the Stock Exchange Review*, Bombay.

Stock Exchange, Bombay, January, 1992.

Teweles, Richard J., Bradley Edward S. and Teweles Ted M., *The Stock Market*, 6th Edition, John Wiley & Sons Inc., New York, 1992.

Uli barri, Carlos A and Schatz bery John, "Liquidity Costs: Screen based trading versus open outcry", *Review of Financial Economics"*, 12(2003), 381-396.

APPENDIX – 6.1

TRADING ON BOLT SYSTEM AT BSE

Trading on the BOLT System is conducted from Monday to Friday between 9:55 a.m. and 3:30 p.m. The scrips traded on the system have been classified into 'A', 'B1', 'B2', 'T', 'S', 'TS', 'F', 'G' and 'Z' groups. The Exchange has for the guidance and benefit of the investors have classified the scrips in the Equity Segment into 'A', 'B1', 'B2', 'T', 'S', 'TS' and 'Z' groups on certain qualitative and quantitative parameters which include number of trades, value traded, etc. The 'F' Group represents the Fixed Income Securities. The 'T' Group represents scrips which are settled on a trade to trade basis as a surveillance measure. The 'S' Group represent scrips forming part of the "BSE-Indonext" segment. The 'TS' Group consists of scrips in the "BSE" segment which are settled on a trade to trade basis as a surveillance measure. Trading in Govt. Securities for retail investors is done under 'G' group. The Exchange also provides a facility to the market participants for on-line trading of odd-lot securities in physical form. With effect from December 31, 2001, trading in all securities listed in equity segment of the Exchange takes place in Compulsory Rolling Settlement (CRS) segment.

This facility of selling physical shares in compulsory demat scrips is called an Exit Route Scheme. This facility can also be used by investors for selling up to 500 shares in physical form in respect of scrips of companies where trades are required to be compulsorily settled by an investors in demat mode.

Listed Securities

The securities of companies which have signed Listing Agreement with the Exchange are traded at the Exchange as "Listed Securities". Baring a few scrips, all scrips traded in the Equity Segment at the Exchange fall in this category.

Permitted Securities

To facilitate the market participants to trade in securities of the companies which are actively traded on other Regional Stock Exchanges but are not listed on the Exchange, the Exchange has in April 2002, decided to permit trading in such securities as "Permitted Securities" provided they meet the relevant norms specified by the Exchange.

Tick Size

Tick size is the minimum difference in rates between two orders on the same side, i.e., buy or sell, entered on the system for a scrip. Trading in scrips listed on the Exchange is done with the tick size of 5 paise.

However, in order to increase the liquidity and enable the market participants to put orders at finer rates, the Exchange has reduced size from 5 paise to 1 paise in case of units of mutual funds, securities traded in "F" group and equity shares having closing price Rs.15/- on the last trading day of the calendar month. Accordingly, the tick size in various scrips quoting upto Rs.15/- is revised on the first trading day of month. The tick size so revised on the first trading day of month remains unchanged. During the month end prices of scrips undergo change.

Computation of Closing Price of Scrips in the Cash Segment

The closing price of scrips is computed by the Exchange on the basis of weighted average price of all trades executed during 30 minutes of the continuous trading session. However, if there is no trade recorded during the last 30 minutes, then the last traded scrip in the continuous trading session is taken as the official closing price.

Compulsory Rolling Settlement (CRS) Segment

As per the directive by SEBI, all transactions in all groups of securities in the Equity Segment and Fixed Income securities listed on the Exchange are required to be settled on T+2 basis w.e.f. April 1, 2003. The settlement calendar, which indicates the dates of various settlement related activities, is drawn by the Exchange in advance and is circulated among the market participants. Under rolling settlements, the trades done on a particular day are settled after a given number of business days. A T+2 settlement means that the final settlement of transactions done on T, i.e., trade day by exchange of monies and securities between the buyers and sellers respectively takes place on second business day (excluding Saturday, Sunday, Bank and Exchange trading holidays) day. The transactions in securities of companies which have made arrangements for dematerialization of their securities are settled in demat mode on T+2 on net basis, i.e., buy and sell positions of a member-broker in the same scrip are netted and the net quantity is required to be settled. However, transactions in securities of companies, which are in "Z" group are settled only on gross basis and the facility of netting buy and sell transactions in such scrips is not available. The Exchange has introduced a new segment named "BSE Indonext" w.e.f. January 7, 2005. "S" group consists of scrips from "B2" group on BSE and companies exclusively listed on regional stock exchanges having capital of Rs.3 crores to Rs.30 crores. All settlement segment are done through BOLT system under S group. The transactions in 'F' group securities representing "Fixed Income Securities" and "G" group representing Government Securities for investors are also settled at the Exchange on T+2 basis. In case of Rolling Settlements, pay-in and pay-out of both funds and securities is completed on the same day. The following table summarizes the scrips in the trading and settlement cycle for scrips under CRS:

Day	***Activity***
T	Trading on BOLT and daily downloading of statements showing details of transactions and margins at the end of trading day. Downloading of provisional securities and funds obligation statements by member-brokers. 6A/7A* entry by the member-brokers/ confirmation by the custodians.
T+1	Confirmation of 6A/7A data by the custodians up to 11:00 a.m. Downloading of final securities and funds obligation statements by members
T+2	Pay-in of funds and securities by 11:00 a.m. and pay-out of funds and securities by 1:30 p.m. The member-brokers are required to submit the pay-in instructions for funds and securities to banks and depositories respectively by 10:30 a.m.
T+3	Auction on BOLT at 11:00 a.m.
T+4	Auction pay-in and pay-out of funds and securities by 12:00 noon and 1:30 p.m. respectively.

Thus, the pay-in and pay-out of funds and securities takes places on the second business day (*i.e.*, excluding Saturday, Sunday and Exchange trading holidays) of the day of the execution of the trade.

Settlement

Pay-in and Pay-out for 'A', 'B1', 'B2', 'T', 'S', 'TS', 'C', 'F', 'G' & 'Z' group of securities

The trades done on BOLT/Exchange by the members in all the securities in CRS are now settled on the Exchange by payment and delivery of securities on T+2 basis. All deliveries of securities are required to be routed through the Clearing House.

The Pay-in/Pay-out of funds based on the money statement and that of securities based on Delivery Order/Receive Order issued by Exchange are settled on T+2 day.

Securities Pay-out

In case of demat securities, the same are credited by the Clearing House in the Pool/ Principal Accounts of the member-broker Exchange has also provided a facility to the member-brokers for transfer of pay-out securities directly to the clients' beneficiation accounts without routing the same through their Pool/Principal accounts in NSDL/CDSL. For this, the concerned member-broker required to give a client wise break up file which is uploaded by the member-brokers from their offices to the Clearing House by the break up given by the member-brokers, the Clearing House instructs depositories, viz., CDSL & NSDL to credit the security Beneficiary Owners (BO) Accounts of the clients. In case delivery of securities received from one depository is to be credited account in the other depository, the Clearing House does an inter depository transfer to give effect to such transfers.

In case of physical securities, the Receiving Members are required to collect the same from the Clearing House on the pay-out.

Funds Payout

The bank accounts of the members having pay-out of funds are credited by the Clearing House with the Clearing Banks on the itself.

In case, if a member-broker fails to deliver the securities, then the value of shares delivered short is recovered from him at the standard/ closing rate of the scrips on the trading day.

7

CLEARING AND SETTLEMENT IN STOCK EXCHANGES

INTRODUCTION

The payment by the customer to the broker for the shares purchased result in transfer and delivery only on the settlement date. Timely settlement of executed deals is the essence of effective management of stock exchanges. In the case of Indian stock exchanges especially exchanges at Bombay and Delhi which have screen based online trading, settlement of transactions depends on the nature of shares, specified or Group A or Cash or Group B shares. In the case of Group A shares, settlement is carried across a series of settlement periods provided a ten per cent margin and mark to market is made. The number of Group A shares which have carry forward facility in the case of Bombay Stock Exchange is 149 and in the case of Delhi, it is 76. The carry forward constitutes forward trading and is known as 'badla' transaction.

The specified shares or Group A shares consists of equity shares which are actively traded. Group B consists of equity shares of the remaining companies listed on the stock exchange whose shares are not so actively traded. In the case of Bombay Stock Exchange B group is subdivided into Bl and B2 including 1086 and 4645 scrips, respectively. A separate group called 'F' Group securities for debt instruments was created by BSE in 1997 by transferring them from B Group.

In the case of 'B' Group or cash shares weekly settlement exists and all stock exchanges are required to set up their own clearing houses. The practice of renewal of contracts in cash shares from one settlement to another is not permitted. The move is intended to prevent illegal 'badla'. In case members fail to deliver shares within eight days auctions are conducted. This measure is intended to prevent price rigging.

SEBI has also set intra day trading limits which would not exceed 33.33 times the base minimum capital deposited with the exchange.

Forward Trading and Speculation

In India forward trading or trading for dealing in shares has been traditional until it was banned in 1969. Since then the facility of carry forward of transactions especially in specified securities has helped to undertake forward trading.

The role of forward trading in stock markets is to supplement the buyers and sellers and make the demand and supply functions continuous so that they interact to produce a smooth price curve. Further, it helps to build a large volume of trade which imparts liquidity to the market. It also lends stability by enabling hedge trading to take place. It is an important instrument for promoting liquidity, price continuity, free negotiability which are indispensable for the efficient and orderly functioning of stock market.

The traditional theory of speculation viewed the economic function of speculation as the evening out of price fluctuations due to changes in the conditions of demand and supply. Nicholoas Kaldor defined speculation as "the purchase (or sale) of goods with a view to resale (repurchase) at a later date, where the motive behind such action is the expectation of a change in the relevant prices relatively to the ruling price and not a gain occurring through their use, or any kind of transformation effected in them or their transfer between different markets."[19] A perfect market and low carrying costs are the two conditions to be met for a good or asset to be the object of speculation. The highly competitive character of the forward market smoothens out price fluctuations and produces an even flow of securities between sellers and buyers. It enables the coordination of the community's current and future expectations through continuous revaluation in the light of the changing demand and supply conditions. It also facilitates larger purchases and sales at short notice and brings about an integration of the price structure at different points of time and between different securities.

In India, forward trading has been instrumental in developing the stock market to its present position. Without speculative activities, no market can work. Even in stock exchanges like NYSE and Tokyo, where

---

19. N. Kaldor, Essays in *Economic Stability and Growth*, Gerard Duckworth & Co. Ltd., 1961.

the facility of the carry-over is not there, there is enough scope for speculative activities in instruments like futures and options. In fact, options were considered for nearly four decades from mid 30's to mid 70's to be adding to the volatility of the market. Studies conducted in this behalf have, however, revealed the utility of the option market. In the absence of any such instruments in the Indian stock markets, forward trading in shares served the purpose. In fact when trading for the clearing was prohibited by the Government of India on 27th June, 1969, stock markets reeled under a long spell of bearish trend. They could recover, however, only when the stock exchange fraternity evolved a type of trading which ostensibly conformed to the letter of the law but in actuality was identical to the type of trading for clearing which was prohibited by the Government. This type of trading subsequently was granted official recognition in 1983 by being called as trading in specified shares.

Excessive speculation can cause wide and sharp fluctuation in prices to the detriment of the market as a whole while defaults shake the very foundation of the functioning of the stock exchanges. It is, however, difficult to state what is a desirable degree of speculation and what is not. Any quantitative approach like the proportion of deliveries to the volume of trading or of the extent of fluctuations to the turnover or trading velocity can be exercises in futility. Paradoxical as it may appear, generally a larger volume is accompanied by a narrower range of fluctuations. It is precisely because of this that the movement of prices on the Bombay Stock Exchange before 1994 was more orderly with oscillations being confined to a narrow groove as compared to other exchanges at that time. A qualitative approach based on an on the spot assessment of the situation was found useful. At BSE the transactions of operators having outstanding business above 0.5 per cent of paid-up capital of a company and of the major ten operators, five on the purchase side and five on sale side in a scrip whose outstanding position was above 2.5 per cent of the paid-up capital of the company were constantly monitored and had proved helpful in tracking down speculative activity.

Expert Study on Trading in Shares (1991)

It has been argued in the Expert Study on Trading Shares (1991) that trading in shares is speculative.[20] It is claimed that system of trading is

20. L.C. Gupta, *Expert Study on Trading in Shares*, Society for Capital Market Research and Development, New Delhi, 1991.

driven by speculation and not by investment. While the difference between speculation and investment is understood by every one in a general way, it is difficult to define them precisely. A cynic once quipped that an investment is successful speculation and speculation is unsuccessful investment. In the study transactions resulting in actual transfer of shares are considered acts of investment and all others are motivated by speculation which lead to wide fluctuation in prices and results in crises. As Kaldor pointed out, the expectation of an impending change in the ruling market price is what distinguishes speculative purchases and sales from other kinds of purchases and sales. Real or sole motive of speculative purchases or sales is expectation of change in their prices.

In this connection it should be noted that all plans to buy and sell shares do not result in investment or actual transfer. It is usual to defer transfer (in the case of non-dematerialized scrips) for at least a year in a bull market. Investors would certainly like to seize an opportunity for capital gains. Option is foreclosed if shares are presented for transfer and registration. The practice in the market is not to fill the purchaser's name in the transfer form at least until the deadline for record date.

Secondly, transactions in the secondary market as in the case of stock exchange do not result in net investment. There is only a transfer of ownership and widening ownership certainly helps the spread of equity cult. However, those including households who buy or sell shares are not making a permanent commitment when buying' a particular scrip even if we assume that a portion of their wealth may be invested in shares. Stock exchanges are driven by both speculative and investment motives. We cannot describe trading as speculation driven or investment driven. Both motives are at play.

Settlement System in Vogue before December 13, 1993

The settlement system in vogue for trading in specified shares is called the badla system. It is akin to trading for clearing with the facility for carrying forward the transactions from one settlement to another. The facility of carry forward provides liquidity to the market and breadth which ensure the absorption of large purchases with minimum fluctuations in prices. Otherwise at the end of the settlement all sales have result in delivery with receipt of money and all purchases have to be taken delivery of with payment for the same.

Badla system has three components: transfer of market position, stock lending and borrowing/lending in money market.[21] It is a way of settling the net position of a broker acquired in the cash market. Badla system[22] allows the transfer of buy or sell positions from one settlement to another. It is a stock lending operation as shares are needed to postpone a sell position as well as a money market operation as finance is needed to postpone a buy position.

Transfer of Market Position

The facility to carry forward the transaction from one settlement to another necessarily means that a purchaser (if he has not already offset his purchase contract by a sale contract in the course of the settlement itself) can either take delivery of shares and pay for the same or alternatively, carry forward his purchase position to the next settlement by reversing his purchase position in the current settlement by a sale transaction at the making up price fixed by the stock exchange authorities (which normally is the closing quotation of the share on the last trading day of the settlement) and paying or receiving as the case may be the difference between his contract price and making up price and creating a fresh purchase position in the next settlement.

Similarly a seller (if he has not already offset his sale contract by a purchase contract in the course of the settlement itself) can either give delivery of shares and receive payment for the sale or alternatively, carry forward his sale position to the next settlement by reversing his sale position in the current settlement by a purchase transaction at the making up prices and receiving the difference between his contract price and making up price and creating a fresh sale transaction in the next settlement.

Badla system enables a trader to play with price expectations, transfer outstanding buy/sell position and not take or give delivery. It constitutes a vehicle of speculation but not the cause. Except in a continuous rolling system, transfer of open positions from one settlement to another have to be provided. Even under a three day recommended by Global Group of Thirty or five day rolling system (which is in vogue in advanced markets), speculators can take and reverse positions every day and take intraday positions. It is better to have price formation activity in the

21. D.C. Anjaria, 'Badla versus Futures and Options', *Economic Times*, May 1993.
22. S. Rangarajan, "Whither Badla System", I,II and III, *Economic Times*, November 15, 22 and 29, 1993.

organized market by providing for position transfers than drive it out into the unorganized one by abolition of badla system.

Stock Lending

Stock lending is a legitimate activity in the US markets. In margin trading apart from margin agreement pledging securities as loan collateral, the customer has to sign a stock-loan consent form. It allows the broker to lend the client's margined securities to others for the purposes of short sales, arbitrage and the like. Badla system facilitates stock lending for short sellers. Short sellers provide liquidity to genuine investors. In a falling market the purchases of short sellers to cover their sales lead to a recovery in prices. In a rising market short sales can arrest further rise.

A short seller is an important participant of a forward market in securities and without him the market cannot function in an orderly and systematic way.

Short Term Finance

Badla operators provide finance to members in need to meet their commitment in the current settlement and transfer their positions to a later settlement. Unless finance against stocks to brokers is liberalized, the ban an badla system will jeopardize the working of the market. Stock markets should be given access to money markets.

The badla system provided for position transfer, stock lending operations and money market borrowing/lending arrangement for stock brokers and investors. Derivatives cannot replace the functions of a badla system. They are a risk hedging instrument.

Committee on Review of Forward Transactions (1995)

The Committee on the review of the present system of forward transactions (Chairman, G.S. Patel) recommended a new scheme for forward transactions which would to a great extent, lead to greater transparency, better disclosures, smooth and disciplined working of the exchanges, control of speculative excesses so that the stock exchanges enjoy better confidence of investors in their fairness, solvency and integrity.

Weaknesses of Badla System

The Committee found that the badla system, lent itself to malpractices and abuses with speculative excesses at time, price rigging, market manipulation, non-reporting of transactions, evasion of margins, neglect of interests of small investors. The defects arose out of the weaknesses and laxity of administration, absence of any satisfactory reconnaissance and surveillance machinery, lack of back-up inspection of the books of accounts of the members, absence of adequate infrastructural facilities, prolonged periods of settlement and resultant delays in deliveries and payments to the investors and overall helplessness of the governing body of the stock exchanges and their inability to meet crisis situations in a prompt and effective manner.

Ban on Badla

The Securities and Exchange Board of India (SEBI) issued on December 13, 1993, an order preventing undesirable speculation in securities following a steep rise in share prices, (BSE Sensitive Index had risen by 32.0 per cent from 2046.90 on November 2, 1993 to 3454.81 on December 13, 1993). A directive to the Bombay, Calcutta, Delhi and Ahmedabad stock exchanges was issued not to permit any further carryover in "specified shares" and to reduce to zero the outstanding carryover position in two settlements. This was, however, subsequently extended by four more settlements. Trading in "specified shares" with carry-over facilities thus came to a halt on March 12, 1994.

Impact of Ban

The abrupt ban on carry forward facility with effect from 13th December, 1993 has resulted in a sharp decline in the turnover on the stock markets. The average daily volume of business at the BSE, which accounted for about 60 per cent of the turnover in the stock markets in India, declined from Rs. 387.78 crores in 1993-94 to Rs.340 crores in the first nine months of 1994-95. In fact, in January 1995, it was just Rs. 140.23 crores.

Another serious impact on the market was the tendency of spreads between bids and offers to widen in a market of declining volumes. The spreads in respect of 91 scrips in the specified group at the BSE as on November 10, 1993, i.e. about a month before the ban on badla trading and as on January 30, 1995 may be compared for the purpose. It may be observed that while the average of the spreads, prior to the ban on badla trading was 1.6 per cent of the price, it increased to 2.7 per cent of the price on January 30, 1995. The spreads have also widened in respect of non-specified securities. The average of spreads in respect of 25 relatively active scrips in the non-specified group as on November

10, 1993 and January 30, 1995 increased from 4.0 per cent to 6.5 per cent. In respect of the less actively traded shares, the gaps between bid and offer prices have increased even further. Mutual fund industry and FIIs, experienced lack of liquidity and were unable to buy and sell shares in desired quantities at reasonable prices. Lack of speculative trades has resulted in the market being rendered narrow and illiquid. It is in fact, the speculative trades continuously emerging at every rise and every fall that are able to absorb continuous orders in the market with relatively smaller bulges in prices. These speculative trades also act as a self-corrective mechanism for the market as a speculative purchase results in a sale when the operator feels that the price may not rise further and he decides to get out of the market.

Similarly a speculative sale will result in a purchases when the seller takes a view that the prices may not decline further and offsets the sale by a purchase transaction. These operations generate liquidity in the market and continuous price formation takes place. After the ban on forward trading, lack of speculative trades have resulted in the turnover of even pivotal scrips falling to less than 5 per cent of the turnover earlier.

The lack of liquidity has also adversely affected FIIs interest because they need quick exit route. FIIs pointed to the Committee that the earlier system provided cash liquidity through a market determined *scripwise* borrowing rate, guaranteed by the brokers' contract. Consequently, forward trading meant increased liquidity by virtue of bringing more players into the market. It meant reduced jobbing spreads. The combination of higher volumes and lower spreads i.e., reduced volatility, in turn helped the cash market.

The Committee was of the opinion that in the absence of a strong and active cash market the carry forward system in one form or the other, should be resumed to impart better liquidity to the stock exchanges without allowing the matters to drift in endless arguments and counterarguments, to the detriment of interests of the investors and the economy. It is to be noted that the carry forward system in the country linking as it does the cash market with the carry forward market in an integrated manner ensures that the cash market which is generally illiquid gets activated automatically and lends itself to better supervision, regulation, control and direction, at the market level.

Implementation of the Committee Report (1995)

Consequent to the Patel Committee Report on the carry forward system, SEBI decided to introduce a revised carry forward system (RCFS) subject the prudential conditions and precautions.

Stock exchanges would be allowed to introduce carry forward system only with the prior permission of SEBI. Screen based trading and systems capability for effective monitoring and surveillance would be a prerequisite. The Executive Director of the Exchange would be responsible for monitoring, surveillance and reporting and he must be empowered in this regard, if necessary, by change of bye-laws, rules and regulations of the exchange. The exchanges would also ensure the submission of timely and regular information to SEBI about various parameters and their implementation.

The transaction would be allowed to be carried forward for a period not exceeding 90 days. While the transaction would be allowed to be squared off upto 5th settlement (75th day), transactions remaining till that day, will have to be settled by delivery or payment, as the case may be.

The financiers funding the carry forward transactions being lenders should not be permitted under any circumstances to square up their positions till repayment of the loan. The shares received by such financiers against these transactions should be deposited and kept in safe custody of the clearing house of the stock exchange or its authorized agent. *Vandhas* or objection memos would be rectified immediately and the *Kapli* system and *Chalu Upla* transactions will not be permitted.

Every member would be required to keep books of record of the source of finance with sub-accounts being maintained in the clearing house.

The carry forward position shall be disclosed to the market, Scrip-wise and broker-wise by the stock exchanges at the beginning of the carry forward session.

The brokers must ensure segregation of client account and own account in accordance with the existing guidelines issued by SEBI.

The stock exchanges should introduce the capital adequacy norm of 3 per cent for individual brokers and 6 per cent for corporates to begin with.

The various margin requirements both for daily and additional for volatile scrips would be levied on a weekly marked to market basis. The Bombay Stock Exchange has since set up systems to introduce revised carry forward transactions, after taking the prior approval.

J.R.Varma Committee Report (1997)[23]

SEBI constituted J.R. Varma Committee in March 1997 to review the Revised Carry Forward System (RCFS). A new Modified Carry Forward System (MCFS) has been recommended by the Committee because RCFS was not a success. The total outstanding position carried forward from one settlement to another at BSE was about Rs.150 crores in all 74 scrips that have the carry forward facility (under RCFS) while prior to the ban on December 13, 1993 the aggregate carry forward position used to be well over Rs.600 crores in the 94 scrips that had carry forward facility at that time. The number of members, 231 who opted for the RCF system on January 15, 1996, had come down to 126.

The recommendations of the Varma Committee were expected to lead to a strong and vibrant badla market, generating liquidity, reducing volatility and providing an excellent medium for hedging.

The detailed recommendations of the Committee include the following: first, abolition of the twin-track system of reporting carry forward and delivery trades; secondly, a uniform margin of 10 per cent on gross basis (instead of 15 per cent on carry forward trades and 7.5 per cent on delivery trades), with daily marking-to-market; thirdly, abolition of the limit of 90 days for carry forward of transactions.

Fourthly, doing away with the requirement of settlement only by delivery after the 75th day; fifthly, dispensing with the limit of Rs.10 crores on badla financing; and six, scrapping the overall limit on carry forward of transactions of Rs. 5 crores.

There are sub-limits of Rs. 3 crores each of purchases and sales, and Rs.50 lakh in respect of an individual scrip and of the overall limit of Rs.7.5 crores, with sub-limits of Rs. 4 crores each for purchases and sales and sub-limits of Rs.1 crore in respect of each individual scrip outstanding at the close of business on any day within the settlement period in respect of speculation transactions.

The Committee observed that badla trading can be misused grossly particularly in the context of computerized trading which enables building up of huge positions easily and quickly. Apart from tight monitoring of positions, deployment of timely and effective corrective measures is required. The Varma Committee remarked as did the Patel Committee that exchanges should be allowed to use all their regulatory

23. M.R. Mayya, "The Future of Carry Forward", *Economic Times*, 2-8-1997.

powers to regulate the market. The measures must preempt the development of any crisis condition.

These powers include suspending carry forward facility whenever the aggregate outstanding position in any security exceeds pre-announced limits; imposition of price corrective measures; fixing differential rates of making-up prices; prohibiting short sales and long purchases; suspending buying-in and selling-out provisions; ordering contraction of outstanding carry forward position; imposition of limits on purchases and sales for speculative business; imposing additional limits on price fluctuations; suspending off-the-floor transactions; fixing maximum and minimum prices; and regulating carry forward charges.

It is also necessary to ensure that the corrective actions that are taken are uniformly and simultaneously made applicable at all stock exchanges that have the carry forward facility.

Modified Carry Forward System (MCFS)

SEBI has accepted the recommendations but has stipulated that screen based on line trading has to be provided by the exchanges opting for MCFS. Actually, the systems of screen based trading and the daily mark-to-market margin should eliminate the risks associated with the old badla system. The exchanges at Bombay, Calcutta and Delhi have opted for MCFS.

Position Limits on Badla

The introduction of position limits and punitive margins of 100 per cent to enforce them were recommended by J.R. Varma Committee on 30.12.1999 to tighten control on badla system practised in some exchanges. The position limits consist of scripwise-market wide limits, scripwise brokerwise limits and brokerwise aggregate limits. The position limits for "scripwise marketwide" at 6 per cent of aggregate market capitalization (one fifth of the floating stock of the market as a whole) on the short (sell) side is recommended. On the long side the position limit of 12 per cent (two-third of the floating stock) has been recommended.

In the case of scripwise, brokerwise limits, the Committee recommended that brokers should not go beyond 3 per cent of market capitalization. The Committee also recommended that badla should be permitted for any period up to a maximum of five days in the rolling settlement regime in contrast to its earlier recommendation of daily badla in rolling.

Ban on Deferral Products

SEBI announced a ban on May 14, 2001 on all deferral products in the cash segment including 'badla' from July 2001 with a view to segregating the cash and futures market and introduced rolling settlement. On December 31, 2001 all the scrips listed on the BSE moved to compulsory rolling settlement mode.

SHORTENING OF SETTLEMENT CYCLE FROM T + 5 TO T + 3 TO T + 2

Rolling settlement on T + 5 basis, which was made compulsory in all stock exchanges for 200 actively traded scrips in BSE and NSE, was extended to cover all scrips from December 31, 2001. The settlement cycle was then shortened to T + 3 from April 1, 2002. The transition from T + 5 to T + 3 took place smoothly without any glitches. In order to derive greater benefits of increased efficiency of the rolling settlement and ensure speedier settlement, the need for contracting the rolling settlement cycle from existing T + 3 to T + 2 was felt. Market participants were intimated about further shortening of the settlement cycle to T + 2 from April 1, 2003.

The operational efficiency has been strengthened through improvement in the clearing and settlement practices and the risk management process. Postponement or clubbing of settlements and bad deliveries have disappeared. The setting up of trade/settlement guarantee funds has reduced the settlement risk for investors. The transaction cost has declined sharply as a result of automated trading, compression of settlement cycle and introduction of dematerialization.

References

Anjaria, D.C., "Badla versus Futures and Options", *Economic Times*, May 1993.

Bombay Stock Exchange, *Profile of Stock Exchange Activities in India*, The Stock Exchange, Bombay, 1970.

Bombay Stock Exchange, *Computerized Settlement System*, The Stock Exchange, Bombay, 1991.

Bombay Stock Exchange, *Technology Perspective*, The Stock Exchange, Bombay, 1991.

Gupta, L.C., *Expert Study on Trading in Shares*, Society of Capital Markets Research and Development, New Delhi, 1991.

Kaldor, N., *Essays in Economic Stability and Growth*, Gerald Duckworth & Co. Ltd., 1961.

Rangarajan, S., 'Whither Badla System', *Economic Times*, November 15, 22 and 29, 1993.

8

DEPOSITORIES

SHARE TRANSFER

Depositories are essentially aimed at facilitating holding of shares and transfer of shares. Share transfer is the process by which the title of ownership to a security on sale or gift is changed in the register of shareholders maintained by the company. In the clearance and delivery method employed in Indian stock exchanges, physical transfer of securities takes place. Transfers are effected through a transfer form (normally valid for one year) duly filled in by the buyer and seller and lodged with the transfer agent or registrar of the company.

The share certificates and dated transfer deed have proved to be a stumbling block to the growth of securities business and entry of foreign financial institutions. It takes too long to get shares transferred, from 3 to 6 months, on top of 3 months to take physical possession of shares. The long range goal in stock exchanges around the world is to eliminate the physical possession of shares. A beginning has been made towards immobilization of securities with the establishment of Stockholding Corporation of India which handles the shares of financial institutions. In addition, the BSE has in association with Bank of India, which currently runs the Clearing House of the Exchange, set up BOI Shareholding Limited. This will initially act as a depository in respect of specified securities involved in carry forward transactions worth Rs.500 crores with the settlement of shares being effected by book entry only. The services of the depository are to be extended to other activities of stock brokers and investors.

The second stage for the nation's stock exchange is to develop a certificateless society as has already been achieved in Norway, Denmark and France. It is pertinent to recall the recent experience of the London Stock Exchange, TAURUS (transfer and automated registration of uncertified stock) which was to replace manual settlement of transactions in shares over two weeks and reduce settlement period for U.K. shares to three days was abandoned in 1993 after six years of work and spending $575 million. As a result of the collapse of Taurus, the trading and settlement system for corporate securities, currently in operation at London Stock Exchange still requires physical delivery of share certificates and stock transfer forms which are then settled on a fortnightly account basis. Failure of Taurus was attributed to managerial factors in letting the software become complicated to meet the requirements of diverse groups.

Recommendations of Technical Group (1993)

A Technical Group appointed by the Finance Ministry to setting up of a modern settlement and depository system has recommended establishment of competitive depositories for securities, a clearing outfit attached to each of them, establishment of an electronic depository, scrapping of stamp duty on transfers and mandatory insurance cover for clients transacting through these depositories.

The group examined two alternatives of moving towards a paperless trading system. One option is immobilization whereby securities are lodged with the depository, with participants having the right to ask for physical scrips when withdrawing from the depository. The other is dematerialization where the entire settlement and depository activity is carried out without any physical scrip whatsoever, with only electronic statements being provided to evidence ownership.

The group concluded that given the widespread preference of Indian investors to hold physical scrips, their general concern for safety with custodians and lack of trust in market intermediaries and' unfamiliarity with new technology, immobilization should be attempted to be ultimate goal. Lodging of securities with the depositories should be entirely voluntary.

Nature of Depository

A depository is an organization which assists in the allotment and transfer of securities and securities lending. It acts as a link between issuers of securities and investors. Shares in a depository are held in the form electronic accounts which are of a dematerialized nature. A depository system is paperless or scripless. The main objective of a depository is to minimize the paperwork involved with the ownership, trading and transfer of securities. The depository and custodial service is an essential component of developed markets and some of the developing markets have also set up depository systems. It benefits the investing public, the issuers of securities, the intermediaries and the markets.

Services Provided by Depository

The depository system provides a wide range of services, primary market services, secondary market services and ancillary services. In the case of primary market services the depository through its participants works as a link between issuers and investors. In the secondary market, the depository through its participants acts as a link between the investor and the clearing house of the exchange to facilitate settlement of the security transactions through book keeping entries. Finally the depository provides ancillary services like collecting dividends, interest and reporting corporate information.

Need for Depository

The large scale irregularities in securities transactions of 1992 exposed the limitations of the prevailing settlement system. It was also realized that a depository could reduce the time between allotment of shares and transfer of entitlements arising out of each allotment which would facilitate the growth of primary market. Finally, the massive amount of paper work associated with transfer of large number of listed companies often gave rise to problems of stolen shares, forged shares posing a threat to security of investment.

Players in the Depository System

There are four principal players which make the dematerialization process possible – a central depository, a depository participant (both these specially set up) the company which offers this facility and of course, the shareholders.

The depository facilitates the transfer of securities through electronic book entry. A depository will interface with the investors through market intermediaries called depository participants. All rights with respect to the securities held in the depository will lie with the investor who have been granted the option of holding securities in a physical or dematerialized form and are also indemnified of any loss caused due to the negligence of the depository or participant.

The Depository Act, 1996

Reduction of settlement risks and of settlement cycles are the basic requirements for upgrading the existing trading system into a modern one. Severe infrastructure bottlenecks have often come in the way of upgrading the Indian clearing and settlement system. These bottlenecks have become more pronounced with a growing number of investors and consequent increase in trading infrastructure to keep up with the flow of paper in settlement cycles and move to rolling settlement. The Depositories Act, 1996 allows for dematerialization (and rematerialization) of securities in depositories and the transfer of securities through electronic book entry. The Act provides for multiple depository system. This will help in reducing settlement risks and removing some of the infrastructure bottlenecks. The dematerialized securities will be fungible, meaning thereby that they will not have any distinctive numbers or specific identification. As the network of depositories expands and the proportion of securities dematerialized increases, the benefits would percolate to the vast majority of market participants. This is expected to lead to better investor service and investor protection.

SEBI and Depositories

The Depositories Act vests SEBI with the powers of registration of depositories and participants and to approve or amend the bye-laws of a depository.

SEBI notified regulations for depositories and participants on May 16, 1996. The regulations stipulate the prerequisites for the sponsors of depository and also the participants. Besides it prescribes procedures to obtain 'certificate of commencement of business', registration of participant, as also the rights and obligations of various entities including depositories, participants, and issuers. SEBI has notified that trades in 104 scrips should be settled only in dematerialized form by May 31, 1999.

After the notification of the SEBI (Depositories and Participants) Regulations, 1996, the National Securities Depository Limited (NSDL) has been set up. The NSDL, sponsored by the IDBI, the UTI and the NSE commenced operation in October, 1996. 13 companies have joined NSDL. Scrips of 5 companies are trading in dematerialized form and the portion for dematerialization is available for scrips in 11 companies. The Depositories Related Laws (Amendment) Ordinance, 1997 was promulgated to remove some lacunae in the Depository Act. This will enable units of mutual funds and UTI, securities of statutory corporations and public sector bonds, to be dealt through depositories.

NSDL will perform the following functions through its various participants: (a) enable surrender and withdrawal of securities to and from the depository (that is, dematerialization and rematerialization); (b) maintain investor holding in the electronic form; (c) effect settlement of securities traded on the exchanges; and (d) carry out settlement of trades not done on the stock exchanges (that is off-market trades).

The depository regulations provide for selection of various categories of market participants as depository participants (DPs). A depository participant is similar to a broker who trades on behalf of shares owner/ investor. He is the representative /agent of the investor. The depository participant will maintain the investors securities accounts and intimate the status of the investor's holding from time to time.

The categories eligible to become depository participants include: public financial institutions, scheduled commercial banks, SFCs, RBI approved foreign banks in India, certified custodians of securities, clearing corporations of stock exchanges, registered stock brokers, and NBFCs. The number of DPs operational as at end of March 1999 stood at 84 which included all custodians providing services to local and foreign institutions. DPs cater at present to investors from about 730 locations across the country. The depository regulations stipulate that agreements should be entered into between the depository and every participant, between participant and every client as well as among depository, issuer company and the registrar.

Benefits to Investors

Dematerialization has speeded up the transfer and ownership of securities. The depository system confers certain benefits to the investors. The more important ones are,

- immediate availability for trading without waiting for delivery
- no possibility of fake certificates or loss of certificates in transit
- no delay in transfers
- no stamp duty on certificates sent for registration
- investors can get loans on demat shares.

Procedure for Dematerialization

The shareholder will have to first open on account with the depository participant (DP) which is similar to opening a savings bank account with a bank. Thereafter he will have to make a request for dematerialization of the shares to the DP. It is to be noted that only the shares of companies offering demat facility can be considered.

The DP in turn will forward the request along with the share certificates to the company concerned. Once the dematerialization takes place, the DP will intimate the shareholder that his shares are now in an electronic form.

NSDL offers the facility for primary market investors to apply for new public issue through demat accounts. To give a boost to the depository system, SEBI has decided to make it compulsory for domestic financial institutions, banks, mutual funds and FIIs, having a minimum portfolio of Rs.10 crores to make settlement through depository with effect from January 15, 1998. Debentures have been exempted from stamp duty in the Union Budget for 1999-2000. The measure would infuse liquidity in the secondary market.

Central Depository Service Limited

A second depository, the Central Depository Service Limited (CDSL) was set up on February 8, 1999 which offers trading in dematerialized form. The depository which has an equity capital of Rs. 100 crores is promoted by Bombay Stock Exchange, Bank of India, State Bank of India, Bank of Baroda and HDFC Bank.

Benefits of Scripless Trading

The introduction of scripless trading in National stock exchange and on-line trading at the Mumbai, Delhi and other stock exchanges have brought in strong elements of accessibility, efficiency and transparency in operations. The payments system has to gear itself to meet the challenges in the new operational environment in the Indian capital market. The reforms introduced by NSE are simultaneously taking place in several other exchanges in the country. At the end of March 1999 nine stock exchanges have established connectivity with NSDL for offering trade in demat securities.

As at the end of March 1999, 84 banks, financial institutions, custodians and brokers had become NSDL participants with more than 4,08,000 accounts of the 375 companies that signed agreements with NSDL for making their securities available for dematerialization. Of the 375 companies, the shares of 365 companies with 80 per cent of market capitalization of all listed companies in the country were available for dematerialization.

Working of Depository System

The number of Companies signed up as at the end of March 2004 were 5,216 on NDSL and 4,810 on CDSL (see Table 8.1). The number of shares demat replaced were 8,36,935 (lakhs) on NDSL and 1,40,100 (lakhs) on CDSL. The number of shares settled under the demat form were 4,38,310 (lakhs) and 975 (lakhs) at NSDL and CDSL respectively; and the total value Rs.2,78,425 crores and Rs.83,715 crores. The market capitalization of companies admitted for demat form was Rs.11,07,084 of companies which have joined NSDL for demat of equity stock and Rs.11,92,263 crores on CDSL. Large number of bond and commercial paper instruments have also been dematerialized. The total value of demated bonds works out to Rs.2,47,268 crores and Rs. 5,623 crores at NSDL and CDSL at end of March 2004, respectively. The size of commercial paper demated stood at Rs.10,455 crores and Rs.396 crores at NSDL and CDSL respectively at the end of March 2004.

The location of depository participants is also presented in Table 8.1. Depository participants of NSDL are available at 242 locations while depository participants of CDSL have their facilities at 108 locatives. Four locations account for 89.2% of NSDL participants; and 97.2% of CDSL participants.

Table 8.1: Working of Depositories (of equity shares only) 2003-04

Particulars	*NSDL*	*CDSL*
	2003-04	*2003-04*
Companies signed up as on March 31	5,216	4,810
Demat: Quantity of shares (lakhs)	8,36,935	1,40,100
Total no. of shares settled in demat (lakhs)	4,38,310	975
Total value of shares settled in demat (Rs. crores)	2,78,425	83,715
Market capitalization of companies in demat (Rs.crores)*	11,07,084	11,92,263
No. of DPs	*Locations*	*Locations*
1	109	59
2	31	21
3	27	10
4-10	49	15
11-20	15	1
21-50	4	1
51-100	5	0
> 100	2	1
Total	242	108

*Capitalization of the companies which have joined NSDL for demat equity shares.

Source: SEBI: *Annual Report*, 2003-04.

References

SEBI, *The SEBI (Depositories and Participants) Regulations,* May 1996 and *Annual Report*, 2003-04.

Reserve Bank of India, *Report on Currency and Finance,* 1996-97, Vol. I and *Annual Report,* 1998-99.

SEBI, *Annual Report,* 2003-04.

9

NATIONAL STOCK MARKET SYSTEM

CONCEPT OF NATIONAL MARKET SYSTEM (NMS)

The concept originated in 1970's to link all markets in order to create economically efficient mechanism for the best execution of transactions and enhance competition among participants in the national markets. U.K. and U.S.A. have implemented it in 1973 and 1978, respectively.

National Market System Abroad

U.K. The first attempt at linking the stock exchanges in the country was made in the United Kingdom. In 1973, the seven exchanges in the United Kingdom and the Republic of Ireland merged to form the International Stock Exchange of the United Kingdom with London as the hub of the intermarket system. Other centres at Liverpool, Belfast, Birmingham, Glasgow, Manchester and Dublin have only trading floors.

U.S.A. In the United States, Congress has determined that the securities market can best be preserved and strengthened through the development of national market system. The system is intended, at a minimum, to link all markets in order to create economically efficient mechanisms for the best execution of securities transactions, increase the availability to broker-dealers and investors of market quotations and transaction information and generally enhance competition among participants in the national markets. The Securities Reform Act of 1975 directed SEC to facilitate the establishment of a national market system.

Elements of National Market System

The basic concept of NMS consisting of a linkage of the markets that would enable customers to receive the best available execution of their orders and market makers and specialists to compete is simple. Six major elements of NMS had been identified by SEC. Some of the elements are facilities that can be regarded as components of NMS while others are changes required in the regulations governing the securities markets. These elements are: (1) a system of public reporting of completed transactions on a consolidated basis; (2) a composite system for the collection and display of bid and asked quotations (composite quotation system); (3) systems for transmitting orders to buy and sell securities and reports of completed transactions from one market to another (market linkage systems); (4) elimination of restrictions on the ability of exchange members to effect over the counter transactions in listed securities (off-board trading rules); (5) nation-wide protection of limit price orders against inferior execution in another market; and (6) rules defining the securities that are qualified to be traded in the NMS.

The SEC left the actual design of the NMS to the securities industry. In 1977, the New York Stock Exchange was the first to develop the Intermarket Trading System (ITS).

ITS is an electronic communications network which links all nine markets of the U.S. to enable market professionals to interact with their counterparts in other markets whenever the nationwise composite quotation system shows better price. ITS commenced operations on April 17, 1978 with the linkage of NYSE and Philadelphia Stock Exchange. During August 1978 four other stock exchanges joined. The National Association of Security Dealers joined ITS in April 1982 through its Computer Assisted Execution System (CAES). The 2,532 issues eligible for trading on ITS at the end of 1992 represented most of the stocks traded on more than one exchange.

The eight regional exchanges in Germany were linked in 1989 nationally under IBIS, a screen-based trading system. Frankfurt which accounts for two-thirds of the turnover of stocks in Germany was linked to other exchanges in Germany.

Regulatory Arrangement

Linking of the stock exchanges into a formal National Stock Market System would require the adoption and application of uniform regulatory arrangement. Such regulatory arrangement would include, (1) coordination and communication of relevant information by stock exchanges in respect of quotation, trading, suspension and resumption, (2) sharing of regulatory information as needed by any party for purposes of their local surveillance and (3) exploration of concerned regulatory initiatives such as development of uniform standards for transactions in scrips listed at multiple centres.

These arrangements have to be formulated and later coordinated by SEBI which is charged with the regulation and development of the stock markets and protection of investors interest.

Objectives of NMS in India

The primary objective of National market system is to provide equal opportunity to all investors in the country irrespective of their location to trade in any security, size of order or the broker through whom the order is routed. National market system affords the opportunity to execute the buy order at the lowest price in any stock market located anywhere in the country and to sell at the highest price prevailing anywhere in the country without any extra cost to the investor. It would ensure price continuity and liquidity. Such a facility necessarily requires multiple listing of companies, providing for markets in the same scrip in different centres and multiple membership of stock exchanges facilitating easy accessibility by same member to different markets with the investor located in one market not being called upon to pay any extra brokerage for execution of his order at another centre and linking up of all these stock exchanges.

The growth of stock market activity has reached a stage in our country where the establishment of a national market system has become necessary. A beginning has been made in this direction in 1987. The five major markets; viz. Bombay, Calcutta, Delhi, Madras and Ahmedabad are linked electronically through PTI stockscan. Quotations of over 500 scrips traded on these exchanges and other market related information are continuously displayed. To really integrate all the stock exchanges and evolve a national market stock system comparable to Inter Market Trading System (ITS) in the USA an electronic routing system based on something similar to Superdot 250 has to be adopted.

PHERWANI STUDY GROUP REPORT (1991)

Review of Operations of Stock Exchanges

The High Powered Study Group on Establishment of New Stock Exchanges (1991) on a review of the operations of the existing stock exchanges identified major areas of concern which directly affect the interest of the investor and have rendered transactions in the capital market to be costly, risky and a dilatory affair. The major areas of concern identified are lack of liquidity, infrastructure facilities, an inefficient and outdated trading system, an outdated settlement system and lack of a single market. Lack of liquidity according to the Study Group arises because markets do not have depth and breadth and no market has been developed for debentures. The trading system according to the Study Group has led to lack of transparency of transactions affecting adversely investor's confidence. The settlement system has been leading to settlement delays and loss in market liquidity. The absence of a single market according to the Study Group has arisen out of the inability of the various stock exchanges to function cohesively, not only in terms of legal structure and regulatory framework but also in terms of trading practices, settlement procedures and jobbing spreads.

National Market System According to Pherwani Committee

The Study Group observed that the establishment of new stock exchanges should be predicated on setting into place a set of conditions that would ensure that exchanges operate efficiently, are liquid and financially viable. The setting up of additional stock exchanges would not serve the purpose of spreading the equity cult or enhancing liquidity in the secondary market. Improvement can be achieved only by establishing closer links between exchanges. An integrated national market system with a three tier stock market structure was recommended by the Study Group. The national market system consists of,

(a) principal stock exchanges comprising the five major stock exchanges at Bombay, Delhi, Calcutta, Madras and Ahmedabad,

(b) regional stock exchanges comprising of other stock exchanges, and

(c) additional trading floors sponsored and managed by either a principal stock exchange or a regional stock exchange.

The Study Group found that for such a nation-wide system to be effective, several support agencies would be required to provide uniform and high quality trading, settlement, clearing and depository services. They are: (i) National Clearing and Settlement Corporation to administer the clearing and settlement functions at a national level, and arrange for payment against delivery, to be set up under the aegis of Stock Holding Corporation of India Ltd. (SHCIL); (ii) Central Depository Trust to eventually usher in scripless trading; and (iii) Securities Facilities Support Corporation which would be entrusted with the task of establishing and maintaining the network.

Benefits to Investors

The Study Group was of the view that the implementation of these measures would benefit investors in terms of lower cost in execution of orders and reduction of risk and time taken for receipt of payment.

Cost: Investors outside the principal metros have to pay brokerage to both local broker and to the broker of the main exchange through whom the order is executed. Further, there is no transparency in the transaction to verify the price at which the deal is executed. After the proposed linking of exchanges, the investors would be able to transact at lower cost and ensure that deals are at right price. The proposed system would also permit close monitoring of transactions by price and quantity.

Risk: Risks in inter market operations include execution of the order at right price, in the best market, delays in communication, malpractices due to the number of intermediaries involved in each operation and delay in receipt of payment. These risks would be eliminated in a formal structure of National Market System. Both efficiency and transparency according to the Study Group would lead to reduction of risks to investors.

Time: The delay involved in receiving payment would be completely eliminated in a National Market System. According to the Study Group the proposed central clearing and settlement system would reduce both risk of intermediation and the delay in completing the transaction irrespective of location.

These three aspects are expected to benefit the investor and lead to improved investor confidence.

National Stock Exchange

The Study Group observed that due to physical constraints, trading in Bombay Stock Exchange was limited to about 900 companies. Out of 2600 listed companies 1700 companies were traded infrequently or not traded at all. It further observed that the exchange was unable to develop a debt market due to shortage of space and unwillingness of members to act as market makers. On account of these factors, the Study Group strongly recommended that a new stock exchange be promoted immediately at New Bombay as a "Model exchange" and to act as a National Stock Exchange. In the opinion of the Study Group NSE would provide access to investors from all across the country on an equal footing and work as an integral component of the national market system.

Evaluation of Study Group Report on Liquidity

Liquidity in BSE is not restricted to shares of 900 companies as stated by the Study Group. Shares of 1400 companies out of 2471 companies listed in 1992 were traded daily out of which securities of 750 companies were traded on a continuous basis.

Table 9.1 presents average daily turnover data of BSE from 1985-86 to 2004-05. Turnover has gone up very rapidly by about 17 times during the period 1985-86 to 1996-97 from about Rs. 30 crores in 1985-86 to Rs. 518 crores in 1996-97. Peaked to Rs. 5405.60 in 2000-01 and declined thereafter. In 2004-05 it was Rs. 2803.9 crores.

There were year to year fluctuations, the latest fall being in 1995-96, when it was Rs.215.79 crores. While there were wide fluctuations since then. They have been at a much higher plateau operations by FIIS and domestic institutional investors were largely responsible.

Table 9.1: Average Daily Turnover on Bombay Stock Exchange (1985-86 – 2004-05)

Year	*Average Daily Turnover (Rs. crores)*
1985-86	29.92
1986-87	67.98
1987-88	39.55
1988-89	82.38
1989-90	127.42
1990-91	189.15
1991-92	332.30
1992-93	239.00
1993-94	387.78
1994-95	292.02
1995-96	215.79
1996-97	517.85
1997-98	1123.50
1998-99	1686.50
1999-2000	3702.80
2000-01	5405.60
2001-02	1161.00
2002-03	1701.00
2003-04	2716.09
2004-05	2803.9

Note: Daily turnover is estimated by dividing annual turnover by185 days (the assumed average number of days the stock exchange trades).

Source: Bombay Stock Exchange, RBI, *Annual Report.*

Reasons for thin trading were discussed at length in Chapter 2. They are narrow capital base, lack of adequate floating stock in the market because of closely held nature of some companies and poor track record of the company. There is no investor interest in these companies. Actually, raising the norm of listing to Rs. 3 crores and quantum of public offer has resulted in regular trading of shares of companies listed since 1989. The solution to the problem of enhancing liquidity of listed shares is to be found in stipulating in listing requirements conditions such as continuous declaration of dividends, minimum percentage of public shareholdings and compulsory market making which have been implemented since by SEBI.

Debt Instruments

Convertible debentures are actively traded in the market. Non-convertible debentures of companies with poor track record fail to develop a market. There are several jobbers dealing in non-convertible debentures. Now that credit rating is made compulsory and interest rates are deregulated the debenture market should undergo a sea change. In 1997, a separate Group called "F" Group Securities for debt instruments was created by BSE by transferring some of the securities from Non-specified "B2" Group.

The union Budget 2006-07 announced the proposal for creation of a single, unified exchange traded market for corporate Bonds. Accordingly, SEBI stipulated that the BSE Limited would set up and maintain the corporate bond reporting platform, the reporting shall be made for all trades in listed debt securities issued by all institutions such as banks, public sector undertakings, municipal corporations, corporate bodies and companies.

Modernization of BSE

The Study Group has ignored the modernization plans of the stock exchanges of their trading and settlement systems. For example, BSE has an ICIM Series 39 Mainframe Computer with a computing capacity of 150,000 trades a day. A large mainframe computer connected to the offices of the members by terminal is proposed to be installed. The computer system will support on-line processing and at the same time, facilitate real-time display of trade information, so as to inject complete transparency to trading. The system installed and the one proposed would render trading and settlement at BSE at par with those of the most developed markets. On-line trading has been extended to by the end of October 1997 to 99 cities. As many as 264 Trading Work Stations have been activated using 235 VSATs. By the end of December 1997 BSE had planned to install 400 VSATs which would cover another 100 cities in the country taking the total number to 250 cities by the end of March 1998.

The system can also be linked to other exchanges (once their modernization plans are completed) to facilitate intermarket trading thus evolving into a national market system. Other stock exchanges need support in terms of finance, technical assistance and guidance.

It is indeed curious that the Study Group has not taken cognisance of the OTCEI and its plans to link up all centres in India. Actually the electronic infrastructure can be shared by all the stock exchanges including OTCEI so that the investors will have the benefit of inter-market trading and the nation the installation of a national market system at an economical cost. Parallel networks are a waste and should be avoided.

Principal Features of the NSE

According to the Study Group listing on NSE would be limited to (a) equity issues of medium companies, (b) debt instruments and (c) public sector units.

The National Stock Exchange is to be promoted by financial institutions and mutual funds. Membership is to be limited 1,000 with an entry fee of Rs. 10 lakhs for individuals and Rs. 25 lakhs for corporate and institutional members. The Study Group estimated the capital outlay for NSE at Rs. 30 crores. The participation of multilateral institutions such as IFC Washington and Asian Development Bank in the capital base of the NSE is contemplated. The introduction of compulsory market makers/ jobbers in the NSE drawn from the institutional members would ensure liquidity according to the Study Group. It is contemplated that the exchange would be completely automatic in terms of both trading and settlement procedures.

The structure of NSE is envisaged to be similar to that of the American Stock Exchange which performs a wholly complementary role to the NYSE system.

While the adoption of National Stock Market System under the supervision of Securities and Exchange Board of India is necessary, the need of having another stock exchange next door to BSE is not justifiable on any rational criteria. Nowhere in the world excepting in the city of New York, is there more than one stock exchange. All the principal stock exchanges in the world, London, Tokyo, Hong Kong, Rio de Janeiro, Frankfurt, Melbourne and Ottawa have only one stock exchange. The only city where there are two stock exchanges is New York. In addition to NYSE, there is the American Stock Exchange set up by curb traders in 1921. The American Stock Exchange is, however, a miniscule market compared to NYSE with a meager 3.9 per cent of the market capitalization of NYSE and a turnover of just 2.8 per cent of NYSE in 1990. The example of American Stock exchange to support the setting up of one in Bombay does not strengthen the case.

Finally, given the financially strong institutional sponsorship a parallel stock exchange in Bombay will definitely fragment the business of BSE. While competition in the case of product markets leads to improvement in quality and reduction in price to the benefit of consumers, in the case of securities markets, it reduces the number of players in each market affecting adversely the degree of competition by reducing the number of transactions in any one of the markets. Stock exchanges do not offer any product for sale. They are only a meeting place to hold an auction and the price is determined by the number of operators who participate in the auction. The fewer the number, the smaller are the number of transactions and less competitive the market. Such a development will have two serious consequences to the detriment of investors. First, the volatility of the market will increase, as the imbalances between supply and demand can only be set right by changes in levels of prices to establish equilibrium between supply and demand. Fragmented markets can absorb large orders for purchase or sale only with wide fluctuations in prices. Secondly, the spread between bid and offer will increase in both the markets penalizing the investor to pay higher price on purchases and realize lower value on sales.

The operations of NSE are covered in an earlier chapter. It has come to occupy a premier position in terms of trading volumes accounting for as much as 40 per cent of total value of securities traded.

References

Bombay Stock Exchange, *National Stock Market System,* 1991.

H.R. Machiraju, "Do we Need a Second Stock Exchange in Bombay", *Financial Express,* 22.9.1991.

Report of High Powered Study Group on Establishment of New Stock Exchanges, June 30, 1991.

"Restructuring the Stock Markets", *New York University Law Review,* November-December, 1991.

10

SELECT STOCK EXCHANGES ABROAD

In this chapter, the working of stock exchanges in U.S.A., Tokyo, London, Germany, France and Hong Kong; and select emerging markets of Asia, Africa and Latin America are presented.

Amsterdam Stock Exchange

Before discussing the stock markets in U.S.A., it may be noted that the oldest stock exchange in the world is the Amsterdam Stock Exchange (ASE) in Amsterdam, Netherlands. It was founded in 1611 to help finance the mercantile activity of Holland. Funds were raised through ASE to finance the exploration of Java archipelago by the United East India Company. During 1996, ASE and the European Options Exchange (EOE) merged to become Amsterdam Exchange (AEX). AEX is a private limited company with shareholders.

In addition to the main market, there is a much smaller over the counter market for domestic unlisted securities. For high growth smaller companies a new market was launched in February 1997.

Hokeman System

AEX has hoekman system similar to specialist system for the retail segment which is organized as a central market for transactions below the whole sale limit. AEX is an order driven market for retail investor with a hoekman for each stock. The wholesale segment is organized so that banks and brokers can trade directly with one another on screen via the Automate Interprofessional Dealing System, Amsterdam (AIDA) and can announce prices nationally and internationally via the Amsterdam advertisement screen called ASSET. The combination of central order driven market for retail investors and wholesale screen for professionals is expected to achieve an efficient and fair market system serving both international wholesale and retail investors.

UNITED STATES OF AMERICA

New York Stock Exchange

Size: The New York Stock Exchange (NYSE) celebrated its bicentennial in 1992. Securities brokers took up trading under a buttonwood tree at 68 Wall street. They reached an agreement on May 17, 1792 to deal with each other and fixed the commission at 0.25 per cent. Since then it has grown to be the world's largest stock exchange.

Board of Directors

NYSE has a Board of Directors with 27 members, 24 of whom are elected by the members and 3 ex-officio, Chairman of the Board, the Executive Vice-chairman and the President. The elected members are divided into two categories, industry directors and public directors. Industry directors include 7 from firms dealing with public, 3 specialists and one floor broker. An additional industry director must be from a specialty company, such as an arbitrage or research firm. To preclude domination of parochial interest in formulation of exchange policies it is provided that half of the industry directors should belong to firms based outside New York. Among the public directors one must be associated with an issuer of NYSE listed securities and one from a financial institution.

Membership

The number of members is restricted to 1366. The NYSE requires that all seats (membership) be owned by individuals. Institutions such as banks and mutual funds are not allowed to own seats because they are the biggest customers of NYSE. Membership (called seat) can be purchased. Seats can also be leased to others who meet the exchange's criteria for regular membership.

Member organizations must have at least one general partner or voting stockholder who is a member of the exchange. The number of members per firm varies from one person operations as a specialist, or $2 broker to large specialist units with 15 to 30 members.

Capital Requirements of Members

A minimum amount of net capital plus a maximum ratio of a net capital (liquid net worth) to aggregate indebtedness is specified under the Securities Exchange Act and NYSE Rules. A broker is considered to be in adequate financial health if his total liabilities do not exceed liquid assets by more than 10 times. Regular reports of capital status are to be submitted to NYSE. Annual audit of net capital by independent public accountants is also required. Supplementary FOCUS reports are required on a monthly and quarterly basis. Further, to protect the public from dishonest acts covering check forgery, security forgery, fraudulent trading and misplacement of securities, partners officers and directors fidelity bonds are required to be carried by members. The size of the coverage is determined by member's capital requirement.

Specialized Functions of Members

Members perform one of several specialized functions. These are commission brokers, floor brokers, floor traders and specialists. Commission brokers are agents on the exchange floor who buy and sell securities for clients of brokerage house. They may also act as dealers for their own positions. Floor brokers (often called $2 brokers) execute orders for commission brokers who have more orders than they can handle. They are free-lance members of the exchange. Much of his business has been siphoned off by the growing use of SuperDot through which orders are routed directly to the specialist bypassing the $2 broker. **Program trading** which involves simultaneous execution of a wide variety of stock orders often near the close has contributed to floor broker's business.

Floor traders or registered traders trade primarily for their own account. They are speculators on the look out for bargains. They sometimes buy and sell the same stock on the same day in order to profit from small price changes. The activity is called day trading. They participate in a customer driven system as opposed to a dealer driven system. They perform a dual function, buy and sell on their own account especially against the market and act as agents by executing orders entrusted to them by the floor trade brokers. They quote and record current bid and asked prices for stocks they are specialists.

Specialists

Their importance to the market is measured by participation rate and specialists involvement in total volume. Participation rate is measured by the sum of shares bought and sold by the specialists acting as principals, divided by twice the total volume of exchange trading. In 1989, they bought and sold 7.96 billion shares for their own account, 9.5 per cent of total purchases and sales in that year. The specialists accounted for 19.9 per cent of total volume in 1990. The exchange volume resulting from member firms and public orders coming together accounted for 80.1 per cent of all exchange volume in 1990.

There has been criticism that specialist function is a monopoly. Each company's share has only one specialist. Only the specialist has the right to make markets in a given share and only a specialist maintains the book for open orders. The markets maintained by specialists remain the first and most liquid in the world. In 1989, 95.9 per cent of all NYSE transactions occurred with either no change in price from the preceding sale or within 1/8 point of that sale. The average bid asked spread was 1/4 point or less for 81.5 per cent of NYSE quotations in 1990.

Specialist's Book

Orders left with specialist by a broker from a member firm are entered in specialist's book or limit order book, which is electronic allowing the information to be displayed at each trading post. Specialist keeps a separate book for each share in which he makes a market. The books are administrative diaries used to record orders to buy and sell that come from customers. If the specialist executes such order later, he receives brokerage fee from member firm whose order was executed.

Specialist as Dealer

In the absence of public orders, he must ordinarily buy or sell shares for his own account at his own risk. When acting as dealer, he may not compete with public orders which always have priority over his own. In addition to filling orders, the specialist is charged with making stabilizing transactions for his own account, buy on down tick, sell on plus-ticks, act as counter to the market trend. By buying in declining markets and selling in rising ones the specialist helps even out the flow of price and keeps the price changes from trade to trade at minimum level. In active shares, there is no problem as there are several participants but in thinly traded shares there is obvious risk that capital will stagnate for considerable period of time before a new buyer appears.

Opening the Market

It is the specialist's duty to open the market at a price that will permit all market orders to be executed, and yet at a price as close as to the previous day's close as possible, so that the market may be as orderly as the situation permits.

Fair and Efficient Market

About 90 per cent of all transactions occur with no change or the minimum variation of 1/8 point. The bid and asked quotations are 1/4 point or less about 65% of the time. Even more remarkable, the average share shows no price change or only 1/8 between 85 and 90 per cent of time. Much of the credit for such smooth price transactions must be given to specialists who continuously stabilize markets by selling from their own accounts when markets are strong and buying when markets are weak.

The role of the specialist remains crucial to the operation of an auction market such as NYSE because he is frequently left to execute various limit orders of brokers who have moved on to other posts. A specialist has an insight into the balance between supply and demand that others lack. He is familiar with current market conditions for the shares in which he deals. This knowledge and his duty to trade so as to maintain orderly markets puts him in a powerful position to influence the trend of prices. This is a factor which has exercised the U.S. Securities and Exchange Commission and to prevent the abuse of the privileged position close surviellance of specialists activities is maintained by NYSE. Monitoring takes place on about eight occasions each year when details of all dealings over one week periods are examined. The exchange scrutinizes the orderliness of the market, the degree of price continuity and the bid-asked spread in order to assess how successfully the specialists function is being performed. The specialist has also to submit to the exchange a weekly report on trades he makes for his own account. Finally, there is a computer surveillance of price behaviour. The computer is programmed to flag unusual price changes and allows the exchange to retrieve data and analyse it for suspicious price movements.

The role of the specialist is governed by the regulations under the US Securities and Exchange Act and NYSE.

Regulations under U.S. Securities and Exchange Act

- Specialist has to maintain an orderly market.
- Specialist may not disclose contents of his book since it contains information that help speculation.
- Specialists can execute only market or limit price orders.
- Any form of manipulation by specialist is unlawful.

Regulations of New York Stock Exchange

- Registration is necessary for specialist activity.
- Trading by specialist is only for maintenance of market. No excessive and unreasonable trading on own account should be undertaken.
- The specialists should have no interest in any pool or trading in the share in which he is registered.
- Specialist can quote only for own account and not from the book in order to maintain closer prices and maintain price continuity.

Registered Representatives

Registered representative's functions involve potential customer contact such as sale and purchase of securities. They are employed by NYSE member firms and have to possess educational and business experience. In 1988, there were 79,075 registered representatives employed by NYSE member firms.

Listed Securities

NYSE has more bond issues listed than stock. At the end of 1990, there were 2912 bonds and 2,284 stock listed. The value of listed bonds include 763 U.S. Treasury Securities, 114 international bank bonds, 53 different foreign government issues and about 2000 U.S. corporate issues. The face value of bonds was $ 1.689 trillion against a market value of $ 1.610 trillion.

Listing and Registration

Listing refers to the procedure for admission to trading on NYSE. Registration refers to the submission of certain financial and business information to the *SEC1*. All securities listed on NYSE must also be registered with SEC[24]. This is in contrast to the position in India where

24. The information required in an SEC registration statement covers the following: (1) Articles of Incorporation; (2) purpose for which the issue proceeds will be utilized; (3) price of public issue; (4) price for special groups; (5) fees to be paid to developers and/or promoters; (6) underwriting fees; (7) net proceeds of issue; (8) data relating to issuers product, history and location; (9) copies of any indentures affecting the new issue; (10) names and remuneration of officers receiving above $25,000 per year; (11) details about unusual contracts such as profit sharing plan; (12) detailed statement of capitalization; (13) balance sheet; (14) income and expenditure statements for three preceding years; (15) names and addresses of issuer's officers, directors and underwriters; (16) names and addresses of investors owning more than 10 per cent of stocks; (17) details about any pending litigation; (18) a copy of underwriting agreement; and (19) copies of legal opinions on matters related to the issue.

no registration is required with SEBI and no financial and business information is required to be submitted to SEBI.

Advantages of Listing

Listing makes a security more marketable since the exchange provides a ready and continuous market. It also lowers financing costs when the company wishes to raise additional capital in future. Listing also aids in the sale of rights by those who wish to sell them rather than exercise them. A ready market for rights makes the privileged subscription a success. Listing also gives a company status and image by having its trading data reported in the daily news. Further widening of the share ownership is possible. Finally, listing helps determination of a fair value which is necessary for tax purposes for the investor as well as the company. Investors are assured of liquidity if the share is listed. There could be greater order flow, narrower spreads and quicker sales. The specialist on NYSE maintains a continuous market. On the other hand in OTC market there is no compulsion on market makers to make a continuous market. Market makers can abandon a stock altogether. Actually OTC market is more liquid for bonds provided the investor deals in institutional quantities.

All listed stock is eligible for margin credit. Listed shares have collateral value for loans from brokers/dealers or banks. Listing on NYSE, confers the advantage of sequential reporting of trades on tape as they occur which gives unparalleled visibility to the investor. Electronic reporting is no match to the tape for clear visibility, actual retail pricing and widespread dissemination.

Listing Requirements of NYSE

The listing requirements of NYSE ensure that the company is in commercial production, has a track record of profitability for three years, has minimum value of tangible assets and market capitalization, adequate floating stock and wide ownership. These requirements are:

1. Pretax income of at least \$ 2.5 million in the most recent year and \$ 2 million during the preceding two years; or an aggregate pretax income of \$6.5 million in the most recent three years, with a minimum of \$4.5 million in the most recent year, (all the three years must be profitable).
2. Net tangible assets of at least \$ 40 million.
3. Aggregate market value of publicly held shares in USA \$40 million.

Chapter–10

4. 1.1 million shares publicly held in the USA.
5. More than 2000 holders of 100 shares or more or total shareholders 2200 and the average monthly trading volume of 100,00 shares for the most recent 6 months.

The alternative listing standards for non-US companies are:

1. An aggregate pretax income of $100 million in the most recent three years with a minimum of $25 million in any one of the three years;
2. Net tangible assets of $100 million worldwide;
3. Aggregate market value of publicly held shares of $100 million worldwide;
4. 2.5 million shares publicly held worldwide; and
5. The number of holders of round lots (100 or more) to be 5000 worldwide.

Apart from payment of fees a listed firm must publish quarterly earnings reports and fully disclose financial information annually.

Trading

NYSE is open for six and half hours every day from 9.30 a.m. to 4.00 p.m. five days a week. Orders can be conveyed by registered representatives to the broker on trading floor who executes the orders on behalf of the customer. Orders can also be processed electronically through SuperDot 250 which is an electronic order routing system linking member firms all over U.S.A. directly to the trading floor of NYSE. The system completes the trading loop within seconds. In 1992 SuperDot processed an average of 180,000 orders per day for 201 subscribers.

Settlement

All transactions are settled within the three day delivery plan. Transactions are due for settlement by the delivery of securities against payment on the third business day after the transaction date. On the settlement date the customer becomes the owner of any securities bought, or gives them up if sold and must pay the brokerage firm by that time. Customers generally leave their securities with the brokerage firm in a street name, the name of the brokerage firm. Brokers mail a monthly statement to the customer showing position as to cash, securities held and funds lent by the brokers. Brokerage houses must settle all their transactions with other brokerage houses or the specialists. The process is facilitated by the clearing house which collects the records of all transactions made by its members during a day verifying both sides of the trades and netting out the securities and money due or to be paid by each member. Clearing and settlement is done through the National Securities Clearing Corporation (NSCC) which is jointly owned by NYSE, AMEX and NASDAQ. All New York's automated trading systems are also linked to the NSCC. Settlement is done with a single cheque with the NSCC for net balance. NSCC system is in turn linked to the Depository Trust Company, the depository of securities to effect by book entry of all transfers in the settlement and clearing process. DTC immobilizes stock and trading is scripless.

NYSE CIRCUIT BREAKERS

After the crisis in 1987 and 1989 NYSE instituted several circuit breakers to reduce volatility and promote investor confidence. Circuit breakers for one or two hours are applied to halt trading if the prices move by specified points . After 2 p.m. New York time if the Dow Jones Industrial Average (DJIA) falls 550 points trading will be halted for half an hour. After 3 p.m. if the 550 point trigger is reached the market will close for the rest of the day.

NASDAQ

Nature

The over the counter securities market in USA is more a way to do business than a place. The market consists of securities houses called broker-dealers located across the country. They buy and sell securities for their own account and risk and they also buy and sell securities for account and risk of others and charge a commission for their service.

The OTC market is a negotiated market rather than an auction market. Prices are arrived at by dealers negotiating with other dealers in order to arrive at the best possible price. Dealers who regularly buy and sell a particular security are said to make a market in that security. There are about 520 active market makers in the system and the average number of market makers per security is 11.0. Before the introduction of computer technology and telecommunication in 1971, OTC market was highly fragmented.

The Automated Quotation System Service of the National Association of Security Dealers began to serve the OTC market from February 8, 1971. NASDAQ is a system with giant computers and special electronic terminals that provide instantaneous bid and asked quotations in over the counter securities. Market makers have to execute trades for at least normal unit of trading. The elaborate communication system allows investors to select among competing market makers instead of being forced to trade with one monopolistic market maker like the specialist on NYSE. While the market makers on OTC sell any given stock at the same price, they compete by offering to execute transactions faster and/or for smaller commission.

The National Association of Security Dealers (NASD) is a voluntary association of security dealers and performs the regulatory function for OTC markets. To become a registered representative or security broker the applicant must apply to NASD and pass a qualifying examination.

OTC execution of NYSE listed stocks by firms who are members of NASD only is referred to as the third market[25]. Fourth market describes direct trading of securities between two parties with no broker intermediary. Generally, the parties involved on either side are institutions.

Size

NASDAQ stock exchange is the second largest stock exchange in the U.S.A. NASDAQ began operations on February 8, 1971. It is a nation-wide electronic screen based trading network blended with market maker competition. More than 50 per cent of the shares traded in U.S.A. are traded in the NASDAQ market. The companies listed on NASDAQ exceed those on all exchanges in the U.S.A. combined. It is also highly automated with more than 60 per cent of the orders executed automatically over the computers at the best prices available.

Before adoption of the central computerized database linking the member firms to provide up to date price and trading information, OTC market since the 1930's served as a nursery for companies maturing into listing on NYSE. Now NASDAQ is so successful that many companies which are fully able to meet the listing criteria of NYSE choose to maintain their NASDAQ listing in preference to graduating to NYSE list. NASDAQ offers smaller, growing companies access to liquid investors. It has supported the highly successful venture capital industry and has been a critical source of funding for the development and rapid growth of biotechnology companies in the USA.

25. The first market is NYSE itself. The second refers to the execution of NYSE listed stocks on one of the regional exchanges.

Listing Requirements

A company must have $4 million in assets, $2 million in capital and surplus, market value of float minimum of $ 1 million, minimum bid price of $ 3 a share and two market makers. Changes were approved in 1997.

Trading Hours

Regular NASDAQ market is open from 9.30 a.m. to 4.00 p.m., Eastern Standard Time (EST). Trading service of NASDAQ International which has been operative since January 1992 allows trading in securities listed on NASDAQ to take place in London for most of the trading day, 3.30 a.m. 9.00 a.m. EST.

Trading

NASDAQ uses a screen based system that centralizes trading information to enable securities firms to compete with one another via the computer. It has an electronic rather than physical trading floor. Trading takes place over the telephone and through automated execution and trading systems. Trades are executed at the prices displayed and size on NASDAQ terminals.

Aqcess which reviews the operation and surveillance of the automated quotation system emphasizes limit orders (orders to buy or sell at prices specified by the customer) and market orders (orders to buy and sell at the prevailing market price). Under the system investors will be able to specify prices or limits for orders to buy or sell stocks. Investor limit orders of up to 3000 shares through Aqcess would be grouped and disseminated publicly in order to foster bids at the best prices. For market orders of 1000 shares better prices are ensured if price movements are not achieved by executing the order at the best displayed prices at the time the order was exposed on the system. Acqucess should contain spreads and benefit investors.

PORTAL: NASD launched in 1990 a global system for trading privately placed nonregistered US bonds and equities.

SOES is a small order (of 1000 shares or less) execution service. Orders are assigned on a rotating basis to market makers offering the best price.

Select Net is another proprietary NASD system which is a screen based trade negotiation service (1990) allowing traders to send orders in NASDAQ securities to specified market makers.

CAES (Computer Assisted Execution System) interfaces with the nation-wide inter-market trading system to execute trades listed on other exchanges.

NASDAQ transactions are settled on three day delivery plan with the NSCC netting out-broker dealer daily positions through continuous net settlement. Processing of transfers in the settlement and clearing process is fully automated by book entry movements in the Depository Trust Company. Delivery and receipt of net position is made by book entry and scrips are immobilized.

AMERICAN STOCK EXCHANGE (AMEX)

Objective

In New York, there is another exchange set up in 1921 which was originally a curb market. American Stock Exchange (AMEX) is a national exchange and stocks listed are distinct from New York Stock Exchange. Amex provides auction market trading. ASE is a voluntary unincorporated association whose primary objectives are to provide a securities market place where high standards of honour and integrity shall prevail and to promote and maintain just and equitable principles of trade and business. ASE has three types of members, regular, associate and allied. ASE has a board of Governors of 21 persons, ten from securities industry and ten represent the public. The 21st is elected by the Board as full time Chairman.

Trading is conducted in open auction market. All trades are made public immediately over a worldwide consolidated tape network. There are no middlemen.

Amex has emphasized foreign securities and in 1996 fifty-four foreign issues were listed. Warrants were listed before NYSE would list them. Since 1975 options were traded on Amex. At the end of 1996, 896 stocks were listed, and volume traded was 5.6 billion shares. The market capitalization of AMEX at $1126.7 billion constituted 15.4% of NYSE market capitalization at the end of 1996.

Listing Criteria

Listing criteria for AMEX are net tangible assets $3 million; market value of publicly held shares $2 million; net income in last fiscal year $300,000; pretax net income in last fiscal year $500,000; number of shares publicly held 300,000; and number of stock holders 9000.

Electronic Trading Systems

There are several electronic systems that share the features of a securities exchange or NASDAQ system. International subscribers use INSTINET (Institutional Networks) to place anonymous bids or offers on a video screen available to all other subscribers. Transactions are executed without either party knowing who the other side is.

Inter Market Trading System

The national market system which is known as Inter Market System discussed at length in Chapter 9 links all nine markets of the USA in an electronic communication network. It displays a nation-wide composite quotation system. In 1992, 2532 stocks were eligible for trading on ITS. Most of them are also listed on NYSE. The share volume on ITS in 1992 was 2.7 billion shares and trades were 2.6 million.

Apart from NYSE, NASDAQ exchange and AMEX, there are five other exchanges in U.S.A., the Boston Stock Exchange Inc.; Midwest Stock Exchange Inc.; Pacific Stock Exchange Inc.; Cincinnati Stock Exchange; and Philadelphia Stock Exchange. All the exchanges are linked together under a system known as the Inter-market Trading System (ITS) to form a national market. ITS facilitates through its composite quotation display system the current quotes as well as the best quote in all the participating markets of all the listed securities. Location confers neither benefit nor a cost. The investor can buy at the lowest price and sell at highest price prevailing in any of the markets.

TOKYO STOCK EXCHANGE (TSE)

Size

The Japanese stock market has a history of over 122 years beginning with the establishment of Tokyo Stock Exchange in 1878.

Of the eight stock exchanges in Japan, three exchanges Tokyo, Osaka and Nagoya are the largest. The Tokyo Stock Exchange in its present form was established in 1949 and accounts for about 80 per cent of trades in both volume and value in Japan. At the end of 1994, there were 1689 companies quoted on the Tokyo Stock Exchange with a market capitalization of 358 trillion yen (or about $3.0 trillion). Tokyo is the second most active exchange in the world right after the NYSE. The 30 actively traded shares account for about 20 per cent of total turnover of 87 trillion yen ($70 billion).

ZARABA

Japan has an auction market and trading is on an open outcry (Zaraba) basis. The domestic stocks are divided into first and second sections. Out of the 1000 stocks in the First Section, 150 most active stocks are traded on trading floor. Trading in all other stocks and all foreign stocks is conducted by computer. From on-line terminals in their offices, official member firms enter buy and sell orders that are received at the exchange. Buy and sell orders are matched on the electronic book entry display screen and confirmation is returned to the trading parties. The information is also recorded on the trade report printer and displayed on all stock quote screens on the trading floor. Prices are established at the start of each trading session on the basis of orders that have reached the floor before the opening of business. Subsequent orders are matched by open auction. Floor trading is restricted to authorized dealers who are members of Japan Securities Dealers' Association.

Regular and Saitori Members

There are two types of members of the exchange, regular members and 'Saitori' members. Regular members pass on orders from investors to the exchange. Saitori members, on the other hand, act only as intermediaries, matching sell and buy orders placed by regular members. Saitori members cannot trade on their own account. Under the constitution of the exchange, the number of regular members is limited to 93 and Saitori members to 4. All members are corporations. The employees of regular members are called trading clerks and conduct business on the trading floor. The employees of the members called intermediary clerks are stationed at trading posts on the floor who match buy and sell orders placed by trading clerks.

Details of all transactions are processed by the exchange's computer system and immediately disseminated to the display screens installed in regular members offices by the exchange's market information system. Under regular settlement which is used for 99 per cent of transactions delivery is due on the third business day following the day of contract; and cash on the day of the contract or following day. Special agreement on the day agreed upon within 14 days, and when issued as determined by the exchange for new and rights. In the Tokyo Stock Exchange, transfer of shares is done electronically via book entry system without involving the physical movement of the scrip. Japan Securities Depository Centre was set up in 1991 and has immobilized share transfer.

Theme Driven Market

It is pointed out that investment decisions in Japan are seldom based on relative PE ratios and industries with low ratio are not expected to out perform those with high ratios. The market it is claimed is theme driven, like companies possessing prime commercial property or having potential for biotechnical innovation. Investors who can identify such themes were able in the past to generate strong returns even during bear phase of the market.

The TSE has also equity, debt and financial futures trading.

UNITED KINGDOM

International Stock Exchange: The United Kingdom has the biggest equity market in Europe. The Stock Exchange in London is the third largest in the world in terms of market capitalization. London Stock Exchange's role as one of the three major stock markets was reinforced by the deregulation of the stock market, the dismantling of fixed commissions and the admission of foreign members after the Big Bang of 1986. UK's regional network established in 1973 is based on six geographical regions represented by six stock exchanges which form the Associated Stock Exchange. London is the hub of the intermarket system.

SEAQ

Trading is fully computerized under the quote driven Stock Exchange Automated Quotation system (SEAQ) based on NASDAQ technology. Exchange members are permitted to trade listed shares directly from their computer terminals. London which has an auction market with trading floor abandoned it and replaced with electronic technology.

Under the SEAQ dealing system, stock exchange member firms act both as market makers, buying and selling shares for their own account, and as agency brokers. Market makers are required to make markets at all times in their registered shares throughout the official trading session. Stocks listed on the Exchange are quoted in normal market size (NMS). There are 12 bands of NMS ranging from 500 shares to 200,000 shares according to each individual stock's average market turnover. Trades in all securities with normal market size (NMS) of 2000 shares or more are subject to immediate trade publication on SEAQ for all bargains upto three times their NMS. Bargains which are larger than three times their NMS are to be published after a 90 minute delay, although these trades must be reported immediately to the exchange.

In 1994, there were 464 overseas companies listed with market capitalization of 1,954.3 million pounds.

Trading and Settlement

Since the abandonment of Transfer and Automated Registration of Uncertified Stock (TAURUS) in March 1993, the trading and settlement system requires physical delivery of shares and transfer forms which are settled on an account basis fortnightly. This has changed in July 1994 to a 10 day rolling settlement. This move is the first phase leading to the introduction of CREST settlement service which was developed by the Bank of England's Task Force on securities settlement in order to reduce the amount of paper work required for the settlement process.

DERIVATIVES

The London International Financial Futures and Options Exchange (LIFFE) was formed by merging in March 1992 London International Financial Futures Exchange (LIFFE) and London Traded Options Market (LTOM). LIFFE is the second most active exchange in the world after CBOT.

GERMANY

Origin

Industry in Germany is still reliant on bank financing and German economy is poorly represented by the stock markets. Market capitalization at end 1994 was 23.6 per cent of GDP Industry is increasingly resorting to equity financing for financing expansion. There are 8 stock exchanges in Germany. The seven regional stock exchanges acquired a 10% share in Deutsche Borse in 1992 and settlement procedures have been centralized.

DEUTSCHE BORSE

Frankfurt Stock Exchange was renamed as Deutsche Borse AG in 1992. Deutsche Borse offers complete service for all transactions in securities and futures from the introduction of an order on the exchange to its settlement. Germany ranks fourth in size globally.

TYPES OF MEMBERS

There are three types of members of the German stock exchanges: credit institutions, official brokers and free brokers. The official brokers (Kursmakler) role is to intermediate in stock transactions and to set official quotations based on buy and sell orders for listed securities that they have executed. The official brokers are supervised by a public body 'kursmakler kammer' which allocates securities to each of them, establishes stock prices and publishes the official list. The free brokers (Freimakler) also act as intermediaries between credit institutions and intervene as brokers in stock exchange dealings.

Trading

A dual system comprising floor and computerized trading is employed. Computerized trading known as IBIS, provided by Deutsche Borse AG and are open to all members of German stock exchanges. IBIS which functions along the lines of voluntary market making caters to institutional investors. Minimum order for share trading is 500 and for bonds DM 1 million. IBIS has been widely accepted and is responsible for bringing the off-exchange trading back to the exchange Transactions concluded within IBIS are automatically transmitted for clearing and settlement.

Banks whose role is universal in Germany provide dealing services and transmit customers orders to the exchange. They act as agents as well as deal on their own account. Banks along with official and unofficial (or free) brokers comprise members of the exchange.

Official brokers are responsible for fixing the official daily price determined for all listed securities once on every trading day in the floor trading system. The price fixed is one at which most orders could be executed. Free brokers can deal only with other stock exchange members. They can trade in any security on their own account.

Orders for highly liquid shares in lots of 50 or multiples thereof can be continuously traded throughout the official trading session.

Settlement

The settlement system of German exchanges was computerized in 1970. DKV, the central depository holds all securities traded on the exchange. Delivery is by book entry. Standard settlement takes place on the second business day after the bargain.

FRANCE

The various stock exchanges in France were replaced in 1996 by Paris Bourse. The Paris Bourse is the national market and the only exchange now in France.

Markets in Stock Exchange System in France

There are three markets within the French stock exchange system. The main listing market is the Cote Officielle which is a cash market. Trading in securities is settled for cash within three days and for active stocks a monthly settlement market. A second market was launched in 1983. For smaller companies which are not listed on the official list or second market the *Marche Hors - Cote* which is an over the counter market. Companies are subject to minimum listing requirement. Transactions are for cash settlement.

Trading

Trading in all securities takes place through the computer order driven trading system (CAC). The electronic trading system allows any securities house to trade all securities listed in France (the trading volume in 1994 was FFR 1.1 trillion). The central on-line trading or CAC system is linked upstream to an order routing system and downstream to a computerized system that disseminates key market data in real time and to the computerized delivery versus the RELIT payment system. The member firms' order books in which orders carried in by the routing system are registered are linked with computers used for quotation. This system called COCA automatically sorts and feeds orders into the CAC computers.

Trading takes place on a continuous basis and the arrival of a new order placed by member firms on behalf of clients or for their own account into the CAC system immediately triggers transactions if maturing order exists on the centralized book. The execution price is the price limit placed on the matching order.

Depending on the volume of trading in a scrip, securities are divided into four quotation groups, Continu A (most actively traded), Continu B (actively traded), Fixing A (less active securities) and Fixing B (all securities traded on the over the counter market). Each quotation group has its own rules of quotation and rules as to maximum daily price fluctuations and halts in trading.

Institutional investors can buy or sell large blocks of share at a predetermined price without waiting for a matching order reaching the central market.

Settlement and Transfer

A fully computerized clearing and settlement system called Relit was introduced in 1990 based on delivery versus payment or the simultaneous exchange of securities and cash on the same day and standard time frame for trade comparisons and settlement. Automatic delivery and payment take place at T + 3 or at the end of the month for securities traded on the monthly settlement market.

HONGKONG

Origin and Size

The Hong Kong Stock Exchange (SEHK) came into existence on October 6, 1986 after consolidating four stock exchanges – Hong Kong Stock Exchange, Far East Exchange, Kowloon Exchange and Kam Ngan Exchange.

Nature

SEHK has an order driven system whereby trades originate from a client order placed at the broker's office. The dealer at the broker's office calls the floor trader at the trading hall who inputs the order into the computer system. In 1993, this semiautomatic system was combined with automatic order matching and execution system (AMS). Stocks are divided into automatic stocks and nonautomatic stocks in the AMS. The order and trade information for both types of stocks are disseminated through Teletext system.

Clearing and Settlement

Clearing and settlement are done on a computerized book entry clearing and settlement system. Settlement is on an T+2 basis.

'China Play' Factor

The Hong Kong market is a highly volatile market and the 'China Play' has been a major factor influencing the market. Hong Kong has been a major beneficiary of the liberalization on mainland China. Trade between China and Hong Kong has gone up at an annual rate of 32 per cent over the past 15 years. The companies listed in HKSE have factories in mainland where labour and other overheads are cheap. Further, mainland companies seek listing on Hong Kong Stock Exchange to take advantage of freedom of access to foreign investors, liquidity and broad investor base.

Foreign Investment

There is no restriction on foreign investment and no limits exist on ownership of domestic companies by foreigners. Profits, dividends and interest can be fully and freely repatriated. The equity market offers outstanding returns for investors.

EMERGING MARKETS

From the view point of attracting foreign institutional investment into the securities of the Indian corporate sector, it is necessary to note the general features of the emerging markets. The stock markets in Malaysia, Taiwan, South Africa, Brazil, Korea, Mexico and Thailand and the conditions regulating foreign institutional investments are briefly presented.

MALAYSIA

The Kuala Lumpur Stock Exchange (KLSE) is significant for the foreign involvement. Of the total equity market capitalization one fifth is held by foreign investors. The KLSE was incorporated in 1973 and is a self regulatory body.

KLSE has a semiautomated trading system (SCORE). Dealing in securities is by member companies. Majority of securities traded are included in the Central Depository (CD) System. Settlement of transactions in CDS prescribed shares is by book entry. Trade settlement is carried out in a batch run at the end of the day. Both the seller's and the buyer's CD accounts are debited and credited on the night of the fifth market day. Buyers have to make payment (credited to CD) by seventh market day and sellers have to deposit (in CD account) shares by the fifth trading day.

There is no withholding tax on dividends in Malaysia. There is no tax on capital gains. There are no restrictions on a nonresident undertaking direct or portfolio investment. Profits, dividends and principal resulting from securities transactions may be freely repatriated subject to completion of exchange control forms for transactions in excess of US $ 39,525.

In December 1995, the Kuala Lumpur Options and Financial Futures Exchange Berhad (KLOFFE) has commenced operations with a Futures contract on the KLSE Composite Index.

TAIWAN

TSE has a fully automated trading system (FAST). The broker enters the details of the order through his terminal into the main computer of the exchange. The basic functions of FAST are to collect orders from brokers, to sort the orders on a price and time priority basis, to execute orders, to log the market price, to send order confirmation reports to brokers and disseminate market information. Trading prices are subject to limits of 7 per cent up or down from the previous trading day's closing price.

Settlement is on a T + 2 basis with the Taiwan Securities Central Depository (TSCD) via its book entry settlement. Stock certificates are immobilized at the TSCD and all trades are settled via book entry on a net settlement basis.

Individual foreigners and corporations are permitted to buy shares directly upto an annual limit of US $ 5 million and US $ 10 million, respectively. Foreign institutions with permission from central bank and securities regulators can buy listed shares upto US $ 600 million.

For investment in Taiwan stock the foreign institutional investor must be among top 500 banks or insurance companies with at least $300 million under management or fund management companies with assets under management of at least $500 million. There were in 1991, 233 qualified foreign institutional investors. FIIs must apply for prior approval from the Stock Exchange Commission to be allowed to invest in Taiwan. FIIs can hold 10% in any listed company and total foreign holding should be below 25 per cent.

Repatriation is allowed. Investment income including capital gains can be repatriated once a year based on certified financial statement and certificate of tax payment.

No capital gains tax is levied but a withholding tax of 20 per cent on dividends and interest exists.

SOUTH AFRICA

The Johannesburg Stock Exchange (JSE) dates back to 1887 and is the only stock exchange in South Africa.

In 1996, trading at the JSE was automated. JSE has an order driven, centralized trading system (JET) with dual trading capacity and voluntary market makers. Market makers voluntarily quote prices and a book for trading orders with special terms is provided. For odd lots a specialist manages an electronic order book against which incoming orders automatically trade. Buying and selling orders are electronically matched in the JET system. Trading in equities is for settlement in 52 weekly accounts each year. Settlement is in the account immediately following the trade date. The net positions due for settlement in each account by member firms are assessed on Friday night and are marked to market which are settled on Monday before deliveries commence on Tuesday.

There are no restrictions on foreign investment and there are no taxes.

On the South African Futures Exchange (SAFEX) futures contracts are traded on the All Share, All Gold and Industrial Indices.

BRAZIL

There are nine stock exchanges in Brazil but the largest and most important being Bolsa de Valores de Sao-Paulo (BOVESPA) and Bolsa de Valores de Rio-de-Janeiro (BVRJ). BOVESPA accounts for two-thirds of transactions. 90 per cent of the trading takes place on the exchanges of Rio de Janeiro and Sao Paulo.

BOVESPA has an auction market through open outcry where trading in stocks and options of 22 actively traded companies is conducted. The computer assisted sessions for other stocks are held simultaneously. Similarly trading in Rio takes place simultaneously on the floor and through the electronic system. Trades may be executed on a cash or forward basis.

Foreign investment by investment companies and investment funds are exempt from corporate tax and capital gains tax. Dividend income is subject to 15 per cent withholding tax. Repatriation is allowed. Of the investment 50 per cent should be in shares of publicly listed companies. Investment companies cannot invest in debentures. The investment in shares is limited to 5 per cent of the voting capital or 20 per cent of total capital of any single company. Further the total value of investment in a single company may not exceed 10 per cent of the company.

KOREA

Nature and Size

Korea Stock Exchange in Seoul is the only stock exchange in South Korea.

Korea has an order driven market where buy and sell orders compete for the best price. There are 38 securities companies which act both as brokers and principals. Customer's order placed with the securities company is electronically transmitted to the stock market automated trading system (SMATS) or to the trading floor. About 99 per cent of trading takes place over SMATS. The exchange operates on a continuous trading basis, on the basis of double auction. Opening prices are determined by all bids and offers submitted to the trading post before the beginning of trading session. A daily price limit of 8 % based on previous day's closing price is set. After the trading hours, transactions are allowed at the closing price.

Transactions are classified into regular way and cash. Regular way transactions have to be settled the same day.

Cash or delivery of shares has to be effected on the basis of the net balance between purchases and sales to the Korean Securities Depository (KSD). Entry of transactions in the brokers books and KSD's books is deemed to be actual delivery.

Foreign Investment Regulations

Foreign investment in a company is allowed up to 20 per cent; and a single foreign investor can own up to 5 per cent of shares outstanding. Foreign investors must register with SEC and appoint a custodian.

Taxes

All investors pay 0.3% tax on the value of their stock sales. Liability to capital gains tax depends on nationality of investor. Nationals of countries with no tax treaties pay 25% on capital gains or 10% of the value of the transaction whichever is lower. They are also subject to 25% withholding tax on dividends and on interest income. Funds invested may be freely repatriated.

MEXICO

The Mexico Stock Exchange (MSE) was established in 1894. MSE is owned by 33 brokerage firms (Casas de bolsa), five of which are foreign. In 1993 significant reforms were implemented mainly directed at increasing investment opportunities through a wider self regulatory scheme and the quotation of foreign instruments on the MSE. The collapse of the Mexican market in 1994-95 triggered the "tequila effect" which hit emerging markets globally.

Total market capitalization in 1996 was US $ 106.2 billion which formed 34.2 per cent of GDP. There were 193 companies listed on the MSE. The global rank of Mexican market was 22nd in 1996. In 1993 Mexican Banking and Securities Commission (MBSC) approved the introduction of a second tier market on the MSE to attract medium sized companies.

Mexico had an auction type market with open outcry. A new automated system (BMV-SENTRA) which connects 53 intermediaries via 180 terminals was introduced in 1996 to trade warrants and about half the stocks listed in the exchange. If price change exceeds 5 per cent trading can be suspended for 30 minutes.

Settlement is on the second business day following the trade in the case of spot transactions. The Institute for the Deposit of Securities (INDEVAL) set up in 1980 functions as a clearing house and depository for securities listed on MSE, eliminating the need for physical transfer. INDEVAL holds 75 per cent of shares traded and the rest by banks which also provide custodial services.

Capital gains are exempt from tax. There is no withholding tax on dividends. Interest is subject to withholding tax which may be reduced by treaty. Foreign investment in MSE ordinary shares in 1996 was $ 31.0 billion.

International Comparison of Stock Markets

Table 10.1 presents a comparative picture of the ten major developed markets and ten major emerging markets on December 31, 1996. The composite index (BSE = 100) based on market capitalization and exchange turnover, worked out by the Bombay Stock Exchange and presented in the Table puts in perspective the relative size of the developed markets as well as emerging markets in terms of the position of the Bombay Stock Exchange. The Table reveals that all the stock exchanges in developed markets were quite large. The exchanges in USA, Japan, and U.K. together accounted for $13.3 trillion of market capitalization and the remaining seven of the developed markets accounted for $ 3.3 trillion of market capitalization. Among the developed markets the highest turnover ratio of 123.2 was registered in Germany. The composite index of 624.8 of Germany would have been much lower but for the high turnover ratio of 123.2 among the developed countries. USA which had a turnover ratio of 92.8 had the highest composite index of 6,713.4 among all the developed and emerging markets on account of the highest market capitalization among the countries listed in the Table. Japan and UK had high composite index reflecting their large market capitalization although their turnover ratio was low.

Table 10.1: International Comparison: Ten Major Developed Markets and Ten Major Emerging Markets (As on 31st December, 1996)

(Amount in U.S. $ million)

Sl. No.	Name of the Country	No. of Listed Companies	Market Capitalization	Turnover (US $ Million)	Turnover Ratio	Composite Index*
DEVELOPED MARKETS						
1.	U.S.A.	8,479	8,484,433	7,121,487	92.8	6,713.4
2.	Japan	2,334	3,088,850	1,251,998	37.1	1,831.6
3.	U.K.	2,433	1,740,246	578,471	36.8	974.0
4.	Germany	681	670,997	768,745	123.2	624.8
5.	France	686	591,123	277,100	49.8	367.7
6.	Canada	1,265	486,268	265,360	62.2	319.5
7.	Hong Kong	561	449,381	166,419	44.2	259.3
8.	Switzerland	213	402,378	392,783	94.0	343.4
9.	Netherlands	217	378,721	339,500	92.4	309.5
10.	Australia	1,135	311,988	145,482	52.2	193.7
EMERGING MARKETS						
1.	Malaysia	621	307,179	173,568	65.5	204.6
2.	Taiwan, China	382	273,608	470,193	204.1	326.4
3.	South Africa	626	241,571	27,202	10.4	110.9
4.	Brazil	551	216,990	112,108	61.5	139.7
5.	Korea	760	138,817	177,266	110.5	137.6
6.	Mexico	193	106,540	43,040	43.6	63.1
7.	Thailand	454	99,828	44,365	36.8	61.0
8.	Indonesia	253	91,016	32,142	40.8	51.8
9.	Philippines	216	80,649	25,519	36.6	44.5
INDIA (BSE)						
	(i) 31.12.96	**5,999**	**122,605**	**109,448**	**87.6**	**100.0**
	(ii) 31.03.97	**5,832**	**129,220**	**346,195**		

$$* \quad \text{Composite Index} = \frac{\text{Exchange Market Capitalization}}{\text{BSE Market Capitalization}} + \frac{\text{Exchange Turnover}}{\text{Bombay Turnover}} /2\times 100$$

as on 31st December, 1996

Source: The Stock Exchange, Mumbai, *Annual Report,* 1996-97.

Chapter–10

The ten emerging markets had a market capitalization of $ 1680 billion. Malaysia, Taiwan, South Africa and Brazil accounted for 62 per cent.

International Comparison by Transactions

Size of the Exchanges: Size of the exchange measured by the number of transactions is presented in Table 10.2. In India while the value of transaction is small by international standards, the number required to be implemented is commensurately large. NSE and BSE are ranked third and fifth respectively in 2003 and 2004.

Table 10.2: Size of Exchanges by Transactions (2003 and 2004)

	2003	*2004*
NASDAQ	1	1
NYSE	2	2
NSE	3	3
Shanghai	4	4
BSE	5	5
Korea	7	6
Taiwan	6	7
Shenzhen	8	8
Deutsche Borse	9	9
London	11	10

Source: Government of India, *Economic Survey*, 2004-05, p.78.

Turnover Ratio

Table 10.3 presents the turnover ratio (per cent) in the equity spot market in 15 countries. Turnover ratio is defined as the one year trading volume divided by market capitalization. Spot market turnover is likely to grow in tandem with market capitalization. India is ranked 12th among the fifteen countries presented in the Table 10.3. Taiwan (163%), China (139%) and Korea (118%) are ahead of India. India turnover ratio is trading in the range of values seen with the developed equity markets such as those of Japan (88%) and the USA (119%).

Table 10.3: Turnover Ratio on the Equity and Spot Market: An International Comparison (November 2003 – October 2004)

Rank	*Country*	*Turnover Ratio*
1	U.K.	165
2	Taiwan	163
3	Turkey	141
4	China	139

contd...

Rank	Country	Turnover Ratio
5	Germany	125
6	Spain	120
7	U.S.A.	119
8	Sweden	118
9	Korea	118
10	Italy	113
11	Finland	112
12	India	107
13	Thailand	98
14	Switzerland	91
15	Japan	88

Source: Government of India, *Economy Survey*, 2004-05.

References

Bombay Stock Exchange, *Annual Report,* 1991-92 and 1996-97, International Finance Corporation, *Emerging Markets 1998 Fact Book,* Washington, May 1999.

Reilly, Frank K, *Investments,* Third Edition, The Dryden Press Fort Worth, Texas 1992.

Shankar V., "Overseas Stock Exchanges", A Systems Perspective, I, II and III, *Handbook of Articles from Bombay Stock Exchange Review,* 1989-91.

Teweles, Richard J., Bradlay, Edward and Tewles, Ted M, *The Stock Market,* Sixth Edition, John Wiley & Sons Inc., New York.

The Guide to World Equity Markets 1991, Euro Money Books.

The Guide to World Equity Market, 1993, Euro Money Books.

Salaman Smith Barney, *Guide to World Equity Markets 1998,* Euro Money Publications.

Government of India, *Economic Survey,* 2004-05.

11

INSIDER TRADING

NATURE AND DEFINITION OF INSIDER TRADING

Insider trading may be defined as sale or purchase of securities by persons who possess price sensitive information about the company on account of their fiduciary capacity. Securities include shares, debentures, rights, index contracts, options and futures in respect of such securities. Insider transactions include also those who receive confidential price sensitive information from insiders who have access to it.

Market Efficiency of Insider Trading

Investors in many countries still think insider trading is a legitimate way to beat the market, not an offence. The essence of investing in stock market is finding an extra bit of information that gives an edge over rivals. In India much of the trading is based on insider information. Some economists argue that insider trading can impart efficiency to the market which is beneficial to the investor. If insiders trade on their information, share prices come to reflect that knowledge. Friedrich Von Hayek recognized that prices acted as signals to uninformed players in a market. The prices are more accurate and react sooner than they would have been had the insider not traded. Accurate prices reduce risk for investors who will then require smaller reward or risk premium for buying the shares. Companies can then raise capital more cheaply and invest more which contributes to economic growth.

Insider regulations should contain two crucial elements. First protection of the integrity of the market and secondly defining precisely items to be protected. The integrity of the market is adversely affected if investors lose sufficient faith in the fairness of the market. They may boycott it. Investors may think that returns have more to do with knowing the right people than informed judgement or even luck. The economic implications of loss of market integrity are less liquidity and a higher cost of capital. Insider regulations must secure the basic belief of investors in the fairness of market.

The second element, defining what information is "inside" and how to punish its disclosure is harder. Insider regulations should encourage companies to make information available quickly to the market. Regulators and shareholders should put far greater pressure on managers to disclose market sensitive news quickly through stock exchange announcements and to use or vote them out when they do not.

Scope of Insider Trading in USA

The growth of the securities market everywhere has been accompanied by the single most unfair and unhealthy practice of insider trading. It damages the integrity of the market. The victim of insider trading is the market itself. Investors will shy away from a market in which they are the last to know. Most of the countries have laws against insider trading.

America has been stamping on insider trading since the 1930's and has intensified it since mid-1980's. US Securities and Exchange Commission (SEC) has treated it as a violation of securities law since 1934. Most European Community countries have now implemented a 1989 EC directive that makes insider trading illegal. The Report of the US Senate Banking and Currency Committee (1934) observed that, "Among the most vicious practices unearthed was the flagrant betrayal of their fiduciary duties by directors and officers of corporations who used their positions of trust and the confidential information which came to them in such position, to aid them in their market activities." The Report adds that "...closely allied to this type of abuse was the unscrupulous employment of inside information by large stockholders who, while not being directors and officers, exercised sufficient control over the destinies of their companies to enable them to acquire and profit by inside information." The U.S. Securities Exchange Commission adopted in 1942 a new rule under which practically anyone could be accused of insider trading. The provisions were used by US Courts to remedy unlawful trading and tipping by persons in a variety of positions of trust and confidence such as underwriters, journalists, lawyers, accountants or government officials.

Directors, Officers and principal stockholders in USA are presumed to have access to information about their companies that is not available to the rest of investing public. Corporate insiders by trading on that information can reap profits at the expense of less informed investors. Insiders are required under SEA 1934 and rules of SEC to disclose their holdings of and transactions involving equity securities of their companies. They are subject to disgorgement of short swing profits arising from purchase and sale of equity shares and are prohibited from engaging in short sales of their company's equity shares. Insiders have to file public reports of their stock ownership and trading activities of the issuer with SEC and any exchange on which issuer's securities are listed. The reporting obligations have come to include since 1991 transactions by insiders in derivative securities.

Shareholders and public investors at large are protected by rule 106-5 against fraud and deceipt in connection with purchase or sale of any security and various other antifraud provisions. Insiders must disclose material facts that are known to them by virtue of their position but that are not known to persons with whom they deal and that, if known, would affect their investment judgement. Failure to disclose constitutes a violation of antifraud provision. If on the other hand disclosure prior to affecting a purchase or sale would be improper or unrealistic in the particular context the insider must forego the transaction. A violation of the "disclosure-or-abstain" rule, when combined with fiduciary duty to disclose, constitutes illegal insider trading.

Outsiders may become fiduciaries of shareholders when they enter into a special confidential relationship in the conduct of a business and are given access to information solely for corporate purposes.

The opportunity for an insider trading arises when the earnings of the company are likely to be affected. Such occasions might be favourable or unfavourable. Favourable occasions are expansion, diversification and takeover. Unfavourable occasions are poor performance of the company resulting in reduction or loss of earnings and amalgamation. In the eighties, takeover mania and leveraged buy-outs swept through USA. The temptation to convert nonpublic information could not be resisted in view of the enormous profit to be made. A simple and common plea in defence was that they overheard a conversation about a takeover while sitting in a restaurant or waiting at the airport. Consequently, the law was amended in 1984 to curb illegal transactions in the market, make the provisions more stringent and penalties more severe to deter would be offenders.

The amendments to the original Securities Exchange Act 1934 carried out through the Insider Trading Sanctions Act 1984 were aimed to serve primarily as a deterrent to insider trading. The civil penalty for insider trading was raised to three times the profit made or loss avoided and the criminal penalty to $ 100,000. The Insider Trading and Securities Fraud and Enforcement Act, 1988 was intended to strengthen and clarify the civil and criminal enforcement provisions of the Insider Trading Sanctions Act, 1984. In addition to expanding the sanctions and the scope of liability, the Act creates a private right of action for market purchasers against market sellers when the seller is not an insider with a duty to disclose but is liable solely on a theory of misappropriating inside information.

Speed Vs. Transamerica Corp.

In the *Speed* case (1952), a tobacco company had a cigarette-tobacco inventory that had greatly appreciated in value during World War II, and this was common knowledge in financial and tobacco circles. It was not known, however, that the controlling shareholder had devised a liquidation plan whereby this appreciated value could be realized in spite of price controls on cigarettes. It was the controlling shareholder's failure to disclose to the plaintiff minority shareholder his intention to liquidate the corporation under this plan that a Federal District Court considered actionable. Without knowledge of the plan, knowledge that tobacco inventories had appreciated was not important.

The judgement found that it is unlawful for an insider, such as a majority stockholder, to purchase the stock of minority stockholders without disclosing material facts affecting the value of the stock, known to the majority stockholder by virtue of his inside position but not known to the selling minority stockholders, which information would have affected the judgment of the sellers. The duty of disclosure stems from the necessity of preventing a corporate insider from utilizing his position to take unfair advantage of the uninformed minority stockholders. It is an attempt to provide some degree of equalization of bargaining positions in order that the minority may exercise an informed judgment in any such transaction. Some courts have called this a fiduciary duty while others state it as a duty imposed by the "special circumstances". One of the primary purposes of the Securities Exchange Act of 1934 ... was to outlaw the use of inside information by corporate officers and principal stockholders for their own financial advantage to the detriment of uninformed public security holders.

Other Countries

Germany passed the financial market bill in 1994 that for the first time made insider trading a criminal offence punishable by upto five years in prison. The insider trading rule apply to all market segments and off exchange trades. France banned insider trading in 1974, Britain in 1980, Switzerland and Japan in the late 1980's and Italy in 1991.

In Britain, insider trading is a criminal offence under the Criminal Justice Act, 1993. The new legislation significantly extends the scope of original law in several directions. Under the new law, it is a criminal offence for an individual who has inside information as an insider, to deal in securities which are "price-affected" securities in relation to that information, or to encourage another person to deal. It is also a criminal offence for such an individual to disclose the information to another person, other than in the proper performance of his employment, office or profession. The dealing in question must either be on a regulated market or it must involve a professional intermediary. The new law does not require an insider to be connected with the issuer to which his information relates. This change significantly expands the number of potential insiders.

Hong Kong curbs insider trading without making it a criminal offence. Any one found guilty of insider trading can be fined up to three times the forbidden profits he made and banned from acting as a company director.

Calculation of Profit or Avoidance of Loss

In the USA, the SEC was of the view that the difference between the actual buying and the selling price should be accepted as the profit made. The courts, however, ruled that this calculation should only consider the stock price at the time of buying and that when the specific information used became public. For example, if a stock was bought at 100 per share and then sold at 200 even though the price was 150 when the information became public, the profit for the insider trader was only 50 and not 100.

Enforcement

The problem with insider legislation is enforcement. Even abroad the enforcers hit-rate is very poor. In the seven year period 1987-1994, London Stock Exchange has referred more than 300 cases of suspected insider dealing to the Department of Trade and Industry. Out of these, there were 50 prosecutions and these produced 23 convictions. In Britain, insiders face unlimited fines and seven years in jail. Since so few are convicted it has not proved to be adequate deterrent. The record of U.S. Securities and Exchange Commission in this regard is much better which currently yields 35 convictions a year. US legislation, firstly, does not have any fancy definition of insider dealing since it provides loopholes to the insider traders. In the U.S.A., the consensus was that SEC should have enough freedom to respond to new market developments and the fringes of what constitutes an offence are "occasionally fuzzy". Insider trading is defined in broad terms and SEC has an option to prescribe new rules and regulations in the future for the purpose of declaring certain transactions illegal.

The law relating to insider trading should make the risk of being caught and punished great enough to deter insider dealing. The effectiveness of U.S. SEC in this regard arises from first, it can deal with securities offences including insider dealing by means of civil action leading to fines, disgorgement of profits or the withdrawal of licenses. For serious offences, criminal action is initiated by federal or state prosecutors with the threat of penal sentence. Criminal proceedings, however, demand high standards of proof. For lesser cases civil action is initiated because it requires lower standards of proof. The regulator negotiates a settlement with suspect under threat of criminal proceedings. SEC, however, enjoys the advantages of civil disciplinary powers and the ability to plea bargain with suspects.

Insider Prosecution in U.S.A.

In the USA, SEC has been prosecuting insider trading violations by extension of the concept of the insider trader. In one of the best known cases SEC Vs Texas Gulf Sulfur (1965-66), the SEC went to court to force the repayment of insider profits not only by those within the company but also by someone who had heard about a huge ore find in the Company's Kidd Creek, Ontario, property.

The SEC had thus extended the doctrine to the 'tippee' as well as the 'tipper'. An analyst who is able to obtain true inside information through personal conversation with corporate insiders would be a 'tippee' and is illegal for him to indulge in trading activity based on such information. In Shapiro Vs. Merrill Lynch a brokerage firm passed on confidential information about the decline in earnings of a company to certain institutional investors who dumped their vast holdings before the results were publicly announced. A Wall Street journal columnist was jailed for four years for buying stock based on information given to him for his column which was not used at all. All these cases are apart from the more celebrated prosecutions of Ivan Boesky, Dennis Levine and Michael Milken in the eighties.

Monitoring

To watch insider activities, monitoring of holding of stocks by insiders is necessary. While Indian Insider Regulations do not provide for it, under the US SE Act, insider holdings have to be reported. An insider in the US is a director, executive officer or a stockholder who owns 5 per cent or more of any class of stock. The names of these parties are filed with the Commission at the time of registration. In addition, anyone who attains this status after registration of the security must file his holdings of stock within 10 days. Changes should be reported. The purpose of this regulation is to enable SEC and shareholders of the company to watch the actions of such holders, who may resort to dealing in their own stocks on the basis of insider information.

Empirical Evidence

A number of studies in USA based on the information published in the SECs official Summary of Securities Transactions and Holdings have found that insiders utilize their monopolistic information to their advantage and earn positive abnormal returns by trading in their firms securities[26]. Several studies have also found that non insiders could earn positive abnormal profits by adopting a strategy of buying (selling) stocks that insiders have bought (sold).

A more recent study[27] of the effects of the U.S. Insider Trading Sanctions Act (ITSA) of 1984 by Eyssell and Reburn found that the Act has deterred corporate insiders from increasing (decreasing) their shareholdings before events that increase (decrease) firm value. The results of the study indicate that before the passage of ITSA insiders exploited their access to nonpublic information by selling shares before

26. Lorie. J.H. and Neiderhoffer V., "Predictive and Statistical Properties of Insider Trading", *Journal of Law and Economics,* (April 1968); Pratt, S.P., and Dever, C.W., "Relationship between Insider Trading and Rates of Return for NYSE Common Stocks 1960-1966" in Lorie J.H. and Breley R. Eds., *Modern Developments in Investment Management,* 2nd Ed. Dryden Press Hinsdale, 111. 1978 Originally quoted in Fuller, Ressell J. and Farrell Jr. James L., *Modern Investments and Security Analysis*, McGraw Hill International Edition, 1987.
27. Eyssell, Thomas and Reburn, James P., "The Effects of the Insider Trading Sanctions Act of 1984: The Case of Seasoned Equity Offerings", *The Journal of Financial Research,* Summer 1993, p. 161-170.

the announcement of equity issues. However, after passage of ITSA insiders no longer displayed this behaviour. Eyssell and Reburn conclude that ITSA has a deterent effect which is more actively concentrated on insiders at the highest level of the firm who are most visible to regulators and other market participants. Eyssell and Rehurn point out that it may be possible to modify the behaviour of some groups of insiders via legislative means. According to them, no empirical study has been undertaken of the transactions by persons or groups not required to register with SEC as insiders but who may have access to non-public information.

The paper by Bin, Ke, Steven, Huddart and Kathy, Petroni provides evidence that insiders possess and trade upon, knowledge of specific and economically significant forthcoming accounting disclosures as long as two years prior to the disclosure[28]. Insiders sales increase three to nine quarters prior to a break in a string of consecutive increases in quarterly earnings. Insider trading takes place quite early, as early as two years because they have knowledge of the unfolding of events. This is more frequent for growth firms. They avoid abnormal selling of stock within two quarters prior to the break.

Definition of Insider in India

SEBI Insider Regulations 1992 defined insider "as any person who is or was connected with the company or is deemed to have been connected with the company and who is reasonably expected to have access by virtue of such connection to unpublished price sensitive information in respect of securities of the company, or who has received or has had access to such unpublished price sensitive information." (See Appendix 11.1)

Scope of Price Sensitive Information

SEBI Insider Regulations define unpublished price sensitive information as any information which relates to

(i) financial results (both half yearly and annual) of the company;
(ii) intended declaration of dividends (both interim and final);
(iii) issue of shares by way of public rights and bonus;
(iv) any major expansion plans or execution of new projects;
(v) amalgamations, mergers and takeovers;

28. "What insiders know about future earnings and how they use it: Evidence from insider trades", *Journal of Accounting and Economics,* 35(2003), p.315-346.

(vi) disposal of the whole or substantially the whole of the undertaking;

(vii) such other information as may affect the earnings of the company and;

(viii) any changes in policies, plans or operations of the company.

Insider Dealing

The SEBI Insider Regulations 1992 prohibit dealing, communicating or counselling on matters relating to insider trading. It is laid down that no insider shall,

(i) communicate any unpublished price sensitive information with or without his request for such information; and

(ii) counsel or procure any other person to deal in securities of any company on the basis of unpublished price sensitive information.

Corporate Governance Measure

To align the interests of the company's shareholders to that of the company's insiders the additional regulation (2007) compels an 'insider' to surrender such profits to the company in any of his or her transaction concerning equity based securities of the company including parents or subsidiary's shares in the event both the buy and sell sides of the transaction are entered into within six months of the other. Insiders would not be able to take advantage of price sensitive information.

Negotiated Deals

SEBI issued guidelines in August 1998 with a view to make corporate deals more transparent and to ensure that no insider trading takes place. A negotiated deal is a transaction having either value of Rs.25 lakhs and more or a volume of not less than 10,000 shares. On settlement of the deals, all negotiated deals must result in delivery of shares. Cancellation of such deals would require prior approval of the stock exchange. The transaction might be settled either through the clearing house or bilaterally as prescribed by the exchange. Cross deals between two clients of the same broker will also be considered as negotiated deals if the size of the transaction is as big as defined.

Negotiated corporate deals have to be reported to the stock exchange within 15 minutes of their finalization. All negotiated deals informed to the exchange and displayed on the screen must include the name of the security, price, quantity, value and name of the brokers involved. Exchanges must arrange for dissemination of information relating to the execution of negotiated deals. In case of a violation of reporting requirements laid down by SEBI, the exchange can prescribe penalties.

Legislative Remedies: Civil and Criminal

As noted above, the Insider Regulations in India prohibit dealing, communicating or counselling on matters relating to insider trading. Violation of these provisions is considered as committing the offense of insider trading. SEBI can launch an investigation and inspection of books of account, other records and documents of an inside trader on the basis of complaints received from investors or intermediaries or *suo-moto* upon its knowledge or information in its possession to protect the interest of investors in securities against breach of insider trading regulations. SEBI after investigation and hearing the insider can give directions to protect the interest of the investors, securities market and due compliance of the SEBI Act, 1992. The directions to inside trader would be, not to deal in securities in any particular manner, prohibit the insider from disposing of any of the securities acquired in violation of the regulations and restraining the insider from communicating or counselling any person to deal in securities. SEBI has also powers to initiate criminal prosecution under Section 24 of SEBI Act of 1992.

How Does Insider Trading Work

A large amount of insider trading in India takes place through broker-management nexus. Managements employ the services of brokers close to them to purchase and sell shares. Since the brokers gain knowledge of the likely trend in scrip price they buy and sell on their own account top. Many of the big brokers are also privy to major happenings in companies. Journalists, government officials and company executives deal on the basis of insider information. The financial institutions and banks also trade on insider information. They regularly buy and sell shares and possess inside information about the company in which they have invested either in equity or as term loans. The mutual funds floated by them can always get a feedback from the other departments about major happenings in the company. Finally, there are brokers who ferret out the advance tax paid by companies to get an idea of the trend in earnings of the company.

TISCO Case

An example (1993) of insider trading relates to Tata Iron and Steel Company (TISCO). The results of operations in 1992-93 were poor.

The pretax profits for half year 1992-93 registered a steep fall to Rs. 50.22 crores from Rs. 278.16 crores (full year) in 1991-92 and Rs. 238.13 crores (full year) in 1990-91. Before the announcement of the half yearly results, there was intense activity in the volume of TISCO shares traded between October 22, 1992 and October 29, 1992[29]. The price of the share registered a sharp fall of 36.7 per cent from Rs. 335 on October 27, 1992 to Rs. 245 on November 6, 1992. It may, however, be noted that SENSEX registered a decline of 8.3 per cent during the same period from 2986.7 on October 27, 1992 to 2756 on November 6, 1992. The sharp fall in prices of TISCO shares and active trading indicate that insiders who had knowledge of poor results of the company had manipulated the market to make large short sales. Bombay Stock Exchange authorities initiated a probe. Small investors were hit badly. The Bombay Stock Exchange authorities claimed that it would not be possible for the exchange to initiate action even if it was proved that insider trading took place in the absence of any law against it. It may be noted that SEBI Insider Regulations were issued on November 19, 1992.

CIPLA (Pharmaceuticals)

A steep rise in the share price (of face value of Rs.100) from Rs.6,900 (high) on 5.11.1993 to Rs.36000 (high) on 31.3.94 of CIPLA, a pharmaceutical company, listed on BSE was registered. The rise in share price was on account of the insider information about the impending issue of bonus shares about which the Bombay Stock Exchange was informed in the third week of January 1994. Although Insider Regulations were laid down in 1992 and SEBI's chairman S. S. Nadkarni declared in March 1994 that CIPLA affair would be examined, no formal investigation to public knowledge was conducted.

Hindustan Lever Limited (HLL) Case

The first ever case investigated by SEBI and orders passed under Insider Regulations, 1992 was the case of Hindustan Lever Ltd. in 1998.

This case relates to the allegation that HLL as an insider purchased the securities of Brooke Bond Lipton India Limited (BBLIL) on the basis

29. Trading volume in TISCO shares,
    22.10.1992 3.26 lakhs shares.
    25.10.1992 3.78 lakhs shares.
    26.10.1992 5.95 lakhs shares.
    29.10.1992 9.99 lakhs shares.
    31.10.1992 Ban on short sales.
Subsequent volume 6.25 lakhs shares.

of unpublished price sensitive information thereby violating Insider Trading Regulations 1992.

HLL is an Indian subsidiary of Unilever Pic. (U.K.) (Unilever) with 51 per cent equity. Unilever also held 50.2 per cent equity of BBLIL. Both these companies were subsidiaries of Unilever. With the announcement of the merger of BBLIL with HLL to the stock exchanges on April 19, 1996 there were allegations in the market and media regarding leakage of information and insider trading. SEBI launched *suo motto* an investigation in April 1997 and gave its verdict on March 11, 1997. SEBI found from investigation, *prima facie,* that

HLL was an "insider" within the meaning of regulation 2(3) read with regulation 2H of the Regulations;

The information about the merger was "unpublished price sensitive information" within the meaning of regulation 2(k) of the Regulations;

By buying eight lakhs shares of BBLIL, prior to the announcement regarding the merger of BBLIL with HLL on April 9, 1996, HLL had violated regulations prohibiting insider trading.

After the consideration of investigation report, SEBI "communicated the findings" on August 4, 1997 to HLL.

HLL had countered SEBI's charge through a reply on 9.9.1997, personal hearing on 17.10/97 and two legal opinions on 19-11-'97 and 27-11-97: That it cannot be considered "an insider" within the meaning of the existing rules. It was in fact a party to the deal.

The news of an impending merger was common knowledge well before the time the deal with UTI took place. Unilever's policy of merging its different entities in India was very well known. Two plantation companies Doom Dooma and Tea Estates got merged earlier. Liptons and Brooke Bond joined together to become BBLIL.

If the impending merger was widely anticipated, it cannot by any stretch of imagination become "unpublished price sensitive" information. Here the specific point is that the merger itself might have been widely anticipated but the time frame (to complete the formalities) and the swap ratio (which would establish the gains or losses of the two different sets of shareholders) were not. HLL has more than once made the argument that on March 25, 1996 when it bought the shares from UTI it was unaware of the swap formula.

Mere news of merger between HLL and BBLIL does not qualify as price sensitive information. The stock prices would react not just because the market is convinced of a merger but on its estimate of swap formula.

Comment

The objective of the share transaction was to ensure that Unilever has a 51 per cent stake in HLL after the merger. HLL had three options.

- Make a preferential allotment to Unilever: this would, in retrospect have been the most straight forward method. It would have involved the subscription by Unilever to a premium preferential issue by the Indian company. Apart from being transparent this would have benefited the Indian shareholders of HLL as well. It is claimed that this route would have been cheaper than the method adopted (HLL purchasing shares from the UTI). The problem here is that funds will normally have to come from abroad to buttress Unilever's stake in the expanded Indian subsidiary.
- A second method was to purchase BBLIL shares from the market. This was ruled out by HLL because it was felt to be practically inexpedient large buy orders pushing up the market and likely problem of deliveries.
- A negotiated deal with the UTI was chosen. Purchase of BBLIL shares by HLL was only an incidental step. After the merger was completed HLL's holdings of BBLIL shares were extinguished. Every BBLIL shareholder received HLL shares on the basis of the agreed swap formula (9 shares of HLL for 20 shares of BBLIL). So the shares purchased from UTI were never meant to be resold. The question of profiting from the trade does not arise, claimed HLL. Although HLL did not profit, it helped in shoring up its parent's stake. In other words, its shareholders' money was used to benefit Unilever. A direct subscription by Unilever would have involved a remittance into India.

SEBI's Order

SEBI in its order observed that HLL was an insider.

- HLL, a company is covered by the definition "person".
- HLL is a person deemed to be connected with BBLIL. Before the merger, HLL and BBLIL had common parentage being subsidiaries of Unilever and had a common management.
- HLL by virtue of its connection was reasonably expected to have access to the information about the proposed merger and as such would also be an insider. HLL received the information independently as one of the principal parties to the transaction as well as a deemed connected person to BBLIL. SEBI observed

that HLL's argument would permit a connected or a deemed connected person to misuse the price sensitive information because he has received the information independently and not by virtue of connection with the company whose shares he has traded in. In SEBI's words, "This would be against all canons of fairness and transparency on the securities markets and no legislation can approve, let alone prescribe it."

Chronology of Trading

A core team including common directors of HLL and BBLIL started on 13-9-1995 evaluation of the merger of BBLIL and HLL. On 5-1-1996 the valuers were short listed. On 17-1-1996 Unilever informed the core team regarding the granting of in principle approval for the merger of BBLIL with HLL. During March 6-15, 1996 the core team deliberated on timing of amalgamation and agreed on the announcement being made on 19-4-1996 and convening the Board meeting on April 22 or 23, 1996.

In the Board meeting on 6-3-1996 HLL decided to buy 8 lakhs shares of BBLIL and shares were purchased on 25.3.96 from UTI which was unaware of the merger for Rs.350.35 per share. The purchase took place a little prior to public announcement of merger on 19-4-1996. On merger of BBLIL with HLL there was no need for maintaining a 51 per cent stake. The purchase was directed toward raising the level of equity holding of Unilever to 51 per cent of the combined HLL. The acquisition of eight lakhs shares of BBLIL from UTI by HLL was motivated to ensure a 51 per cent holding for Unilever in the merged company. The transaction was founded upon and affected on the basis of unpublished price sensitive information about the impending merger.

LOSS OR GAIN

Gain to Unilever

Unilever in order to raise its holding in HLL (after its merger with BBLIL) would have been required to bring in about Rs. 45-50 crores (including about Rs.28 crores spent on purchase of 8 lakhs shares) in foreign exchange. Instead HLL, the Indian subsidiary of Unilever, depleted its resources to acquire 8 lakhs shares before the announcement of merger and 4.73 lakhs shares after the announcement of merger. In the corporate world, normally to acquire holding upto 51 per cent, the promoters or holding companies, perforce, spend substantial amounts. In this case, the holding company, that is HLL, acquire holding upto 51 per cent. This way, while, on one hand, HLL did secure an advantage for its holding company, that is, Unilever, on the other, the deal(s) caused a loss of foreign exchange of about Rs.50 crores to the country.

HLL as the subsidiary company depleted its resources to enable its holding company, that is, Unilever, to gain increased shareholding in the composite company after merger of two subsidiaries. The subsidiary company (HLL before merger) spent sizable funds out of its resources to purchase shares which were to be extinguished and that too for the benefit of its holding company (that is, Unilever). In a fair and transparent markets, adhering to high regulatory standards, such a practice is abhorrent and would be treated against the interests of the ordinary shareholders.

Loss to UTI

The loss may be calculated on the basis of the difference between the value of UTI holding if it had not sold eight lakhs shares and the amount it received. On a 20:9 swap ratio UTI would have received on the finalization of merger 3,60,000 shares whose market value was Rs.48.83 crores (at the rate of Rs. 1356 per share) which is Rs.20.38 crores more than what UTI actually got from the sale of eight lakhs BBLIL shares from HLL.

The second method of calculation of loss to UTI is the difference in market prices between March 1996, (Rs.356 plus premium) and December 1996 (Rs.356 plus premium). This was Rs.38 per share which for the entire deal of 8 lakhs shares would amount to Rs.3.04 crores.

SEBI concluded that HLL as an insider purchased eight lakhs shares of BBLIL on the basis of unpublished price sensitive information and had therefore violated Insider Trading Regulations.

SEBI directed HLL to compensate UTI to the extent it suffered disadvantage or incurred loss. The losses range from Rs.3.04 crores – 20.83 crores. However to be conservative and fair it was decided to place the likely loss to UTI at Rs.3.04 crores. This amount was calculated on the basis of difference between the market prices of the shares of BBLIL sold by UTI to HLL after the announcement of the merger and prior to the announcement of merger. SEBI also ordered the prosecution of five directors who were aware of the impending merger was price sensitive information along with HLL.

Direction of Appellate Tribunal

HLL appealed on April 2, 1998 to the Securities Appellate Tribunal against the order of SEBI in March 1998. The Securities Appellate

Tribunal passed the Direction on July 14, 1998 absolving HLL of the insider trading charge and struck down SEBI's order of prosecution against five HLL directors and payment of compensation of Rs.3.04 crores to the Unit Trust of India.

The Securities Appellate Tribunal on July 14, 1998 upheld HLL's view that the news of a possible merger was "generally known" because it had been widely speculated and reported in the media. The Appellate Tribunal therefore concluded that there was no reason to prosecute the company and its directors.

The appellate authority said, "An order of prosecution should be based on conclusive determination of all aspects of insider trading and on specific justification in terms of the gravity of the offence. For these reasons, we hold that SEBI is not justified in ordering the prosecution of the appellants."

It is also held that SEBI did not have the power to grant compensation to any party. More specifically, in the HLL case, UTI which is a well-established and qualified investor, could not but have known about the impending merger given the wide reporting in the media. Further, UTI had not expressed any grievance about the transaction for two years and had in fact sold more BBLIL shares to HLL in December 1996. It made a complaint only in April 1998, after the SEBI order was issued and HLL had appealed to the Securities Appellate Tribunal.

The order also said, "Since the possibility of merger appears to have been generally speculated about and was probably already discounted by the market, this information is not likely to have significantly impacted on the price at which the transaction was concluded with UTI in March 1996. This is further corroborated by the fact that UTI continued to sell BBLIL shares in the market after the merger at prices close, to the price at which they had sold shares to HLL in March 1996."

Comment

Under the SEBI Act, 1992, SEBI has general powers under Section 11 B to make orders in the interests of investors in securities and securities market and specific powers under Section 15 G of the Act to levy penalty for insider trading. SEBI in the past has ordered refund of moneys or confiscated or impounded proceeds of public issues under provisions of Section 11 B. Section 15 I lays down adjudication in cases of contravention of rules by broker, market intermediaries, mutual funds, asset management companies besides insider trading and other issues (Section 15 A to H). SEBI has been using the adjudication procedure where there is no urgency for relief or respondents are few. But adjudication is time consuming and would take years for investors to get relief. Further personal appearance before SEBI is necessary.

The appellate authority has said that SEBI had no power in the HLL case to take action under provisions of Section 11 B of SEBI Act and should have gone in for adjudication under Section 15 G. It has to be noted that there is a specific provision for adjudication (Section 15 I) and penalty for insider trading (Section 15 G). The question of speed in providing relief and need for personal appearance are not material in insider trading cases. Where a specific provision (15 G for insider trading) and procedure (15 I for adjudication of insider trading) exist they have to be followed.

A further point is about compensation versus penalty. The appellate authority held that SEBI cannot levy penalty under Section 11 B. As the Act reads insider trading proceedings have to be initiated under Section 15 G and penalty has to be levied as contemplated although a modest one of below Rs.5 lakhs. SEBI chose to use provisions of Section 11 B and awarded a compensation of Rs.3.04 crores which the Securities Appellate Tribunal held that SEBI had no power. It decided that 15 G should have been used, adjudication and penalty. The Securities Appellate Tribunal however has not commented that Unilever had raised its stake for free. The amount spent by HLL to acquire shares of BBLIL belonged to the entire body of shareholders. The gain in shareholding accrued to just Unilever. Finally, HLL was an insider unto itself (which was agreed by the appellate authority) and the gains of insider trading were used for private gain of Unilever.

SEBI TO MOVE BOMBAY HIGH COURT

It is reported (3.9.1998) that SEBI is likely to move the Bombay High Court against a statement made in its order by the Securities Appellate Tribunal (SAT) in the HLL Insider Trading Case. The SAT stated that "It was not open to SEBI to initiate investigations under the Insider Trading Regulations and then without passing an order under those regulations, taking recourse to the general powers given to it under Section 11 of the SEBI Act for awarding compensation." SEBI will be questioning the statement.

References

Ernest Block, *Inside Investment Banking, Dow Jones,* Irwin, Illinois, 1986.

Eyssell, Thomas H. and Reburn, James P., "The Effects of the Insider Trading Sanctions Act of 1984: The Case of Seasoned Equity Offerings" *The Journal of Financial Research,* Summer 1993, pp. 61-70.

Fuller, Russell J, and Farrell Jr., James L., *Modern Investments and Security Analysis,* McGraw Hill International Edition, 1987.

Gemavat Sanjeev, "Insider Trading", *The Chartered Accountant,* July 1993.

Lorie J. Hand Niederhoffer, "Predictive and Statistical Properties of Insider Trading", *Journal of Law and Economics,* April, 1968.

Pratt, S.P. and Devere, C.W., "Relationship between Insider Trading and Rates of Return for NYSE Common Stocks, 1960-1966" in Lorie, J.H. and Brealey, R., eds. *Modern Developments in Investment Management,* 2nd ed., Dryden Press, Hinsdale, 111, 1978.

Securities and Exchange Board of India *(Insider Trading) Regulations.* 1992.

Ke, Bin, Huddart, Steven and Petroni, Kathy, "What insiders know about future earnings and how they use it: Evidence from insider trades", *Journal of Accounting and Economics,* 35 (2003), p. 315-346.

Manne, Henry G., *Insider Trading and The Stock Market,* The Free Press, New York.

APPENDIX 11.1

INSIDER TRADING

Securities and Exchange Board of India Bombay, 19th November, 1992

Securities and Exchange Board of India (Insider Trading) Regulations, 1992

No. LE/6308/92 in exercise of the powers conferred by section 30 of The Securities and Exchange Board of India, Act 1992 (15 of 1992), the Board with the previous approval of the Central Government, hereby makes the following regulations, namely:-

CHAPTER – 1

PRELIMINARY

SHORT TITLE AND COMMENCEMENT

1. (1) These regulations may be called the Securities and Exchange Board of India (Insider Trading) Regulations, 1992.

   (2) These regulations shall come into force on the date of the publication in the Official Gazette.

Definitions: 2. In these regulations, unless the context otherwise requires:-

(a) "Act" means the Securities and Exchange Board of India Act, 1992 (15 of 1992);

(b) "body corporate" means a body corporate as defined under section 2 of the Companies Act, 1956 (1 of 1956);

(c) "connected person" means any person who –

   (i) is a director, as defined in clause (13) of section 2 of the Companies Act, 1956 (1 of 1956) of a company, or is deemed to be a director of that company by virtue of sub-clause (10) of section 307 of that Act or

   (ii) occupies the position as an officer or an employee of the company or holds a position involving a professional or business relationship between himself and the company and who may reasonably be expected to have an access to unpublished price sensitive information in relation to that company;

(d) "dealing in securities" means an act of buying, selling or agreeing to buy, sell or deal in any securities by any person either as principal or agent;

(e) "insider" means any person who, is or was connected with the company or is deemed to have been connected with the company, and who is reasonably expected to have access, by virtue of such connection, to unpublished price sensitive information in respect of securities of the company, or who has received or has had access to such unpublished price sensitive information;

(f) "investigating authority" means any officer of the Board or any other person, not being a firm, body corporate or an association of persons, having experience in dealing with the problems relating to the securities market and who is authorized by the Board under Chapter III;

(g) "officer of a company" means any person as defined in clause (30) of section 2 of the Companies Act, 1956 (1 of 1956) including an auditor of the company;

(h) "person is deemed to be a connected person" if such person —

(i) is a company under the same management or group of any subsidiary company thereof within the meaning of section (IB) of section 370, or sub-section (11) of section 372, of the Companies Act, 1956 (1 of 1956) or sub-clause (g) of section 2 of the Monopolies and Restrictive Trade Practices Act, 1969 (54 of 1969) as the case may be; or

(ii) is an official or a member of a stock exchange or of a clearing house of that stock exchange, or a dealer in securities within the meaning of clause (c) of section 2, and section 17 of the Securities Contracts (Regulation) Act, 1956 (42 of 1956) respectively or any employee of such member or dealer of a stock exchange;

(iii) is a merchant banker, share transfer agent, registrar to an issue, debenture trustee, broker, portfolio manager, Investment Advisor, sub-broker, Investment Company or an employee thereof, or, is a member of the Board of Trustees of a mutual fund or a member of the Board of Directors of the Asset Management Company of a mutual fund or is an employee thereof who have a fiduciary relationship with the company;

(iv) is a member of the Board of Directors, or an employee, of a public financial institution as defined in Section 4A of the

Companies Act, 1956; or (v) is an official or an employee of a self Regulatory Organization recognized or authorized by the Board of a regulatory body: or (vi) is a relative of any of the aforementioned persons; (vii) is a banker of the company,

(i) "relative" means a person, as defined in section 6 of the Companies Act, 1956 (1 of 1956),

(j) "stock exchange" means a stock exchange which is recognised by the Central Government under section 4 of the Securities Contracts (Regulation) Act, 1956 (42 of 1956);

(k) "unpublished price sensitive information" means any information which relates to the following matters or is of concern, directly or indirectly, to a company, and is not generally known or published by such company for general information, but which if published or known, is likely to materially affect the price of securities of that company in the market —

(i) financial results (both half-yearly and annual) of the company;

(ii) intended declaration of dividends (both interim and final);

(iii) issue of shares by way of public rights, bonus, etc.;

(iv) any major expansion plans or execution of new projects;

(v) amalgamation, mergers and takeovers;

(vi) disposal of the whole or substantially the whole of the undertaking;

(vii) such other information as may affect the earnings of the company;

(viii) any changes in policies, plans or operations of the company.

CHAPTER – 2

PROHIBITION ON DEALING, COMMUNICATING OR COUNSELLING

Prohibition on dealing communication or counselling on matters relating to insider trading

3. No insider shall –

(i) either on his own behalf or on behalf of any other person, deal in securities of a company listed on any stock exchange on the basis of any unpublished price sensitive information;

(ii) communicate any unpublished price sensitive information to any person, with or without his request for such information, except as required in the ordinary course of business or under any law; or

(iii) counsel or procure any other person to deal in securities of any company on the basis of unpublished price sensitive information.

VIOLATION OF PROVISIONS RELATING TO INSIDER TRADING

4. Any insider who deals in securities or communicates any information or counsels any person dealing in securities in contravention of the provisions of regulation 3 shall be guilty of Insider trading.

CHAPTER – 3

INVESTIGATION

BOARD'S RIGHT TO INVESTIGATE

5. (1) Where the Board, on the basis of written information in its possession, is of the opinion that it is necessary to investigate and inspect the books of account, other records and documents of an insider for any of the purposes specified in sub-regulation (2), it may appoint an investigating authority for the said purpose;

(2) The purposes referred to in sub-regulation (1) may be as follows:

(a) to investigate into the complaints received from investors, intermediaries or any other person on any matter having a bearing on the allegations of insider trading; and

(b) to investigate suo-moto upon its own knowledge or information in its possession to protect the interest of investors in securities against breach of these regulations.

Procedure for investigation

6. (1) Before undertaking an investigation under regulation 5, the Board shall give a reasonable notice to insider for that purpose.

(2) Notwithstanding anything contained in sub-regulation (1), where the Board is satisfied that in the interest of investors or in public interest no such notice should be given, it may by an order in writing direct that the investigation be taken up without such notice.

(3) On being empowered by the Board, the investigating authority shall undertake the investigation and inspection of books of accounts and insider against whom an investigation is being carried out shall be bound to discharge his obligations as provided in regulation 7.

Obligations of insider on investigation by the Board

7. (1) It shall be the duty of every insider, who is being investigated to produce to the investigating authority such books, accounts and other documents in his custody or control and furnish the authority with the statements and information relating to the transactions in securities make within such time as the said authority may require.

(2) The insider shall allow the investigating authority to have reasonable access to the premises occupied by such insider and also extend reasonable facility for examining any books, records, documents and computer data in his possession of the stock-broker or any other person and also provide copies of documents or other materials which, in the opinion of the investigating authority are relevant.

(3) The investigating authority, in the course of investigation, shall be entitled to examine or record statements of any member, director, partner proprietor and employee of the insider.

(4) It shall be the duty of every director, proprietor, partner, officer and employee of the insider to give to the investigating authority all assistance in connection with the investigation, which the insider may be reasonably expected to give.

Submission of Report to the Board

8. The investigating authority shall, within one month of the conclusion of the investigation submit an investigation report to the Board.

Communication of Findings etc.

9. (1) The Board shall after consideration of the investigation report communicate the findings to the insider and he shall be given an opportunity of being heard before any action is taken by the Board on the findings of the investigating authority.

(2) On receipt of the explanation, if any, from the insider, the Board may call upon the insider to take such measures as the Board may deem fit to protect the interest of investors and in the interest of the securities market and for due compliance with the provisions of the Act, rules made thereunder and these regulations.

Appointment of Auditor

10. Notwithstanding anything contained in regulation 5, the Board may appoint a qualified auditor to investigate into the books of account or the affairs of the insider;

Provided that, the auditor so appointed shall have the same powers of the inspecting authority as stated in regulation 5 and the insider shall have the obligations specified in regulation 7.

Directions by the Board

11. On receipt of the explanation, if any, from the insider under sub-regulation (2) of regulation 9, the Board may without prejudice to its right to initiate criminal prosecution under section 24 of the Act, give such directions to protect the interest of investors and in the interest of the securities market and for due compliance with the provisions of the Act, rules made thereunder and these regulations, as it deems fit for all or any of the following purposes; namely;

(a) directing the insider not to deal in securities in any particular manner;

(b) prohibiting the insider from disposing of any of the securities acquired in violation of these regulations;

(c) restraining the insider to communicate or counsel any person to deal in securities.

Appeal to the Central Government

12. Any person aggrieved by an order of the Board under these regulations may prefer an appeal to the Central Government.

[F.No.LE/6308/21]

G.V. Ramakrishna

Chairman,
Securities & Exchange Board of India

APPENDIX 12.1

CHAPTER – 4

Chapter 4 was inserted by SEBI on February 20, 2002 acting policy on disclosures and internal procedure for prevention of insider trading. The norms specify disclosure standards and trading restrictions on directors/officers and designated employees of the company; appointment of a compliance officer; and limited access to confidential and price sensitive information.

12

STOCK MARKET INDICATOR SERIES

INTRODUCTION

Price movements for the market as a whole are measured by market indicator series. The indicator series constitute a composite report on market performance. One popular type of indicator series is an index.

Uses of Market Indicator Series

Firstly, market indicator seriess constitute a bench mark to judge the performance of an individual portfolio. Any investor should be able to derive a rate of return comparable to the market by randomly selecting a large number of shares and debentures from the total market.

Secondly, indicator series help investors develop index portfolios. Several academic studies have revealed that money managers consistently outperformed a market indicator series on a risk adjusted basis over time. Investment in a portfolio that emulates the market portfolio should help in consistently doing better than the market. The development of index funds which are portfolios designed to track the performance of specified market indexes over time is based on this idea.

Thirdly, the indicator series are used as proxies for the share or debenture markets while examining the factors that influence aggregate price movements. They are also used to analyze the relationship among stock and bond returns of different countries and stock price movements. Market analysts and portfolio managers also use the indicator series to analyze the past movements in them to predict future.

Finally, to compute the systematic risk (which is the relationship between the rate of return for the security and the rate of return for a market portfolio of risky assets) for an individual security, the returns on that security must be related to those for an aggregate market index that serves as a proxy for the market portfolio of risky assets.

Definition of an Index

A price index such as the stock market index is an average of changes in the price of the individual securities in the market. It reflects the overall price or return movements of a group of securities. Movements in an index are determined by sample, weighting and computational procedure.

Sample is normally generated by random selection or by a non-random selection technique designed to incorporate desired characteristics. In the case of a stock market index desired characteristics are used to select sample shares rather than by completely random selection. Major criterion for selection are market activity, due representation to various industrial groups and to the major stock exchanges.

Weighing

In compiling an index number, three principal weighing schemes are used. These are price weighed, value weighed and equally weighed schemes. Stock market indices are constructed on the basis of anyone of the schemes. Although the terms average and index are used interchangeably, technically stock market price indexes are more refined methods of measuring changes in the level of stock prices than are the averages especially over long periods. Such price indexes use base periods that vary from index to index whereas averages are merely a weighed or unweighed arithmetic mean of a group of stocks. Further, indexes are weighed by one of the three methods discussed here such as multiplying the number of shares outstanding for each stock by the price of the stock.

PRICE WEIGHED SERIES

Price weighed series are calculated as an arithmetic average of the current prices of the sample securities. It is an arithmetic average of current prices. Dow Jones Industrial Average (DJIA) is the best known and is the oldest of the stock market indicator series. The DJIA is a price weighed average of 30 large well known industrial stocks listed on NYSE. The index is derived by totalling the current prices of 30 stocks and dividing the sum by a divisor adjusted to take account of stock splits and changes in the same over time. In India, the index number compiled by Reserve Bank of India which was discontinued in 1998 was a price weighed series.

Economic Times Index

Economic Times ordinary share price index is a simple arithmetic average of the price relatives[30] of 72 scrips. Price relatives for each day are obtained by dividing the daily quotations by the corresponding average prices of the base year 1984-85. No specific weights have been assigned. Adequate representation has been given to large stock exchanges (Bombay, Delhi, Calcutta, Madras, Ahmedabad, Pune and Kanpur), larger industry groups, the number of scrips listed in each industry group, the number of scrips listed for trading in each stock exchange and their paid-up capital. The criteria for selection of scrips was active trading measured by frequency of price change and the magnitude of price fluctuations.

No adjustment is made for dividends.

Adjustment for bonus issue is made by multiplying the base year price by number of shares held and dividend bonus issue. Adjustment for rights issue is made by calculating the estimated ex-rights price

$$Er = \frac{Cr + (f + p) / 1 + p}{Cr}$$

Cr = last cum rights price,
r = rights ratio,
f = face value of share,
p = premium per share.

Another example of a price weighed index is Nikkei Dow Jones Average which is an arithmetic average of prices of 225 stocks on the first section of the Tokyo Stock Exchange.

Value Weighed Series

Value weighed series is an indicator calculated as the total market value of the securities in the sample. It is based on the initial total market value of all stocks in the sample which is assigned a base index value of 100. From trading day to trading day a new aggregate market value is computed for all securities in the index and compared to the initial base value. The percentage change is multiplied by the beginning index value to obtain the indicator for the day.

30. A price relative is simply the stock price of this week divided by stock price of last week. If the stock price of this week is Rs. 330 and the stock price of last week was Rs. 315 then the price relative is 330/315 = 1.047619.

$$\text{Index}_t = \frac{P_t\, Q_t}{P_b\, Q_b} \times \text{Beginning index value}$$

The value weighed index adjusts automatically stock splits (bonus issues) and other capital changes because the decrease in the scrip price is offset by an increase in the number of shares outstanding. The importance of individual scrips or the weight of each scrip in the sample is proportional to the total market value of the sample. Companies with large market capitalization have a greater impact on the index than the same change for small companies.

Standard and Poor 500 Series

Standard and Poor (S&P) in U.S.A. was the first company in U.S.A. to employ a market value index. S&P computed separate indexes for industrial stocks, utilities and transportation firms along with a 500-stock composite index with 1935 to 1937 as a base period. Subsequently, base period was shifted to 1941-43. The series underwent significant changes in 1976.

Other indexes which are compiled on the basis of value weighed method are NYSE Indexes for different sectors covering all listed stocks. NASDAQ series (including all domestic listed stocks, 3967 in 1990), American Stock Exchange's price change index, Wilshire 5000 equity index published by Wilshire Associates of Santa Monica, California including stocks listed on NYSE (82 per cent weight), Amex (4 per cent) and OTC (14 per cent) and Dow Jones Equity Market Index covering 700 stocks in 82 industry groups listed on NYSE, Amex and OTC. Other US stock market series are Russell Indexes, the Russell 3,000 (US stocks representing 97 per cent of the US equity market), Russell 2000 (consisting of smallest 2000 in the Russell 3000 index) and Russell 1,000 (consisting of largest US stocks by capitalization).

In the U.K., Financial Times Actuaries share index covering stocks listed on the London Stock Exchange relate current market capitalization of each index to its market capitalization at the base date adjusting for capital changes.

NSE 50/S&P CNX NIFTY

The National Stock Exchange (NSE) on April 22, 1996 launched a new equity index – the NSE-50. The new index, which replaces the existing NSE-100 index, is expected to serve as an appropriate index for the new segment of futures and options.

The NSE-50 comprises 50 companies that represent 20 broad industry groups with an aggregate market capitalization of around Rs.1,70,000 crores. The new index covers about one-third of the total market capitalization. This is expected to give the index a very high hedging effectiveness making it suitable for future and options trading.

All companies included in the index have a market capitalization in excess of Rs.500 crores each and have a reasonably high level of liquidity.

The base period for the index is the close of prices on November 3, 1995 which marks one year of completion of operations of NSE's capital market segment. The base value of the index has been set at 1000.

The new index will be published daily, and will also be made available on real-time basis on the NSE's trading system during the market hours shortly.

NSE-50, *i.e.*, Nifty has been rechristened as S&P CNX Nifty with effect from July 28, 1998.

NSE MIDCAP Index

The NSE Midcap Index or the Junior Nifty (NSE-50 Midcap Index) comprises 50 stocks that represent 21 broad industry groups and will provide proper representation of the midcap segment of the Indian capital market. The new index is expected to have high hedging effectiveness for portfolios having midcap companies and will also be appropriate for index based derivatives.

The base period for the index is November 4, 1996 which signifies two years of completion of operations of the capital market segment of the NSE. The base value of the index has been set at 1000.

Besides the information of Nifty for the benefit of investors, the NSE will publish periodically the weightages of every security included in Junior Nifty, volatility of the index, rate of return on the index and liquidity measures of the constituent securities. The Junior Nifty will be published daily to begin with and will be made available on a real time basis on the NSE's trading system during market hours.

The midcap index set will be mutually exclusive of the Nifty securities set, its review will be on the same lines as Nifty. The index committee of the NSE, consisting of eminent personalities in the field of finance such as mutual funds, trading members and academicians will review the performance of Junior Nifty along with Nifty at the quarterly meetings.

Selection of the constituents of Junior Nifty is based on market capitalization and liquidity (impact cost). In the case of market capitalization, all the companies to be included in the index will have a market capitalization of Rs.200 crores or more and all selected securities will bear a weight in the index in the proportion of their market capitalization.

For inclusion in the Midcap Index, the securities should have high amount of liquidity defined in terms of trading frequency and cost of executing a transaction in all constituent securities in proportion of their weightages on immediate basis at any point in time.

Junior Nifty securities will be required to fully satisfy the required execution on 85 per cent of the trading days at an impact cost of less than 2.5 per cent. The impact cost of the select set for approximately Rs.25 lakhs transaction size is an average of 0.80 per cent for the period June to November 1996. The total market capitalization of the select Midcap Index set works out to be Rs.22,539 crores.

BOMBAY STOCK EXCHANGE

SENSEX, National Index, BSE 200 and Dollex

The Sensitive Index, National Index, BSE 200 and Dollex compiled by the Bombay Stock Exchange are value weighted series. They follow the methodology used by Standard & Poor in USA.

NATIONAL INDEX

BSE National Index covers equity shares of 100 companies from both the specified and non-specified lists of the five major stock exchanges, Bombay, Delhi, Calcutta, Ahmedabad and Madras, with 1983-84 as the base year. The criteria for selection of scrips was market activity, due representation to various industrial groups and to the major stock exchanges. The National Index while including 30 scrips of the BSE sensitive index has another 70 scrips selected on all-India basis depending on their market activity. Out of these hundred scrips, 19 are quoted on Bombay only, 79 are quoted on BSE besides other exchanges while the remaining two scrips are quoted only on other exchanges.

The selection of the base year, 1983-84, was guided by the price stability during that year and the proximity to the current period.

The prices of the shares included in the index are weighed by the number of shares outstanding so that they influence the index in proportion to their respective market importance. The current market value for any particular share is obtained by multiplying the price of the share by the number of shares outstanding. The index for a day is calculated as the percentage of aggregate value of the equity shares of all the companies in the sample on that day to the average market value of the equity shares of the same companies during the base period. This method has the necessary flexibility to adjust for price changes caused by the issue of right and bonus shares.

SENSEX

SENSEX was first compiled in 1986. It is market capitalization-weighed index of the equity of 30 companies from both specified and non-specified groups selected on the basis of market activity and representation of major industries. Several global equity benchmarks are based on this method. The base year chosen for SENSEX was 1978-79 and the exchanges covered Bombay, Delhi, Calcutta, Ahmedabad, Madras and Bangalore. Being a sensitive index it covers all market leaders. It is weighted in favour of highly capitalized companies.

Base changes are in effect proportional adjustments in the base year average market value to offset price changes in market values upon which the index is based. Base year average is changed as per the formula,

$$\text{New base year average} = \text{old base year average} \times \frac{\text{New market value}}{\text{Old market value}}$$

Table 12.1 presents the list of 30 companies whose share prices are included in compiling SENSEX.

Shift to Free Float Methodology (September 1, 2003)

SENSEX was shifted to free float methodology with effect from September 1, 2003. The free float capitalization methodology of index compilation is regarded as an industry best practice globally. All major indices MSCI, FTSK, S&P and Dow Jones use free float methodology.

Free Float Methodology

The level of SENSEX at any point of time reflects the free float market value of 30 companies stocks relative to a base period. The market capitalization of a company is determined by multiplying the price of its stock by the number of shares issued by the company. Free float market capitalization takes into consideration of the proportion of total

Table 12.1: Share of Companies Listed in SENSEX

Code	*Name*	*Beta Values*	*Coefficient of Determination (R^2)*	*Avg. Daily Volatility (%)*	*Returns (1 year) (%)*	*Weightage (%) in SENSEX as on 30-12-05*
500410	A.C.C.	0.75	0.28	1.45	60.35	1.22
500490	Bajaj Auto	0.79	0.24	1.70	107.58	2.52
532454	Bharti Televentures	0.96	0.26	1.98	54.37	3.89
500103	BHEL	1.02	0.31	1.90	139.44	2.55
500087	Cipla Ltd.	0.76	0.20	1.75	53.90	1.31
500124	Dr. Reddy's	0.74	0.19	1.78	52.08	1.06
500300	Grasim Ind.	0.78	0.29	1.50	9.29	1.76
500425	Gujarat Ambuja Cement	0.88	0.25	1.82	47.76	1.48
500010	HDFC	0.85	0.21	1.91	72.28	4.97
500180	HDFC Bank	0.78	0.22	1.73	35.11	13.13
500182	Hero Honda	0.79	0.18	1.92	59.51	1.4*
500440	HINDALCO	0.98	0.32	1.78	34.67	2.3*
500656	Hindustan Lever	0.91	0.27	1.83	21.86	3.55
532174	ICICI Bank	1.17	0.37	1.99	68.93	8.98
500209	Infosys Technologies	1.12	0.50	1.64	39.30	10.46
500875	ITC Ltd.	0.83	0.27	1.65	70.56	6.73
500510	Larsen & Toubro	0.89	0.24	1.87	115.53	4.37
532500	Maruti Udyog	1.07	0.33	1.95	67.46	1.08

Contd...

532555	National Thermal Power	0.69	0.23	1.51	32.58	2.34
500312	ONGC	0.90	0.35	1.58	51.15	4.38
500359	Ranbaxy Lab.	0.69	0.12	2.06	–26.43	1.60
500325	Reliance	1.08	0.51	1.58	74.24	9.06
500390	Reliance Energy	1.04	0.35	1.83	15.58	1.0*
500376	Satyam Computer	1.28	0.46	1.97	80.22	3.59
500112	State Bank of India	1.11	0.45	1.72	37.96	3.47
532540	TATA Consultancy	0.89	0.28	1.74	28.41	2.65
500570	TATA Motors	1.21	0.41	1.98	40.53	2.65
500400	TATA Power	1.08	0.36	1.88	22.51	1.08
500470	TATA Steel	1.16	0.43	1.84	4.73	2.75
507685	Wipro Ltd.	1.27	0.48	1.89	50.42	2.49
SENSEX		1.00		1.03	51.31	

Beta = Co-variance (SENSEX, Stock)/Variance(SENSEX)

R^2 = $(\text{Correlation})^2$

Avg, Daily Volatility = One standard deviation of daily returns of individual stock price for last

Returns = % variation in the stock price over last one year

Source: The Bombay Stock Exchange.

Chapter–12

shares issued by the company that are readily available for trading in the market. It generally excludes promoters' holdings, government holding, strategic holding and other locked in shares which are not available for trading in normal course. Market capitalization of each company in the index is reduced to the extent of its readily available shares in the market.

The general guidelines for selection of constituent scrips in SENSEX are quantitative and qualitative criteria.

Quantitative Criteria

1. **Final Rank:** The scrip should figure in the top 100 companies listed by Final Rank. The final rank is arrived assigning 75% weightage to the rank on the basis of six-month average full market capitalization and 25% the liquidity rank based on six-month average daily turnover and six-month average impact cost.
2. **Trading Frequency:** The scrip should have been traded on each and every trading day for the last six months. Exceptions can be made for extreme reasons like scrip suspension, etc.
3. **Market Capitalization Weightage:** The weight of each scrip in SENSEX based on six-month average free capitalization should be at least 0.5% of the index.
4. **Industry Representation:** Scrip selection would take into account a balanced representation of the listed the universe of BSE. The index companies should be leaders in their industry group.
5. **Listed History:** The scrip should have a listing of at least 3 months on BSE. However, the commit the criteria under exceptional circumstances.

QUALITATIVE CRITERIA

Track Record

In the opinion of the Committee, the company should have an acceptable track record.

ADVANTAGES OF FREE FLOAT

A free float index reflects the market trends more rationally since it takes into consideration only, those shares that are available for trading. It makes the index more broad based by reducing the impact of few companies. The impact of top five companies in SENSEX has been reduced after shift to free float. Table 12.2 presents the free float bands (20). Free float factor is a multiple with which market capitalization of a company is adjusted to arrive at the free float market capitalization. A free float factor of say 0.55 means that only 55% of the market capitalization of the company will be considered in the index calculation.

Table 12.2: Free-Float Bands

% Free-float	*Free-float factor*	*% Free-float*	*Free-float factor*
>0-5	0.05	>50-55	0.55
>5-10	0.10	>55-60	0.60
>10-15	0.15	>60-65	0.65
>15-20	0.20	>65-70	0.70
>20-25	0.25	>70-75	0.75
>25-30	0.30	>75-80	0.80
>30-35	0.35	>80-85	0.85
>35-40	0.40	>85-90	0.90
>40-45	0.45	>90-95	0.95
>45-50	0.50	>95-100	1.00

Source: The BSE *Adjustment for Bonus, Rights and Newly Issued Capital.*

- **Adjustments for Rights Issues:**

  When a company, included in the compilation of the index, issues rights shares, the free-float market capitalization of company is increased by the number of additional shares issued based on the theoretical (ex-right) price or proportionate adjustment is then made to the Base Market Capitalization.

- **Adjustments for Bonus Issue:**

  When a company, included in the compilation of the index, issues bonus shares, the market capitalization of the company does not undergo any change. Therefore, there is no change in the Base Market Capitalization when the 'number of shares' in the formula is updated.

- **Other Issues:**

  Base Market Capitalization Adjustment is required when new shares are issued by way of conversion of company by mergers, spin-offs, etc., or when equity is reduced by way of buy-back of shares and corporate restructuring.

- **Base Market Capitalization Adjustment:**

  The formula for adjusting the Base Market Capitalization is as follows:

  New Base Market Capitalization

  $$= \text{Old Base Market Capitalization} \times \frac{\text{New Market Capitalization}}{\text{Old Market Capitalization}}$$

  To illustrate, suppose a company issues right shares which increases the market capitalization of the company by say, Rs.100 crores. The existing Base Market Capitalization (Old Base Market Capitalization) of Rs.2450 crores and the aggregate market capitalization of all the shares included in the index before the adjustment is, say Rs.4781 crores, the "New Base Market Capitalization" will then be:

  $$\frac{2450 \times (4781 - 100)}{7481} = \text{Rs.2501.24 crores}$$

This figure of 2501.24 will be used as the Base Market Capitalization for calculating the index number.

National Index

The compilation and publication of an index series called BSE National Index was started on January 3, 1989. Since there is little difference in prices of index scrips between exchanges an account of uniform trading period and instantaneous availability of information, the prices of BSE are taken to calculate the index which was redesignated BSE 100. BSE 100 is calculated on free float methodology effective from April 5, 2004. The index covers 100 companies based on market activity, due representation of various industry groups and trading activity. The base year 1983-84.

BSE 200

A new broad based index reflecting market trends in a more effective manner and providing a better representation of a large number of equity listings, market capitalization and emerging industry groups was launched by BSE on June 6, 1994. The index was also designed to build index based futures contract in due course.

Coverage The equity shares of 200 selected companies from the specified and non-specified lists on BSE have been included in sample for "BSE-200". The selection of companies was primarily done on the basis of the market capitalizations of the listed scrips on the exchange. In addition, the market activity of the companies indicated by the volumes of turnover and certain fundamental factors were considered for the final selection of the scrips.

The financial year 1989-90 was chosen as the base year for the price stability exhibited during that year and due to its proximity to the current period. The method of compilation like the earlier two indices of, BSE is free float effective August 19, 2005.

BSE Bankex

Since bank stocks are emerging as a major segment in the equity markets, BSE considered it important to design an index exclusively for bank stocks. The index is computed on the basis of the globally accepted free float methodology. Earlier BSE had launched its first free float index on TMT stocks now popularly known as the BSF. TECk Index.

Features

BANKEX will track the performance of the leading banking sector stocks listed on the BSE.

BANKEX is based on the free float methodology of index construction.

The base date for BANKEX is 1st January 2002.

The base value for BANKEX is 1000 points.

BSE has calculated the historical index values of BANKEX since 1st January 2002.

12 stocks which represent 90 per cent of the total market capitalization of all banking sector stocks listed on BSE are included in the Index. The index is disseminated on real time basis through BSE On Line Trading (BOLT) terminals from June 23, 2003.

BSE TECk Index

Going by the trading pattern, around 68% of the turnover on the stock exchanges is taking place in TMT sector stocks. These stocks collectively account for 23% of the total market capitalization. The investment interest in technology stocks continues unabated.

Scrip selection criteria for BSE TECk Index: Scrips classified under information technology, media and telecom sectors that are present constituents of BSE-500 index would form the eligible universe.

Trading Frequency: Minimum of 90% trading frequency in preceding six months.

Market Capitalization: Scrips with a minimum of 90% market capitalization coverage in each sector based on free-float final rank will form the index.

Buffers: A buffer of 2% both for inclusion and exclusion in the index is considered so that movements in and out of the index are minimized. Eg. A company can be included in the index only if it falls within 88% coverage and an existing index constituent cannot be excluded unless it falls above 92% coverage. However, the above buffer criterion is applied only after the minimum 90% market coverage is satisfied.

Why BSE-TECk Index?

The TMT sectors have seen heightened activity in the last couple of years and the stock valuations of the companies in these sectors have witnessed unprecedented volatility. This led to a strong bull run in the TMT stocks in 1999 and early 2000. The market subsequently witnessed the most unexpected sell-off in the stocks of the TMT sectors which led to a huge market capitalization erosion on the bourses and scared away genuine investors. It is felt that in the absence of a proper benchmark, the performance of the TMT sectors remained inadequately tracked. In order to fill this void, the BSE-TECk index is being positioned as a reliable index for benchmarking the performance of the TMT sectors. Globally a lot of investment is being committed to the TMT sectors. Even in India, the last 2 years have seen a lot of international and local money flowing into the TMT sector. The TMT sectors is currently dominating the trading pattern on the bourses worldwide. In India, the TMT sectors account for around 68% of the total daily turnover. With a lot of domestic retail money committed to the TMT sectors and existence of many mutual funds dedicated to one or more of the TMT sectors in India, a need for a quality benchmark to track the performance of such funds has been long felt.

BSE-PSU Index

Bombay Stock Exchange Limited launched "BSE-PSU Index" on Monday June 4th 2001. The index consists of major Public Sector Undertakings listed on the Exchange. The BSE-PSU index is displayed on-line on the BOLT trading terminals nation-wide. The BSE-Public Sector Undertaking (PSU) Index is a stock index that will track the performance of the listed PSU stocks on the Exchange.

Objective

An Index Tracking the performance of listed equity of PSU companies.

A suitable benchmark for the Central Government to monitor its wealth on the bourses.

Index Specifications

The Base Date for the BSE-PSU Index would be 1st February 1999 when the BSE-500 was launched. Being a subset of BSE-500, the BSE-PSU Index will ensure a reasonable history of how the Central

Government wealth fluctuated on the bourses. The Base Value for the BSE-PSU Index has been set at 1000 to ensure adequacy in terms of Daily Index movement.

SCRIP SELECTION CRITERIA FOR BSE PSU INDEX

Qualification Criteria

For consideration/scrips for inclusion in BSE PSU index, Public Sector Undertaking refers to any undertaking wherein the Central Government holding is equal to or more than 51%. Since BSE PSU index is a subset of BSE-500 index, scrips that form part of BSE-500 index will automatically be included in BSE PSU index.

BSE Mid-Cap and BSE Small-Cap Index

BSE introduced the new index series called 'BSE Mid-Cap' index and 'BSE Small-Cap' index to track the performance of the companies with relatively small market capitalization that would exclusively represent the mid and small cap companies listed on the Stock Exchange. BSE-500 index – the broad based index that is considered as a BSE Composite index represents more than 93% of listed universe. The movement of BSE-500 index used to get influenced by companies with large market capitalization and with the result, the need for a separate indicator to capture the trend in the specific class of companies (with lower market capitalization) was felt. BSE Mid-Cap and BSE Small-Cap index would prove to be a great benefit to the investing community as they would truly capture the movement of the segments they represent (mid and small).

Salient Feature of these Indices are:

Base year of these indices would be 2002-2003.

Base index value would be 1000 for each of these indices.

Based on a free-float methodology, constructed on 80%-15%-5% method whereby top 750 companies by average market capitalization and liquidity are categorized under large, mid and small cap segment respectively from the list of eligible universe of BSE.

BSE Mid-Cap tracks the performance of scrips between 80% and 95% of 750 companies and BSE Small-Cap index tracks the performance of remaining 5% scrips (95-100%).

Number of companies in each of these indices would be variable. On the date of launch (April 11, 2005), these indices comprised of 231 and 425 companies in BSE Mid-Cap and BSE Small-Cap index respectively.

Table 12.3 presents the indices highlights and Table 12.4 the indices watch.

Table 12.3: Indices Highlights (March 3, 2006)

Indices	*Close*	*52 Week High*	*Low*	*Market Capitalization (Rs. Crores)*	*Turnover % to Total Mkt Cap*	*(Rs.% to Crores) Total Turnover*	
SENSEX	10,595.43	10,626.78	6,134.86	646,679.07	23.36	1,004.28	23.29
BSE-100	5,554.94	5,559.51	3,310.14	883,435.53	31.91	1,552.76	36.01
BSE-200	1,327.69	1,327.69	821.02	1,002,404.33	36.21	1,957.66	45.40
BSE-500	4,232.73	4,232.73	2,610.50	1,129,518.58	40.80	2,438.05	56.53
BSEMIDCAP	4,918.03	4,918.03	2,976.29	204,772.98	7.40	784.72	18.20
BSESMLCAP	6,244.06	6,422.74	3,518.82	57,851.14	2.09	556.86	12.91
DOLLEX-200	493.30	498.46	313.16	—	—	—	—
BSE TEC/c	2,520.60	2,522.60	1,549.57	185,626.97	6.71	194.16	4.50
BSE PSU	5,728.79	5,749.62	3,992.52	700,799.72	25.31	277.95	6.45
BSE AUTO	5,252.13	5,252.13	2,546.16	95,872.82	3.46	287.42	6.66
BANKEX	5,251.56	5,331.37	3,504.33	135,195.99	4.88	104.72	2.43
BSECG	7,709.00	7,716,32	3,138.16	84,491.65	3.05	247.65	5.74
BSE CD	3,224.48	3,351.37	1,411.44	5,675.12	0.20	75.09	1.74
BSE FMCG	2,000.26	2,011.94	1,022.50	94,556.73	3.42	87.55	2.03
BSEHC	3,613.94	3,648.02	2,426.10	65,240.03	2.36	109.90	2.55
BSE IT	3,746.18	3,826.43	2,346.47	138,249.57	4.99	124.74	2.89
BSE METAL	7,609.79	7,609.79	5,279.17	55,118.33	1.99	192.23	4.46
BSE OIL & GAS	4,470.10	4,560.59	2,931.98	111,699.15	4.03	196.39	4.55
Total				2,763,373.16	—	4312.5	100

Note: The market capitalization of all the indices is free float market capitalization except for BSEPSU.

Source: BSE

Table 12.4: Indices Watch (March 6, 2006)

Index	*Open*	*High*	*Low*	*Current Values*	*Previous Close*	*Change (Pts)*	*Change (%)*
SENSEX	10,616.99	10,738.64	10,616.99	10,734.04	10,595.43	138.61	1.31
BSE-100	5,565.04	5,629.23	5,565.04	5,627.00	5,554.94	72.06	1.30
BSE-200	1,330.01	1,345.40	1,330.01	1,344.79	1,327.69	17.10	1.29
BSE-500	4,240.10	4,288.46	4,240.10	4,286.51	4,232.73	53.78	1.27
BSE MIDCAP	4,928.41	4,990.07	4,928.41	4,985.72	4,918.03	67.69	1.38
BSE SMLCAP	6,263.72	6,322.90	6,263.72	6,318.50	6,244.06	74.44	1.19
BSE TECk	2,523.16	2,544.88	2,523.16	2,535.50	2,520.60	14.90	0.59
BSE PSU	5,738.97	5,834.95	5,738.97	5,823.99	5,728.79	95.20	1.66
BSE AUTO	5,262.04	5,350.93	5,262.04	5,345.88	5,252.13	93.75	1.78
BSE BANKEX	5,260.74	5,301.06	5,260.01	5,266.42	5,251.56	14.86	0.28
BSECG	7,749.94	7,835.89	7,749.94	7,770.90	7,709.00	61.90	0.80
BSE CD	3,245.12	3,292.51	3,239.00	3,268.22	3,224.48	43.74	1.36
BSE FMCG	2,000.80	2,037.11	2,000.80	2,029.90	2,000.26	29.64	1.48
BSEHC	3,619.01	3,677.60	3,619.01	3,663.41	3,613.94	49.47	1.37
BSE IT	3,746.67	3,796.74	3,746.67	3,781.20	3,746.18	35.02	0.93
BSE Metal	7,637.58	7,935.94	7,637.58	7,933.33	7,609.79	323.54	4.25
BSE Oil & Gas	4,482.36	4,549.20	4,482.36	4,549.92	4,470.10	76.82	1.72

Chapter–12

Dollex

BSE launched on May 27, 1994 two new index series, Dollex along with BSE 2001. The BSE-200 on any day reflects the growth in the market value on that day over the base period 1989-90 with both the current market value as well as the base value expressed in rupee terms. It was felt that there should be an index by which these growth values can be measured when the investment and return are expressed in dollar terms, particularly in the present context of the increased willingness shown by foreign investors and growth in the number of foreign financial institutions in the country. This became possible by the introduction of a dollar linked version of the 'BSE-200' in which the formula for calculating the BSE 200 is suitably modified to express the current and base market values in dollar terms by dividing the current rupee market value by current rupee conversion rate and the base value by a constant average rupee-dollar conversion rate in the base year.

An ORG survey (March 1998) revealed that the BSE SENSEX remained the most popular index with approval from 66 per cent of retail and 92 per cent of institutional investors and the NSE 50 is second with 18 and 7 per cent respectively. On reliability, 56 per cent of institutional investors are for BSE 30 and 29 per cent for NSE 50. Knowledge level is also high for SENSEX with 84 per cent institutional investors being aware of current levels, and 56 per cent about the NSE 50.

To provide for still broader, segment specific and sector specific indices BSE 500 index and 5 sectoral indices were introduced in 1999.

BSE 500 and Sectoral Indices

Bombay Stock Exchange Limited has compiled a new index, BSE-500, consisting of 500 scrips in its basket with effective from August 9, 1999.

BSE-500 index represents nearly 93% of the total market capitalization on Bombay Stock Exchange Limited. This means BSE-500 index ideally represents total market. This index represents all 20 major industries of the economy. The BSE-500 index had been calculating on a full market capitalization methodology and effective August 16, 2005 calculation methodology was shifted to a free-float methodology in line with SENSEX.

Simultaneously, BSE also started 5 sectoral indices viz. BSE IT Sector index, BSE FMCG Sector index, BSE Capital Goods Sector index, BSE Consumer Durables Sector index and BSE Healthcare Sector index. All these sectoral indices are calculated and displayed on the BOLT system on a real time basis.

Unweighed Price Indicator Series

In the unweighed price indicator series, all stocks are equally weighed regardless of price or value. The unweighed index is affected equally by the performance of each security in the sample regardless of price or market value. The stock's market value and the price level does not have an impact because percentage changes alone are important. In computing percent change, a geometric average is taken rather than an arithmetic average. The series is sensitive to the short movements of the market and is not an appropriate long term measure of market returns to evaluate portfolio performance.

Examples of equally weighed or unweighed series are University of Chicago Series and Value Line Composite Average based upon equally weighed geometric average of the percentage changes for approximately 1700 issues (out of which 80 per cent are listed on NYSE).

The computation of Value Line Composite Average gives it some characteristics of weighed average and its expression as a percentage of 100 could well qualify it as an index rather than an average or at least as a hybrid. Adjustments incorporate daily net percentage price changes for each stock as well as stock dividends and splits.

Another example is the Financial Times ordinary share index of 30 heavily traded blue chip stocks listed on LSE. It is a geometric average of the rates of return for the 30 stocks.

Trends in Share Prices

Share prices during the period 1984-85 – 1998-99 have shown an upward trend except in the years 1987-88, 1995-96 and 1998-99 which registered a bear phase. Table 12.2 presents index number of share prices of Bombay Stock Exchange (SENSEX and National) and Reserve Bank Index Number of Security Prices.

The stock market buoyancy in 1985-86 was set off by the Union Budget for 1985-86. The announcement of incentives for export promotion, widespread rains in deficit areas, raising of margins on bears and reduction of margins on bulls, the beneficial impact of long term fiscal policy on FERA, tea, leasing and surtax paying companies, liberalization in industrial licensing policy extending also to FERA and MRTP companies, declaration of liberal bonus issues by certain companies and good corporate news, hike in fertilizer prices and expectations for saving and investment oriented budget for 1986-87 sustained the rise in share prices. The stiff daily margins imposed by

Stock Exchange authorities in Bombay and Calcutta had only a marginal impact in containing the speculative rise in equity prices.

Equity prices on major stock exchanges moved erratically during greater part of 1986-87. This was in part corrective to the disproportionately high buoyancy experienced earlier in 1985-86. Adverse factors were disturbances in certain parts of the country, disappointing corporate news, payment crisis on BSE arising from over trading and building up of long position in certain scrips by leading member brokers, searches of premises of leading brokers of BSE by Income Tax authorities and budget proposals falling short of market expectations. The imposition of corporate tax on a minimum of 30 per cent of book profits of companies depressed market sentiment.

On the other hand, good monsoon, good corporate news, success of India Fund launched by UTI aided market sentiment. Reduction of gap between bonus issues, clearance of Rs.400 crores mega convertible debenture issue, announcement about enactment of comprehensive legislation for orderly regulation of stock exchanges and rationalization of the tax system and the comfortable position of the economy had a favourable impact on market sentiment. The net result was an increase of 15.67 per cent in SENSEX in 1986-87.

The decline in 1987-88 of 19.9 per cent in the SENSEX, 9.6 per cent in National Index and 10.1 per cent in RBI Index was on account of several adverse factors such as drought, political uncertainty and law and order problems.

During 1988-89 the capital market experienced considerable buoyancy on account of the improvement in the basic economic fundamentals and better performance of private corporate sector. These factors are reflected in the improvement of SENSEX by 35 per cent during the year. Share prices rose sharply over the year more than regaining the losses in previous year when SENSEX declined by 19.9 per cent.

In 1989-90 SENSEX moved up by 18.9 per cent. Factors which had a favourable effect were fiscal reliefs in excise and customs duties, formation of new government at the Centre and expectations of continuation of pragmatic and liberal policies by the new government and the budget for 1990-91. Financial institutions which had emerged as major players on the market played a positive and stabilizing role in their operations.

The buoyancy witnessed in the share prices in 1989-90 continued further till October 1990 resulting in a gain in the SENSEX of 43.9

per cent in 1991-92. The market reflected the ready policy response to a series of macro-economic imbalances accentuated by the Gulf crisis, depletion of foreign exchange reserves and uncertainties in the economy.

The stock markets in 1991-92 were a scene of an unprecedented bullish frenzy. The market scaled unbelievably high levels with the trend getting more accentuated during the last quarter, January-March 1992. After the presentation of budget of 1992-93, during March 1992 prices soared.

The considerable increase in the activities of the secondary markets is reflected in turnover, market capitalization and price earning ratio. The average monthly turnover of the BSE at Rs.5,881 crores during 1991-92 was almost twice as that of previous year (Rs.3,001 crores). BSE market capitalization at Rs.2,76,434 crores was more than three and half times that at the end of March 1991 (Rs.75,348 crores) BSE SENSEX price earning ratio (monthly average) rose to 26.1 in 1991-92 from 19.3 in 1990-91.

The stock markets during the most part of 1992-93 remained subdued. The high level of equity prices reached towards the end of March and beginning of April 1992, could not be sustained once the irregularities in transactions involving banks, financial institutions and stock brokers came to light. After April 1992, stock markets experienced continuous decline in share prices till the middle of August 1992. After a short recovery in September 1992, equities once again drifted downward till January 1993. The rise in share prices in February 1993 proved to be short lived.

The subdued trend in stock market is reflected in the major indicators of the BSE, market turnover, market capitalization and price earning ratio. The average monthly turnover of Rs.3307 crores during 1992-93 was 36.3 per cent lower than the previous year (Rs.5981 crores). Market capitalization at Rs.2,10,952 was 34.8 per cent lower than in 1991-92 (Rs.3,23,363 crores). PE ratio for SENSEX which was 52.6 in April 1992 declined to 29.3 in March, 1993.

In 1993-94, there was an underlying favourable sentiment pushing up the prices in the stock markets. Market sentiment which was subdued till the end of July 1993 improved in August 1993 on account of large scale purchases by FIIs, favourable monsoon and assurance from the government that investors' interest would be protected against attached shares. There was also improvement in balance of payments position and fairly high level of foreign exchange reserves. The markets retreated in March 1994 after the brokers were directed by SEBI to square up their outstanding positions as on March 11, 1994 on account of the ban on carry forward transactions. FIIs withdrew following the rise in interest rates in U.S.A. The SENSEX rose by 0.1 per cent. National index, 3.8 per cent and RBI index number security prices declined by 8.0 per cent. The first half of 1994-95 witnessed a bullish sentiment on account of the encouraging corporate results for the financial year 1993-94; sustained buying support of FIIs as also of domestic financial institutions and mutual funds and the onset of a normal monsoon. Since the middle of September 1994 equity prices drifted downwards due to profit taking by domestic institutions, interest rate developments abroad and the consequent deceleration of support from FIIs and weakening of GDR prices in international market. The year 1994-95 registered a gain of 37.1 per cent in SENSEX, 38.26 per cent in National index and 46.2 per cent in RBI Index Number of security prices.

Equity prices remained bearish almost during the whole of 1995-96. There was lack of buying support from domestic financial institutions and FIIs, high domestic interest rates and problems associated with reintroduction of carry forward trading. There was, however, a strong recovery in equity prices towards the end of 1995-96 aided by an upsurge in net investments by FIIs. The year registered a decline of 17.3 per cent in SENSEX, 19.44 per cent in National Index and 22.6 per cent in RBI Index Number of security prices.

The share prices in 1996-97 showed a buoyancy in the first quarter due to higher level of investment support from the FIIs and anticipation of a favourable budget in July 1996; the second phase from mid July to mid December was characterized by subdued conditions on account of high interest rates, introduction of minimum alternate tax and lower net investment by FIIs; and in the final phase especially towards the close of the year the market recovered partially on account the favourable budget, 1997-98. Security prices measured by SENSEX rose by 5.5 per cent, National Index 1.41 per cent and registered a decline of 3.6 per cent in terms of RBI Index Number of Security Prices.

Equity prices which staged a recovery in the first four months of 1997-98 on account of the larger inflow of FII investment and favourable budget suffered a set-back between August 1997 and mid-February 1998 reflecting a slowdown in industrial production and absence of FII interest in the wake of South East Asian crisis. Between mid-February and March 1998, the stock markets staged a smart recovery on account of renewed investment interest by FIIs and expectations of favourable budget. On a point to point basis SENSEX gained 532 points (15.8%)

from 3210 to 3893 during 1997-98. On an average basis, the index registered an increase of 9.9%.

During 1998-99, subdued conditions set in during May to October on account of reversal of market optimism surrounding the budget, the imposition of economic sanctions, downgrading by international rating agencies, the continuing industrial slowdown, the problem with the US 64 scheme of the UTI and uncertainties on account of crises in major South East Asian Markets, Russia and Brazil and outflows on account of FIIs. It was only in November 1998 and March 1999, that share prices recovered in terms of the US decision to ease sanctions and issue of guidelines by SEBI for buy-back of shares and revival of FII buying interest. On an average basis, the index declined by 13.6 per cent over the year. During 1999-2000 share prices have continued the bullish momentum with the SENSEX moving from 3739 at the end of March to 5533.98 on January 4, 2000. A significant part of the appreciation was accounted by select stocks belonging to the software and pharmaceutical sectors. During 1999 the S & P CNX Nifty index gained around 67.4% and closed at 1480 points.

The largest increase in prices was registered in 1985-86 under all the three indices followed by the increase in 1991-92, 1992-93 and 1994-95. The popular impression that the markets registered largest gains ever in 1991-92 seems to be based on the absolute size of the SENSEX number rather than gain measured by per cent increase in the number. The record gain in the index was registered in 1985-86 when National Index registered an increase of 87.04 per cent, Sensitive index 84.51 per cent and RBI index 63 per cent. In all the fifteen years (1984-85 – 1998-99) inflation measured by increase in index of wholesale prices was lower than the gain in equity prices except in five years in 1987-88, 1993-94, 1995-96, 1996-97 and 1998-99. Equity has proved to be a good hedge against inflation. As compared to a doubling of wholesale prices, share prices have gone up by more than fifteen times. These trends it may be noted are not in consonance with the trends observed in the stock markets abroad. For instance in 1990 stock markets in India recorded a gain of about 40 per cent whereas Morgan Stanley Capital Internationals World Index fell by 18.6 per cent on account of rising interest rates (influencing bonds yields), economic slow down and Gulf crisis. America's main share index, Dow-Jones rose by more than three times (save the brief plunge in October 1997) between 1990 and 1998. More so since 1994 when the markets began to show "irrational exuberance". Higher asset prices since 1994 have added no less than $12 trillion to households' (nearly half of American households own shares in some form) apparent wealth.

Since mid May 2003, the stock markets recorded a sustained rally and SENSEX has marched past several historical milestones to reach the current level of 12,513 (May 2006). On NSE the S&P CNX Nifty hit 3,720 various factors like good monsoons, encouraging quarterly results by major corporates, strong institutional support, especially by FIIs, positive trends in international markets, sector specific factors and strong macro economic fundamentals along with the appreciation in the rupee contributed to the buoyant market sentiments which supported the rally. The dramatic drop on May 17, 2004, reflected political uncertainties as well as adverse investor sentiment in many other emerging market economies. Gaining a speedy recovery from the decline SENSEX gathered momentum.

The rally in 2004-05 was spread across mid cap and small cap companies. BSE-500 increased by 21.9% during 2004-05 as compared to an increase of 88% in the SENSEX. Market capitalization of BSE increased by 41.11% during 2004-05 reflecting increase in prices as well as listing of new securities. The P/E ratio of BSE SENSEX was higher than the other emerging market and volatility remained higher than most of the international stock markets.

Volatility and Dispersion of Share Prices

The volatility and dispersion of share prices during the period 1986-87 – 2004-05 are presented in Table 12.5 and the average is presented for 1986-87 – 1992-93, 1993-94 – 1998-99 and 1999-2000 – 2004-05 to distinguish the impact of badla abolition from 1993-94 year and entry of FIIs after liberalization. First the average coefficient of variation which measures volatility prices may be noted. The coefficient was higher at 12.66 in the period 1986-87 – 1992-93, than in 1993-94 – 1998-99 when it was 11.07 of variation and 1999-2000 – 2004-05 when it was 11.4. The years 1988-89, 1990-91, 1991-92 and 1992-93 have also witnessed wide fluctuations in dispersion of index in terms of the range between high and low. The dispersion in the index of ordinary share prices in the years 1990-91, 1991-92 and 1992-93 was higher than the average of 371.75 for the seven year period. In the latest period 1999-2000 – 2004-05 the dispersion is highest in the 19 year period covered in the Table. In the years, 1999-2000, 2003-04 and 2004-05 the dispersion was higher than average of 2032 in the six year period.

Table 12.5: Volatility and Dispersion of Share Prices (1986-87 – 2004-05)

Year	*Coefficient of Variation*	*Dispersion*
	(Per cent)	*(The range)*
1986-87	3.65	3.83
1987-88	4.82	40.00
1988-89	16.36	121.10
1989-90	5.90	93.70
1990-91	14.66	258.60
1991-92	27.04	948.50
1992-93	16.21	764.80
Average for the seven year period (1986-87 – 1992-93)	**12.66**	**371.75**
1993-94	19.99	661.60
1994-95	8.81	486.00
1995-96	6.74	331.20
1996-97	11.21	430.70
1997-98	7.90	1338.00
1998-99	11.80	1517.00
Average for 1993-94 to 1998-99	**11.07**	**704.08**
1999-2000	13.20	2689.00
2000-01	8.80	2001.00
2001-02	7.20	1142.00
2002-03	4.80	679.14
2003-04	23.00	3270.08
2004-05	11.20	2409.93
Average for six year period (1999 – 2000 – 2004-05)	**11.40**	**2032.00**

Source: Reserve Bank of India, *Annual Report* 1990-91, 1991-92, 1992-93 and 1996-97, 1998-99, 2002-03 and 2004-05.

In 1991-92, the dispersion in the index was 3.7 times the range of previous year (258.6) and about 2.5 times the average for the seven year period, 1986-87 to 1992-93; and in 1992-93, the dispersion was lower than previous year but 2 times the average for the period 1986-87 – 1992-93.

The average coefficient of variation in the succeeding period 1993-94 – 1998-99 was significantly higher than average of 11.07 only in one year, 1993-94 (19.99). The dispersion in the index for ordinary shares was higher than average of 704.08 in 1997-98 and 1998-99. While the coefficient of variation in the two periods was not too high, the average dispersion was higher in the second period than in the first. In the latest six year period, the coefficient of variation was lower at 11.4 than in the first period (1986-1993), the dispersion is much higher in 2003-04 and it reached the peak at 3,270.08 (60% above the average for the period).

Risk Free Return

Table 12.6 present yields on 10 year Government Securities and real return for 22 countries published in Economic Times (August 31, 2005). The analysis by ET Intelligence Group of risk free real return across the world showed that India is the only major country save China that currently (August 2006) offers negative risk free real returns on investment. India's risk free real return on investment is minus 1.9% next to China's minus 1.1%.

Table 12.6: G-Sec Yields, Inflation and Real Return

	10 year G Sec Yields	*Inflation Rate*	*Real Returns*
	A	*B*	*(A + B)*
Philippines	13.44	6.0	7.44
South Africa	8.87	4.8	4.07
Malaysia	5.09	1.3	3.79
Britain	4.95	1.6	3.35
Hong Kong	4.13	0.9	3.23
Sweden	4.34	1.2	3.14
Australia	5.60	2.5	3.10
Denmark	4.15	1.1	3.05
Canada	4.67	2.0	2.67
Switzerland	2.72	0.5	2.22
Germany	4.03	2.0	2.03
Japan	1.57	–0.3	1.87
Thailand	4.95	3.1	1.85
US	4.26	3.0	1.26
Singapore	3.38	2.3	1.08
Spain	4.28	3.3	0.98
Korea	4.13	3.6	0.53
Czech Republic	3.50	3.2	0.30
Indonesia	7.39	7.2	0.19
Poland	2.60	2.5	0.10
China	2.69	3.8	–1.11
India	6.04	7.94	–1.90

Source: Bombay Stock Exchange, *National Index of Security Prices and SENSEX,* October 1992.

Reserve Bank of India, *Report on Currency and Finance,* 1989-90, 1990-91 and 1997-98, *Annual Report,* 1994-95, 1995-96 and 1998-99; *Bulletin,* October 1991.

Government of India, *Economic Survey,* 1991-92 and 1997-98.

Risk free is defined as returns from government securities adjusted to inflation. Ten year government bonds are actively traded around the world and offer accurate direction in which interest rates are headed. From the yield on 10 year government instrument the current inflation rate was subtracted to arrive at the risk free real returns. India's current yield in August 2005 was 6.04% and inflation rate 7.94% leaving the year return at (–)1.9%.

References

Bombay Stock Exchange, *BSE National Index of Equity Prices,* October, 1992.

Bombay Stock Exchange, *Annual Report,* 1996-97.

Economic Survey, 1991-92 and 1996-97

Fosback, Norman, G., *Stock Market Logic* 1994, Dear Bosh.

Fortune, India, October, 1992.

R.R. Nair, "BSE Index Numbers or equity prices", *Handbook of Articles from Stock Exchange Review,* 1989-1991, BSE, January, 1992.

Reilly Frank, K., *Investments,* Third Edition, The Dryden Press, Fortworth, Texas, 1992.

Reserve Bank of India, "Index Number of Security Prices - New Series", (1980-81 = 100), *Bulletin* July, 1985. *Annual Report* 1990-91 – 1992-93, 1994-95, 1995-96, 1998-99, 2003-04 and 2004-05 and *Report on Currency and Finance,* 1989-90, 1990-91 and 997-98, Vol. I.

Teweles Richard J., Edward S. Bradley and Teweles Ted M., *The Stock Market,* 6th Edition, John Wiley & Sons, Inc., New York, 1992.

13

TRADING IN DERIVATIVES*

DERIVATIVES: NATURE AND GROWTH OF GLOBAL MARKETS

Derivatives are financial instruments which are derived from equities, bonds, currencies and commodities. Annual turnover in derivative financial instruments including options and futures traded on international organized exchanges rose from 146 million contracts in 1986 to 453.9 million in 1992 and 6,145 million in 2004[31]. The notional amount outstanding in 2004 was $46.6 trillion.

Further, warrants, swaps, swaptions, collars, caps, floors, circuses and scores of other products are collectively known as derivatives. All these constitute tools for the management of financial risk. Hedging strategies or insurance depends on the use of derivatives, especially options. Financial regulators around the world are worried about derivatives, since the biggest traders and counter parties are banks. Interest rate futures accounted for 39.0% of the total ($46.6 trillions); and interest rate options for 52.8%. Over the counter derivatives (two-thirds of them interest rate swaps) were $221.3 trillion in 2004 compared to only $500 billion at the end of 1986. Interest rate swaps (mainly banks) accounted for 66.6%, and interest rate options (12.3%). Trading in derivatives often exceeds transactions in the markets for the underlying securities or currencies.

---

* Index futures were introduced in India June 2000, index options in June 2001, stock options in July 2001 and stock futures in November 2001 both in the BSE and NSE.

31 Bank for International Settlements, *Annual Report* 1992-93 1997-98, *International Banking and Financial Market Developments,* November 1999 and June 2005.

The volatility in financial market has led to a boom in derivatives. The former Chairman of America's Federal Reserve, Alan Greenspan thinks that this kind of financial innovation is good for the global economy. It makes the financial system more flexible, promotes economic growth and allows better control of risk. On the other hand, Warren Buffet, America's famous investor called them "financial weapons of mass destruction." They can be misused and their complexity foils any rules for their regulation.

Derivatives are used by banks, securities firms, companies and investors to hedge risks, to gain access to cheaper money and to make profits. According to a poll in 2003 around 90% of world's 500 biggest companies now use derivatives. Derivatives are likely to grow even at a faster rate in future. They are first of all cheaper to trade than the underlying securities, be they bonds, currencies, commodities or equities. Exchanges around the world have met the demand by designing new standardized contracts. With the increasing volume of products tailored to the needs of particular customers, trading in derivatives has increased even in the over the counter markets.

The popularity of derivatives is also to be traced to simple familiarity and more sophisticated ways of pricing and managing business risks. Finally, the growth of derivatives was influenced by easing of legal, fiscal and regulatory restrictions on the use of derivatives. In Britain Unit Trusts are allowed to invest in futures and options. The capital adequacy norms for ranks in the European Economic Community demand less capital to hedge or speculate through derivatives than to carry underlying assets. Derivatives are weighted lightly than other assets that appear on banks' balance sheets. The size of these off-balance sheet assets which include derivatives is more than seven times as large as balance sheet items at some American banks causing concern to regulators.

Characteristics of Derivatives

The three key characteristics of financial derivatives are;

(1) Their value is derived from an underlying instrument such as stock index (futures and options based on them), currency or interest rates.

(2) They are vehicles for transferring risk.

(3) They are leveraged instruments.

Users of Derivatives

Derivatives are used by corporations to hedge currency risk and inventory risk. They are used by individual investors for speculation, hedging and yield enhancement. Institutional investors (mutual funds, pension funds and insurance companies) for hedging, asset allocation, yield enhancement and to avail arbitrage opportunities. Finally, dealers (securities firms, market makers and banks) use them for hedging, position taking, exploiting inefficiencies (arbitrage) and earning dealer spreads.

In this Chapter, Stock Index Futures and Options are discussed. It may be noted that in the global derivatives markets, options on single equities continue to grow more rapidly than those on large indices, reflecting the high trading cost of traditional contracts on indices and the increasing preference of institutional investors for instruments offering a more closely tailored exposure[32]. On the other hand in India index derivatives are favoured. In 2004, they accounted for 33% of equity derivatives trading. It is held that when market sophistication grows beyond trading futures on individual stocks, there will be greater share of index derivatives as opposed to individual stock derivatives, greater share of contracts expiring beyond the near month (longer dated contracts) and greater share of options as opposed to futures[33].

STOCK INDEX FUTURES

Origin Trading in stock index futures based on value line index commenced on February 24, 1982 on the Kansas City Board of Trade previously known as the mart for hard winter wheat, the staple of America's bread baking industry. Two months later, the Chicago Mercantile Exchange began offering futures on the S&P 500 and NYSE followed with a contract on its Composite Index, offered on its subsidiary, the New York Futures Exchange. The Stock futures contract based on S&P 500 index is the most successful one. Other futures exchanges are Chicago Board of Trade in U.S.A., London International Financial Futures Exchange, (LIFFE), Germany's DTB and Tokyo Financial Futures Exchange's Topix Future. In 1997, the German, Swiss and French (MATIF) financial Exchanges proposed to develop a joint computer based European Derivatives Market. They will do this by

32 BIS, *Annual Report*, June 1998.

33 Government of India, *Economic Survey* 2003-04, p.71.

building electronic links between their stock markets. This move has been abandoned by London and Frankfurt exchanges joining together[34].

Activity in Futures Market

The value of stock market index futures traded on organized exchanges was $42.0 trillion in 2004 and the outstanding stock index futures traded on regulated futures exchanges amounted to $634.3 billion[35].

Nature

Stock index futures track a stock market index and are concerned with the changing value of the markets rather than of individual stocks in those markets. The market is the combined number and weighings of stock in the underlying index. The stock index futures give the investor the ability to hedge systematic risk. They are a means of hedging against or profiting from swings in the market.

Definition

Stock index futures contract is an agreement to buy or sell a specified amount of an underlying stock index traded on a regulated futures exchange for a specified price for settlement at a specified time in future. A stock index future is an indicator for a cash settlement of a futures contract. The difference between stock index futures and most other financial futures contracts is that settlement is made at the value of the index at maturity of the contract. The monetary difference between assuming position in futures contract and the price of that contract at close out or settlement determines the profitability of the position. Stock index futures are settled in cash rather than by delivery of the underlying asset. Investors choose to close out their position prior to delivery period specified in the contract. Even hedgers prefer to close their futures position and then buy or sell the asset in the usual way. Closing out a position involves entering into an opposite trade to the original one.

In a stock index futures contract, there is no obligation to hold it to its maturity date. Open positions can be eliminated by taking an equal and opposite position in the market at any time after the initial futures transaction.

Futures require a small margin. All stock index futures are large, $500 times the index value. Trading is done on a margin averaging less than 5 per cent of current contract values. These amounts range from $3,500 to $6,000. In a futures contract the loss can exceed the original margin commitment.

34 The *Economist*, July 11, 1998.

35 Bank for International Settlements, *Quarterly Review*, June, 2005, p. 104.

The terms of a futures contract are revised everyday to maintain a zero market value for the contract. The aspect of the futures contract that is revised everyday is the futures price. The difference between the futures price yesterday and today multiplied by the number of futures outstanding is credited or debited to the account.

Futures and Options

Futures should be distinguished from options. Futures create an obligation to make or take delivery at some future date while options confer a right but not the obligation to do the same. Premium paid on options is nonrefundable. No payment is involved for futures. Future contracts are larger, valued at $500 times the index value, whereas most popular index options have a $100 multiplier.

Options on futures contracts are a hybrid which combine the limited risk nature of the option with the profit potential of the futures contract. Options set a range within or outside which a position proves profitable while a futures contract establishes a price.

Prerequisites for Futures Trading

Before choosing a financial instrument such as the stock index future the futures exchange should after extensive research to establish that a forward market exists, it would enjoy the support of dealers and other industry participants, the likelihood that adequate price volatility will attract speculation and the market requires a formal risk shifting mechanism.

Aspects of Futures Contract

The contract should specify the asset in clear and unambiguous terms. The contract specifies the amount of the asset that has to be delivered and the delivery month. The delivery months vary from contract to contract and are chosen by the exchange to meet the needs of the market participants. Financial futures often have delivery months of March, June, September and December. Contracts trade for the closest delivery month.

Price Quotes

Price quotes for financial futures are in terms of dollars and one 32nd of a dollar. The exchange lays down daily price movement limits to prevent large price movements because of speculative excesses. If the price moves down by an amount equal to the daily price limit, the contract is said to be limit down; and if it moves up by the limit, it is said to be limit up. A limit move is equal to the daily price limit and could be in either direction. Position limits, specifying the number of contracts a speculator can hold are stipulated to prevent speculators from exercising undue influence on the market.

Participants in Futures Market

The participants/investors in the futures market fall into three categories. Hedgers, speculators and arbitrageurs. Hedgers are those who have certain commitment independent of any transactions in the futures market and they enter the market in order to reduce the risks arising out of their commitments. Futures are considered more useful for institutional investors because they are large and allow for a greater use in hedging. Speculators have no commitment and they assume risks by entering the market. Hedgers and speculators can be buyers or sellers of futures but in both cases, it is the speculators who assume risks and the hedgers who get rid of them.

The scope for arbitrage, buying spot and selling futures simultaneously and holding the stock until the date of delivery arises when the difference between futures price and current price ensures a riskless profit. Arbitrage differs from hedging in that the ordinary hedger enters the futures market to reduce risk on a commitment which occurs independently of the existence of a futures market; and an arbitrageur assumes risk which he would not have assumed if the facilities of the forward market did not enable him to pass them on, on advantageous terms. The possibility of arbitrage sets an upper limit to the futures price in relation to the spot price.

The theory of normal backwardation explains the relationship of futures price to current price. There is no limit to backwardation (when stocks in relation to turnover are normal) to the extent to which the futures price may fall short of the current price; and there is a limit to the contango (which develops in terms of excess stocks and also low spot prices) in that futures price cannot exceed the current price by more than the cost of arbitrage, which is the sum of interest plus carrying costs. Arbitrage prevents futures price from rising above expected price minus risk premium[36].

For efficient functioning of futures markets, speculators are necessary because the volume of business done by genuine hedgers at any given time is too small thus limiting liquidity necessary for efficient market. Hedgers are generally to be found on the same side of the market. The speculators along with traders and arbitrageurs are needed to take the other side of some of these trades. They provide a continuous liquid market which reduces transaction costs and without them the futures market would not function. But speculators could also increase volatility in asset prices which imposes its own costs on the economy.

---

36 Kaldor, N., *Essays in Economic Stability and Growth*, Gerald Duckworth & Co. Ltd., 1961.

Arbitrage would be done in spot and futures markets. Stable and reliable spot market is required for concluding genuine investment processes. Speculation prevents futures price from falling below expected price minus risk premium. Hedging is predominantly on the selling side and their net sale of futures is taken up by speculators. The hedgers will *sell* futures if the futures price is equal to or *higher* than expected price minus risk premium; whilst speculators will *buy* futures if their price is equal to or *lower* than expected price minus risk premium. When hedgers are predominantly sellers of futures, the buying of futures by speculators therefore prevents the futures price from falling below expected price minus risk premium; whilst arbitrage prevents it from rising above this level. When expectations are not uniform transactions will take place not only between hedgers, arbitrageurs and speculators but between speculators, who could be bears or bulls. Bull speculators will be *buyers* of futures and bear speculators will be *sellers* of futures. In real world where expectations differ, we can only say futures price will reflect the expected price subject to the provision that it cannot exceed the current price by more than the cost of arbitrage.

Stock Index Futures and Risk

There are two broad categories of risk associated with stock market investment. The first category relates to the individual stock and is referred as unsystematic risk. Unsystematic risk covers all risks which are unique to the stock. The other category known as systematic risk is that portion of the total variability in the returns to a stock that is caused by factors which are beyond the control of the company and which simultaneously affect the prices of all other stocks. Total risk, unsystematic + systematic risk is commonly measured in terms of variation from the expected return to the stock. The standard deviation from the expected return is used to show how stock diversification can reduce and eventually eliminate the unsystematic component of total risk. If two stocks are not perfectly positively correlated a combination of the two would produce a portfolio standard deviation which would be less than weighted average. This is the essence of stock diversification. If we combine ten to fifteen randomly chosen stocks, unsystematic risk can be diversified away.

Stock index futures contain only systematic risk and they are used to manage exposure to market risk.

Beta: Beta indicates the sensitivity of a stock's value to market movements. Beta measures a stock's sensitivity to systematic risk. The beta of any given portfolio will be weighted average of the betas of the individual stocks in the portfolio. A market index will generally have a weighted average beta of 1 or close to 1.

The beta of a portfolio can be altered to insulate it from the downturn in a market or take advantage of a temporary rally. To increase the portfolio responsiveness in expectation of a market rally low beta stocks may be sold and high beta stocks may be purchased in their place to increase the portfolio beta from say 0.8 to 1.3. A far easier and less costly method would be to use Stock Index Futures to achieve the desired change. The number of futures required to achieve desired change is given,

$$\text{Number of futures to achieve desired change} = \frac{\text{Portfolio Value} \times (\text{desired beta} - \text{current beta})}{\text{Value of Index}}$$

This strategy is used when investors, traders or portfolio managers wish to alter the exposure of their portfolios to take advantage of temporary market movements.

Basis Risk It is the spread risk similar to that encountered in all futures versus security trades. The risk is the likelihood of the spread between futures contract and the underlying index will change adversely during the life of the hedge so as to reduce the profitability of the strategy. It is the difference between the spot price of an asset and the futures price. Basis risk arises out of the hedger's uncertainty as to what the basis will be at maturity of the hedge.

For investment assets, the basis risk tends to be less than for commodities for consumption. This is because arbitrage leads to a well defined relationship between the futures price and the spot price of an asset. The basis risk for an investment asset arises mainly from the uncertainty as to the level of risk free interest rate in the future. Basis risk can lead to an improvement or worsening of a hedger's position. In the case of a short hedge, if the basis strengthens unexpectedly, the hedged position improves whereas if the basis weakens unexpectedly the hedgers position worsens. In the case of a long hedge if the basis strengthens unexpectedly the holder's position worsens whereas if the basis weakens unexpectedly hedger's position improves.

Basis risk increases as the time difference between the hedge expiration and the delivery month increases. Delivery month should be as close as possible to but lower than the expiration of the hedge.

The basis in a hedging situation is,

Basis = Futures price – Spot price

If the asset to be hedged and the asset underlying the futures contract are the same, the basis should be zero at the expiration of the futures contract. Prior to expiration, the basis may be positive or negative. When the underlying asset is a stock index the futures price is greater than the spot price and the basis is negative.

When a spot price increases by more than the futures price, the basis increases. This is known as strengthening the basis. When the futures price increases by more than the spot price, the basis declines. This is known as a weakening of the basis.

Hedging The standard hedging formula is,

$$\text{No. of futures contracts} = \frac{\text{Portfolio Value} \times \text{portfolio beta}}{\text{Value of futures contract}}$$

When the portfolio is fully hedged, it is risk free and would earn no more than a risk free return.

The aim of hedgers is to use futures market to reduce a particular risk they face. A perfect hedge is one that completely eliminates the risk. In real world, perfect hedges cannot be constructed.

The objective of using a futures market to hedge risk is to neutralize it as far as possible. There are short hedges and long hedges. A short hedge requires a short position in futures market. It is appropriate when the hedger already owns an asset and expects to sell it at some time in the future. It can also be used when a hedger does not own an asset right now but knows that the asset will be owned at some time in the future. Where a long position is taken in a futures contract they are known as long hedges. It is appropriate when a company/investor knows it will have to purchase a certain asset in the future and wants to lock in a price now. They can be used to partially offset an existing short position. A part of the risk in shorting a certain stock is related to the performance of the stock market as a whole. The investor can neutralize this risk by taking a long position in index futures contract. Hedgers with long positions usually avoid any possibility of having to take delivery by closing out their positions before their delivery period.

Minimum Variance Hedge Ratio

The hedge ratio is the ratio of the size of the position taken in futures contracts to the size of the exposure.

Hedge ratio that minimizes the variance of the hedger's position, h*

$$h^* = p \frac{\sigma S}{\sigma F}$$

where Δ S! is change in spot price S, during the life of the hedge;

Δ F! change in futures price, F during the life of the hedge.

σ S : Standard deviation of Δ S

σ F : Standard deviation of Δ F

P : Coefficient of correlation between Δ S and Δ F.

The parameters P, σ F and σ S in equation are estimated from historical data on Δ F and Δ S. The optimal hedge ratio h* is the product of the coefficient of correlation between Δ S and Δ F and the ratio of standard deviation of Δ S to the standard deviation of Δ F. The variance of the value of hedger's position depends on the hedge ratio chosen. The optimal hedge ratio h* is the slope of best fit line when changes in the spot price Δ S is regressed against changes in futures price Δ F.

The optimal number of contracts, $N^* = \rho \frac{\sigma S}{\sigma F}$

where S : value of position being hedged

F : Future contract price

The variances σ S, σ F and ρ will denote standard deviation of and coefficient of correlation between S and F respectively.

The optimal number of contracts N* is given by

$$N^* = \beta \frac{S}{F}$$

where S is the value of portfolio

F : the price of a futures contract

β : the relationship between the return on a portfolio of stocks and the return on the market.

When a stock index futures contract is used to hedge a portfolio position or position in individual stock the optimal number of futures contracts is equal to the beta of the position times the ratio of the value of the portfolio to the futures contract price.

The hedger's position grows only at the risk free interest rate. Hedging can be justified if the hedger feels that, that individual stocks are properly picked but is uncertain about the performance of the market as a whole. A hedge using stock index futures removes the risk arising from market moves and leaves the hedger exposed only to the performance of the portfolio relative to the market. Hedging may also be undertaken if the hedger is planning to hold a portfolio for a long period of time and requires short term protection in an uncertain market situation. Sometimes futures contracts are used to change the beta of a portfolio to some value other than zero.

Rolling the Hedge

When there is no liquid futures contract that matures later than the expiration of the hedge a strategy known as rolling the hedge forward may be appropriate. This involves entering into a sequence of contracts. Rolling the hedge works well if there is a close correlation between the changes in futures prices and changes in spot prices.

Marking to market has an effect on the performance of the hedge. It means that the payoff from futures contract is realized day by day throughout the life of the hedge rather than all at the end.

Pricing Stock Index Futures

The fair value of a futures contract relative to the underlying asset is determined by the cash and carry trade. Arbitrage plays beneficial role in maintaining this relationship. For an investor to be indifferent to owning futures contracts or stocks in exact proportion to the index, the price of the futures contract must be equal to the price of buying and carrying such stocks from the stock settlement date to the maturity date of the futures contract. The cost of carry element in owning stocks which is the financing cost minus the present value of the dividend determines the fair value of the futures contract. The fair value of the futures contract will be higher than the underlying index to the extent of this cost of carry element. The fair value premium is,

Index value × (financing rate – present value of dividend yield) t

where t is the proportion of the year from the stock settlement date to the maturity date of the futures contract. The fair value of a stock index futures contract is a function of dividend yield and stock financing costs.

NEWS PAPER QUOTES OF FUTURES

Futures quotations from The Wall Street Journal of May 5, 2004 are presented in Table 13.1. In the Table futures financial quotations can be found. These refer to the trading that took place on May 4, 2006. The quotations for index futures under Indexes give the underlying futures contract, the exchange it is traded on, the contract size, the maturity month, volume, prices, (open, high and low) settlement price (the average of the prices at which contracts were traded immediately before the bell signalling the end of the trading for the day) and change (in the settlement price from the previous day). The settlement price is used, for calculating daily gains and losses and margin requirements.

Table 13.1: Futures Price Quotes (May 4, 2004)

Futures

Finance						***May 04, 2004***		
High	Low	Date	Open	High	Low	Settle	Chg	Open Int
3-MO Eurodollars Deposits (CME)								
$1 million-pts of 100 pct.								
98.88	98.34	May 04	98.78	98.82	98.77	98.80	+ 0.1	89,222
98.85	91.77	Jun 04	98.67	98.70	98.58	98.67	...	823,073
98.81	98.50	Jul 04	98.52	98.53	98.51	98.53	...	39,615
98.75	98.37	Aug 04	98.38	98.39	98.37	98.38	...	1,430
98.74	91.70	Sep 04	98.25	98.30	98.19	98.26	...	873,785
98.53	91.61	Dec 04	97.79	97.87	97.71	97.81	+ 0.1	758,291
98.26	91.38	Mar 05	97.32	97.42	97.25	97.33	+ 0.1	603,509

Est vol ...: prew vol 672,061 : open int 5,790, : – 18,825

5 Yr. Treasury (CBT)
$ 100,000 prin–pts & 32nds & a half 32nd

114-06	109-19	Jun 04	109-29	110-105	109-19	109-265	–0.25	1,074,012
113-00	107-17	Sep 04	108-20	108-225	108-14	108-18	0.25	98,815

Est vol 409,724: prev vol 267,983: open int 1,172,827: +7,220

10 Yr. Treasury (CBT)

$100,000 prin-pts & 32nds & a half 32nd

116-185	107-13	Jun 04	110–16	111-03	109-31	110-095	–0.65	1,272,457
115-095	108-205	Sep 04	109-03	109-22	108-24	108-285	–0.65	166,424
113-045	107-15	Dec 04	107-15	107-155	107-15	107-155	–0.65	2,364
Est vol 772,967: prev vol 508,475: open int 1,441,245: +4,039								

US Treasury Bonds (CBT)

(6 pct-$100,000-pts & 32nds of 100 pct)

116-13	102-09	Jun 04	107-07	107-28	106-11	106-21	–17	472,617
114-30	101-31	Sep 04	105-27	106-15	105-02	105-10	–17	38,441
113-12	100-30	Dec 04	104-25	104-28	104-02	104-02	–17	1,307
Est vol 270,236: prev vol 117,126: open int 512,547: –2,047								

S&P Comp. Index (CME)

250 × Index

1162.30	930.30	Jun 04	1115.80	1127.50	1111.50	1115.50	–.50	562,923
1159.00	839.20	Sep 04	1115.80	1115.80	1112.00	1114.50	–.50	21,881
1138.50	840.20	Dec 04	1115.80	1115.80	1114.20	1114.20	–.50	2,738
Est vol 38,322: prev vol 37,290: open int 587,915: –1,147								

Chapter–13

DJ Inds (CBT)

$10 × Dow Jones Industrial Average

10715	9678	Jun 04	10300	10374	10245	10278	–14	43,683
10557	9985	Sep 04	10280	10295	10255	10260	–14	867
Est vol 6,675: prev vol 8,196: open int 44,564: +272								

NASDAQ 100 Index (CME)

$100 × Index

1555.50	1366.00	Jun 04	1414.00	1439.00	1410.00	1419.00	+4.50	80,694
1500.00	1405.50	Sep 04	1425.00	1438.00	1421.50	1421.50	+4.50	26
Est vol 14,858: prev vol 15,853: open int 80,724: –1,239								

Source: The Wall Street Journal, May 5, 2004

Index Options ***May 04, 2004***

S&P 100 Close: 547.15

Strike	Calls			Puts		
Price	May	Jun	Jul	May	Jun	Jul
460	r	r	r	0.05	r	1.50
470	r	r	r	0.10	0.60	r
480	r	r	r	0.10	0.60	r
485	r	s	s	0.10	0.80	r
490	r	r	r	0.15	s	s

Contd....

500	45.00	r	48.30	0.25	1.55	r
505	r	r	s	0.30	1.70	3.90
510	r	r	r	0.55	r	s
515	r	r	s	0.75	2.85	5.70
520	r	30.00	r	1.10	3.50	s
525	r	r	s	1.55	4.00	7.50
530	22.50	r	r	2.15	r	s
535	17.10	r	s	3.30	4.90	r
540	10.00	15.50	19.70	4.80	7.50	s
545	7.20	12.50	s	7.00	9.20	15.00
550	4.50	9.00	r	9.50	11.50	s
555	2.70	7.20	s	11.00	13.90	16.20
560	1.50	5.40	r	16.00	16.40	s
565	0.75	3.50	s	19.50	19.00	22.70
570	0.45	3.00	r	r	26.00	r
575	0.20	1.60	s	r	37.00r	s
580	0.15	1.00	3.50	r	r	r
585	0.10	0.60	s	r	r	s
590	0.05	0.35	r	r	r	r
595	0.05	r	r	r	r	r

Prev call vol. 25,970   Call open int. 171,110

Prev put vol. 21,135   Put open int. 210,489

S&P 500   Close: 1119.55

Chapter–13

Strike	Calls			Puts		
Price	May	Jun	Jul	May	Jun	Jul
1050	r	r	r	1.30	6.60	12.50
1060	61.50	s	s	1.50	s	s
1065	r	s	s	2.00	s	s
1070	51.00	s	s	2.40	s	s
1075	46.00	54.00	65.00	3.10	10.00	18.90
1085	s	r	s	s	11.90	s
1100	32.80	34.50	46.00	8.50	18.00	22.80
1110	20.50	r	s	11.60	20.00	s
1115	16.00	25.00	s	12.50	21.90	s
1120	12.60	22.00	s	16.10	24.50	s
1125	9.70	19.50	28.20	18.00	26.50	34.00
1130	8.60	17.00	s	21.40	29.40	s
1135	6.00	s	s	22.50	s	s
1140	4.80	15.00	19.70	22.50	36.60	r
1145	4.10	s	s	35.00	s	s
1150	2.80	8.80	15.10	35.90	40.30	r
1155	2.00	7.60	s	38.00	43.30	s
1160	1.50	8.00	s	45.00	r	s
1165	1.40	s	s	r	s	s
1170	0.45	s	s	r	s	s

Contd....

1175	0.40		3.60	7.80	57.00	54.00	r
1180	0.35		s	r	s	s	s
1185	0.25		s	r	s	s	s
1190	0.30		s	r	s	s	s
1200	0.25		1.40	3.50	r	r	86.50
Prev call vol.32,927							Call open int. 1,200,404

Prev put vol.91,594 Put open int. 2,017,763

Nasdaq 100 Close: 1422.11

Strike	Calls			Puts			
Price	May	Jun	Jul	May	Jun	Jul	
1100	r		r	r	r	1.20	r
1150	r		r	r	r	1.90	5.40
1175	r		r	r	r	r	7.70
1200	r		218.00	r	r	3.50	9.20
1225	r		r	r	1.00	5.00	11.20
1250	r		r	r	1.00	7.80	r
1275	r		155.00	r	1.70	8.00	18.00
1300	122.00		r	r	2.70	13.50	r
1325	102.00		r	r	4.70	17.00	r
1350	74.50		r	r	6.10	20.70	35.00
1375	52.20		69.50	r	11.00	r	42.50
1400	39.00		62.50	69.80	18.00	34.00	r

Contd....

Chapter–13

1425	24.00		51.00	58.80	26.30	45.70	r
1450	14.10		33.00	r	36.80	63.50	76.20
1475	7.00		26.30	40.10	50.10	79.00	r
1500	3.40		16.00	27.70	92.00	95.50	r
1525	1.85		8.60	r	104.00	114.50	r
1550	0.50		7.00	14.40	128.60	134.50	r
1575	0.50		3.30	r	r	r	r
1600	0.30		r	5.90	r	r	r
1625	0.20		r	3.90	r	r	r
1650	0.05		r	r	r	r	r
1675	0.10		r	r	r	r	r
1700	0.20		0.50	0.50	r	r	r
1750	r		R	0.50	r	r	r

rev call vol.4,206 Call open int. 84,150

Prev put vol.7,154 Put open int. 17,921

DJ Inds (1/100) Close: 103.17

Strike Price	Calls May	Jun	Jul	Puts May	Jun	Jul	
88	r		r	r	r	r	0.35
94	r		s	r	0.05	s	r
96	7.60		r	r	0.10	0.45	r
98	5.00		r	r	0.25	0.80	r
99	r		r	r	0.15	r	r

Contd....

100	3.50	r	r	0.35	1.05	r
101	r	r	r	0.55	1.40	2.15
102	1.75	2.60	r	0.80	1.35	r
103	1.05	1.90	2.60	1.20	2.05	2.85
104	0.60	1.80	r	1.80	2.65	r
105	0.45	1.00	r	2.50	r	r
106	0.20	0.80	1.30	3.40	r	4.10
107	0.10	0.50	1.05	r	r	r
108	r	0.40	0.75	4.90	r	r
109	r	r	0.60	r	6.30	r
110	r	r	0.35	r	r	r
112	r	r	0.15	r	9.00	r
116	r	r	r	r	13.00	r

Prev call vol. 6,466 — Call open int. 274,210

Prev put vol. 11,694 — Put open int. 327,238

Japan Index — Close: 123.25

Strike	Calls			Puts			
Price	May	Jun	Jul	May	Jun	Jul	
120		3.60	r	r	r	r	r
125		0.95	2.35	r	r	r	r

Prev call vol. 68 — Call open int. 5,043

Prev put vol. … — Put open int. 3,823

Source: The Wall Street Journal, May 5, 2004

Chapter–13

Trading in Stock Options (May 04, 2004)

An option is a contract permitting (but not requiring) a purchase or sale of stock at a given price (the "strike") by a specified date. A "call" is a purchase option: a "put" is for a sale. The lists of gainers and losers comprise only options that traded as $1 or above both yesterday and in the previous session. "Pr" and "Chg" are the price and change of the underlying stock.

Most Active Options

Company	*Date*	*Strike*	*Ty*	*Exc*	*Vol*	*Pr*	*Chg*	*% Chg*	*Pr*	*Chg*
Nasd 100 Tr	May 04	36.00	c	ACIXP	77,749	0.40	..	...	35.28	+0.18
Nasd 100 Tr	Jun04	33.00	p	ACIXP	49,510	0.45	–0.05	–10.2	35.28	+0.18
Nasd 100 Tr	Jun04	39.00	c	ACIXP	47,386	0.10	...	...	35.28	+0.18
Nasd 100 Tr	May04	35.00	p	ACIXP	46,743	0.60	–0.10	–14.2	35.28	+0.18
Nasd 100 Tr	Sep04	38.00	c	ACIXP	46,580	1.05	+0.10	+10.5	35.28	+0.18
Nasd 100 Tr	June04	34.00	c	ACIXP	35,838	2.10	+0.15	+7.6	35.28	+0.18
Nasd 100 Tr	May04	38.00	p	ACIXP	30,921	2.75	–0.10	–3.5	35.28	+0.18
Nasd 100 Tr	Sep04	36.00	c	ACIXP	25,644	1.85	+0.10	+5.7	35.28	+0.18
Semi HTr	May04	35.00	c	ACIXP	22,965	1.60	+0.30	+23.2	35.78	+0.62
Nasd 100 Tr	May04	34.00	p	ACIXP	20,641	0.25	–0.10	–28.4	35.28	+0.18

Volume Comparisons

	Call Volume	Call Op Int	Put Vol	Put Op Int
American Stock Exchange	449,206	54,000,000	316,200	41,800,000
Boston Options Exchange	24,363		15,955	
Chicago Board Options Exchange	698,925	71,328,186	467,344	59,753,743
International Securities Exchange	774,655	62,329,658	545,051	51,539,100
Philadelphia Stock Exchange	292,941	51,038,893	191,458	41,255,900
Pacific Stock Exchange	198,783	65,104,846	127,597	52,742,296
Total	2,438,783		1,663,605	

Company	Date	Strike	Ty	Exc	Vol	Pr	Chg	% Chg	Pr	Chg
VimpelC	May 04	90.00	c	ACX	3	9.00	+7.40	+62.5	97.48	+11.75
VimpelC	Jun 04	100.00	c	ACX	155	4.80	+3.80	+80.0	97.48	+11.75
VimpelC	May 04	85.00	c	ACX	22	12.30	+9.10	+284.4	97.48	+11.75
VimpelC	Jul 04	100.00	c	ACX	64	6.70	+4.75	+243.5	97.48	+11.75
Mobile Tel	May 04	110.00	c	C	20	6.60	+4.65	+238.4	116.06	+14.86
VimpelC	Jun 04	95.00	c	ACX	13	6.60	+4.60	+230.0	97.48	+11.75
Givenimg	May 04	35.00	p	ACX	624	4.20	+2.85	+211.0	30.90	–5.53
Mobile Te	Sep 04	110.00	c	C	7	17.70	+12.00	+210.6	116.06	+14.86
GenProbe	May 04	35.00	c	ACP	236	3.40	+2.30	+209.1	38.22	+4.32
ChiMerc	Jun 04	115.00	p	ACIX	10	3.80	+2.55	+203.9	121.30	+3.02

Chapter–13

Company	*Date*	*Strike*	*Ty*	*Exc*	*Vol*	*Pr*	*Chg*	*% Chg*	*Pr*	*Chg*
Silcn Lab	May 04	40.00	c	ACI	20	8.30	–450.20	–98.2	48.46	+1.32
Silcn Lab	May 04	30.00	c	ACI	20	17.30	–451.20	–96.3	48.46	+1.32
Mobile Tel	May 04	110.00	p	C	40	1.90	–9.10	–82.7	116.06	+14.86
VimpelC	May 04	90.00	p	ACX	430	1.00	–4.50	–81.8	97.48	+11.75
VimpelC	May 04	95.00	p	ACX	127	1.95	–8.45	–81.2	97.48	+11.75
Macrvsn	May 04	22.50	p	ACP	727	1.05	–4.35	–80.6	22.74	+5.18
Mobile Tel	May 04	105.00	p	C	46	1.95	–5.55	–74.0	116.06	+14.86
EvgrnRes	Oct 04	40.00	c	ACP	20	1.00	–1.75	–63.6	38.99	–1.64
VimpelC	Jun 04	85.00	p	ACX	80	1.95	–3.15	–61.8	97.48	+11.75
Mandalay	May 04	55.00	c	ACIXP	129	1.70	–2.60	–60.5	55.41	–3.46

c–call, p–put, A–American Stock Exchange, B–Boston Options Exchange, C–Chicago Board Options Exchange, I–International Securities Exchange, P–Pacific Stock Exchange, X–Philadelphia Stock Exchange

Source: *The Wall Street Journal*, May 05, 2004.

In the case of S&P 500, (the underlying futures contract) CME, (the exchange) contract size (250 × index) maturity month (September 04, 2004) volume (38.322) prices (open 1115.80, high 1115.80, low 1112.0) settlement price (1114.50) and change in settlement price (0.50).

Convergence of Futures Price into Spot Price

Futures price converges to the spot price of the underlying asset when delivery month approaches. If futures price is above the expected futures spot price (contango) there is an expectation that futures price will decline. Similarly, if the futures price is below the expected futures spot price (normal backwardation) there is an expectation that the futures price will rise. If hedgers tend to hold short positions and the speculators tend to hold long positions the futures price will be below the expected spot price to compensate speculators for the risks they are bearing. Speculators will only trade if there is expectation that the futures price will rise over time. If hedgers tend to hold long positions while speculators hold short positions, the futures price must be above the expected futures spot price. To compensate speculators for risks they are bearing, there must be an expectation that the futures price will decline over time.

Marking to Market

The exchange organizes trading so that contracts defaults are minimized. The system of marking to market requires the investor to deposit funds in a margin account. The *initial margin* is deposited at time the contract is first entered into and is marked to market at the close of trading on each subsequent day. When there is a decrease in futures price, the margin account of an investor with a long position is reduced and the investor's broker has to deposit the difference. Similarly when there is an increase in futures price, brokers for parties with short positions pay money to the exchange and brokers for parties with long positions receive money from the exchange. A *maintenance margin* is also set to ensure that margin account does not become negative. If the balance in margin account falls below initial margin the investor receives a margin call and is expected to top up margin account to the initial margin the next day.

To satisfy the initial margin requirement an investor can deposit securities with the broker. The effect of marking to market is that a futures contract is settled daily rather than at the end of its life. The investor's gain is added to the margin account and the loss is subtracted bringing the value of the contract to zero. A futures contract is in effect closed out and rewritten at a new price each day.

Margin requirements are lower in the case of day trades and spread transactions. A day trade is a trade where the trader informs the broker that the position will be closed the same day. Short position is offset by long position and long position by an offsetting short position later in the day. If the trader simultaneously takes a long position in the contract corresponding to one month and a short position in a contract corresponding to another month, it is a spread transaction.

Clearing House

The clearing house of the exchange acts as an intermediary in futures transactions. It guarantees the performance of the parties to each transaction. The clearing house has members to whom the brokers channel their, business. The members are required to maintain a margin account with the exchange which is known as clearing margin. The margin accounts of members are adjusted for gains or losses at the end of each trading day in the same way as margin accounts of investors. The members have to make an initial margin but no maintenance margin. The account balance for each contract at an amount equal to original margin times the number of contracts outstanding. The main task of clearing house is to keep track of all transactions that take place during a day so that it can accumulate the net position of each of its members. Most exchanges use net margining. The net basis allows long positions entered into by clients be offset by the total of all short positions entered into by clients. Clearing house members have to add funds to its margin account at the end of the day or withdraw them depending on the number of contracts and price movements during the day. The purpose of margining system is to reduce the possibility of market participants sustaining losses because of defaults. The system has been very successful in eliminating losses from defaults.

Trading

All stock futures trading is done on margin averaging less than 5 per cent of current market values. A large proportion of stock index futures transactions in exchanges where they are traded are purely speculative since a great deal of leverage is available from trading such instrument. Trading in futures is a zero sum game. At any given moment, there is going to be gain for one and loss for another. Exchanges should check malpractices to ensure that investors do not lose money. With a futures position the loss can exceed the original amount.

Institutional investors find futures useful mainly because of size. A futures contract at $500 times the index at 395 would have a value of $187,500. A $1 million portfolio could be hedged by selling 10 contracts assuming the portfolio had a beta of 1.

A 10 per cent market decline would also result in a similar decline in the short futures contract. The loss in value on the portfolio is offset largely by profit in the futures market. Stock index futures are settled in cash. There are no specialists in futures exchanges. Long options have to be paid in full which are small amounts. All stock futures trading is done on margin averaging less than 5 per cent of current contract values ranging from $3500 to $6000 per contract. In the case of long stock or option position the original deposit represents the maximum possible loss but with a futures position the loss can exceed the original margin commitment.

Program Trading

Program trading is resorted to by institutional investors to reallocate their assets or align their portfolios with a chosen index. Index arbitrage consists of dealing with index futures as well as underlying securities whenever there is a gap between their prices. A trader utilizing index arbitrage identifies a group of stocks within one of the indexes that move closely in line with the value of the index. When there is an increase in the value of the index compared to the underlying shares, futures are sold short and underlying securities are purchased locking in a price differential between the two. Conversely, when futures prices are low compared to prices of underlying securities, the process is reversed. The trading is risk free because gaps between prices will be closed by arbitragers buying in the cheap market and selling in the high. Since gaps do not persist for long time the transactions must be executed on the trading floor with split second precision. Preprinted order tickets that need only to be time stamped at point of entry and employment of $2 brokers are resorted to handle the flood of orders that program trading entails.

Index trading releases large order volume leading to wild price swings in the averages and the underlying stock. This is especially so on dates when index options and futures expire forcing an immediate alignment of closing prices with the actual indexes. Securities included in the index basket fall prey to the pernicious practice and may experience fall in prices discouraging investors from committing capital.

Trading Irregularities

Futures markets operate efficiently and in public interest most of the time. Investor groups sometimes try to corner the market. The investor with a hedge of long position exercising some control over supply do not close out its position, the number of outstanding contracts may exceed the supply and the holders of short position would not be able to deliver and become desperate to close out their position. The result is a large rise in futures and spot prices. Regulators deal with this type of abuse by increasing margin requirement, imposing strict position limits, prohibiting trades that increase a speculator's open position and forcing market participants to close out their position.

Volatility

Dealing spreads in futures markets tend to be lower than in the underlying physical securities markets enhancing the appeal and accessibility of stock index futures as tools for market speculation. The study by FED\SEC\CFTC shows that derivatives have no impact on volatility and academic analysis indicates a reduction in volatility.

October 1987 Crash

The stock market crash on Wall Street was remarkable in the extent and the speed in which value was eroded and in the extent of the dislocation of relative economic values. The arbitrage of stock index futures prices against prices in the underlying activity known as program trading was central to this price action. It was decoupling of the economic value of the futures contract from the value of the underlying index facilitated tumbling values in the overall market. A few large sell orders brought about a swift market decline which was worsened by the authorities move to halt trading late in day. The authorities move to close the exchange led to panic selling of both stocks and futures and brought about at one stage 20 per cent discount on S&P 500 futures contract relative to its underlying index. Arbitrageurs could not move into restore the economic value of the futures vis a vis underlying stocks for fear of market closure. Where derivative markets remained open, relative economic values were quietly restored after Black Monday.

Table 13.2 presents the features of exchange traded stock index futures.

Table 13.2: Features of Exchange Traded Stock Index Futures

Liquidity	Most liquid are the ones based on established indexes. Liquidity is best in front contracts.
Maximum maturities	Liquid contracts trade on a quarterly cycle with front contracts trading simultaneously.
Deal size	Fixed contract sizes.
Trading costs	Brokerage costs plus initial and variation margin.
Price quote	Open outcry on floor of the exchange. Prices quoted on an index basis.
Margin leverage	Deposit and variation very high.
Credit risk	Clearing House assumes all credit risk.
Market risk	Risk is the systematic risk of the market as given by the index tracking efficiency plus tracking error. Exposure to overall market movements.
Documentation	Authority to deal.

Disclosures and Fair Value Accounting

Since stock index futures are an off balance sheet item, the balance sheet of a company would not disclose the exposure.

Stock index futures on account of their being marked to market and not valued at cost, could create significant volatality in a firm's profit. In USA, the accountants would like the derivatives including futures marked to market. However Federal Reserve is against it, because it would impart considerable volatality in firm's profit.

The Financial Accounting Standards Board (FASB) Standard (January 1999) requires the recognition of changes in the value of derivatives in their quarterly earning reports and list them as assets or liabilities with fair market value in the year end balance sheet. Any fluctuations in the value of derivatives can be offset by changes in the values of future cash flows, assets or liabilities for which they serve as hedges.

Accounting and Tax

In the US contracts that are entered into for hedging purpose are treated differently from those entered into for speculative purposes. Speculative transactions are marked to market for both accounting and tax purposes. In the case of hedging transaction gains or losses arise only when the contract is closed out or when delivery is made.

Report of the Committee on Derivatives (1998)

The value of stock index futures would be influenced by the movement in the underlying basket of shares. The latters value would be influenced by the movements in the underlying basket of shares. Investors can trade in standard lots of such an instrument. The Committee emphasized the importance of having a hedging facility in the market. Hedging is required where there already exists a related commercial position which is exposed to risk of loss due to price movement. Mutual funds and investors with portfolios of any size require hedging. According to the Committee hedging is the key aspect of derivatives and also its basic economic purpose. The Committee recommended that legal restrictions should be removed on use of derivatives by financial institutions for purposes of hedging their investment exposures.

Merits of Index Futures

According to the Committee, the merits of index futures are:

- Institutional and other large equity holders need a portfolio hedging facility. Hence, index-based derivatives are more suited to them and more cost-effective than derivatives based on individual stocks. Even pension funds in the US are known to use stock index futures for risk-hedging purposes.

- Stock index is more difficult to manipulate than individual stock prices, more so in India, and the possibility of cornering is reduced. This is partly because an individual stock has a limited supply which can be cornered. Of course, the manipulation of stock index can be attempted by influencing the cash prices of its component securities. While the possibility of such manipulation is not ruled out, it is reduced by designing the index appropriately. There is need for minimizing it further by undertaking cash market reforms.

- Stock index futures enjoy distinctly greater popularity and are, therefore, likely to be more liquid than all other types of equity derivatives as shown by the international experience.

- Stock index being an average, is much less volatile than individual stock prices. This implies much lower capital adequacy and margin requirements in the case of index futures than in the case of derivatives on individual stocks. The lower margins will induce more players to join the market.

- In the case of individual stocks, the positions which remain outstanding on the expiration date will have to be settled by physical delivery. This is an accepted principle everywhere. The futures and the cash market prices have to converge on the expiration date. Since index futures do not represent a physically deliverable asset, they are cash settled all over the world on the premise that the index value is derived from the cash market. This, of course, implies that the cash market is functioning in a reasonably sound manner and the index values based on it can be safely accepted as the settlement price.

- Regulatory complexity is likely to be less in the case of stock index futures than for other kinds of equity derivatives such as stock index options or individual stock options.

REGULATION OF THE DERIVATIVES MARKET

Self Regulatory Organization

As far as regulation is concerned, the Committee has suggested derivative exchange be a self-regulatory organization. Since the day-to-day regulatory requirement would be of a different nature compared to anything so far on stock exchanges, the SRO concept form the start may create the right market structure. SEBI would be the overall regulator, with the authority to approve the laws and regulations of the exchange and specific derivative contracts (such as products based on NSE-50, BSE SENSEX or CRISIL-500).

While expressing the view that an independent exchange may be in order for derivatives, the Committee has in view of the cost of creating the necessary infrastructure, recommended that existing stock exchanges could start derivatives trading. But a set of strict entry barriers have been prescribed and derivatives trading will have to be a separate division with its own governing council. The members of the Governing Council of the Exchange should not be part of the derivatives council. Given the entry barriers and systems specified, the NSE and the BSE may be best placed to launch the futures system.

Clearing Corporation

The recommendations to set up a clearing corporation to collect margins and provide a guarantee as counter-party, the margin systems, capital adequacy and exposure limits provided should ensure that the trading system has **the** right checks and balances.

Members

As far as members are concerned a minimum number of 50 has been prescribed. Perhaps keeping in mind the general perception about the complex nature of the derivatives market, all brokers/dealers would have to pass a certification programme to be organized by SEBI. A minimum net worth requirement of Rs.3 crores and the suggestion that the regulations should be more stringent for the derivatives market than the cash market should ensure that serious players enter the fray. But the net worth requirement could, at least partly, be represented by a value for trading rights on the derivatives exchange. Even the NSE, which has no concept of seats in the regular market, could use this route on derivatives to create a higher degree of interest and responsibility among market players.

As far as the marketing of derivative products is concerned, the recommendation that a risk disclosure document should be given to the client should ensure that both parties enter into the transaction with their eyes open. The proposal that every client should be registered with the broker/dealer and provide an authorization from the Board of Director's/Trustees should also place a reasonable restriction on the process.

Survey of Potential Participants

The Committee conducted a survey of potential participants on key issues such as risk need, favoured instrument and status of the participant. Out of the 300 questionnaires sent 37.3 per cent responded. The break up of respondents (112) were 59.8 per cent brokers, 8.0 per cent merchant bankers, 8.9 per cent mutual funds (10), 12.5 per cent banks and financial institutions and 10.7 per cent (FIIs). The case for futures was based on the needs of mutual funds and investors. Out of 32 mutual funds only 31.2 per cent or 10 responded. About 85 per cent identified systematic risk as the cause of most concern, and the need for various instruments was identified as index futures, closely followed by stock index options and options on individual stocks, the instrument favoured by potential participants was stock index futures, and about 70 per cent indicated their status of participation as hedgers followed by brokers.

The questionnaire has not sought any information about the respondents hedging needs or investment activities.

Hedgers and Stock Index Futures

The proposal for introduction of stock index futures is mainly based on the need for hedging. It was noted above that the questionnaire did not seek to establish the hedging needs or investment activities. Unless there is demand for hedging and sufficient interest among investors for trading in equity futures the proposal would not be successful. Several countries including Argentina, Chile, Uruguay and Mexico have failed. The introduction of stock index futures requires a large market with substantial volatility. There must be sizeable cash market to impart liquidity to the futures market. There should be genuine demand for hedging by a large number of investors. The index stocks are held by government or multinationals or a few development financial institutions. They are not interested in short term trading or investment gains. The genuine portfolio investors do not hold any significant amount of index shares which would need hedging. Actually, the shares available to public are few and varied. Even tracking the index portfolio would not be efficient because the shares do not have high correlation with the index. If hedgers are few and are on same side there would not be any need to offset the possible risks or liquidate another hedge as a result of change in their positions in the cash markets. As with other futures contracts, the market cannot exist only for the hedgers. There must be an opposite side of every transaction. Stock index futures have a strong appeal to speculators because of low margin (great leverage) and the potential to make large gains.

Representative Index

Finally the index should be representative of the market and should be understood by investors. In the case of Chicago Board of Options Exchange which created a new index when Dow Jones did not allow it to adopt its index, the index did not work. However, NSE introduced futures on NSE 50 and BSE on SENSEX.

Futures Launch by NSE

The National Stock Exchange (NSE) is expected to launch derivatives trading between October 15 and November 15, 1998. To begin with, NSE plans to start futures on its most popular index NSE-50 (NIFTY) and subsequently on its other broad based stock indices. The net worth of a trading member is proposed to be Rs.1 crore. The minimum size of the contract would be Rs.l lakh. The composition of the NIFTY may change in order to represent a fair view of stock market trends. NSE has entrusted the task of recomposing NIFTY to Indian Index Services and Products. A training programme on derivatives trading for its members' staff is proposed to be organized.

Futures Launch by BSE

The Bombay Stock Exchange announced on July 22, 1998 that it would launch derivatives trading based on the SENSEX. The membership criteria in terms of net worth of a trading member is proposed at Rs.50 lakhs. The transaction charges would be a flat rate of Rs.5 on all contracts up to a maximum value of Rs.3.5 lakhs.

Interest Rate Futures

Banks and primary dealers were permitted to undertake transactions in exchange traded interest rate derivatives. In June 2003, initially only interest rate futures have been introduced and banks were allowed to hedge interest rate risk inherent in the government securities portfolio. Harmonizing the regulatory, legal and prudential treatment of OTC and exchange traded interest rate derivatives is yet to be implemented. Futures contracts are based on notional 10-years Government of India bonds, notional 91 days treasury bills and 10-years zero coupon bonds.

OPTIONS

Nature and Definition

Options on stocks are one of the derivative instruments. "Options are marketable securities, that give their owner the right but not the obligation to buy or sell a stated number of shares (usually of a particular security at a fixed price within a predetermined time period."[37] Options provide a contractual right to purchase or sell at a stated price subject to certain conditions, such as the length of time for which this right is exercisable. The basic characteristics of options are limited loss, high leverage potential and limited life. Losses are limited to the amount paid for the option while enjoying much of the profit potential of the underlying security. A small sum is needed to obtain high profits. The life of option expires on the expiration date.

Put and Call Option

There are two basic types of options, the put option and call option. A call is an option to buy securities. A put is an option that gives its owner the legal right to sell shares to someone else.

Straddle, Strip, Spread and Strap

There are four other kinds of options which are a combination of puts and calls. A straddle is a combination of put and call giving the buyer the right to either buy or sell stock at the exercise price. If the price of the stock fluctuates sufficiently, the buyer may exercise both the put and call portions of the straddle. A strip is two puts and one call at the same period. A spread consists of a put and a call option on the same security for the same time period at different exercise prices. A strip is two calls and one put at the same contracted exercise price and for the same period.

Options in U.K.

The concept of options is not a new one and they have been traded for a number of years. Reports of their use in England go as far back

37. Francis. J.C., *Investments: Analysis and Management,* Fifth Edition, McGraw Hill International Edition, p. 634.

as 1694, some 80 years earlier than the founding of the London Stock Exchange. In the seventeenth century, tulip bulb options were common in Holland. They were useful to growers in reducing their exposure to price fluctuations. In the absence of any regulatory mechanism the tulip bulb option market was totally undisciplined. There were no financially sound option endorsers to guarantee that writers would fulfil their contracts. When the market broke in 1663, a number of puts were wiped out. The losers were neither willing nor able to meet their commitments. In London organized trading in puts and calls on securities began late in seventeenth century. In view of the Dutch experience and since they were considered speculative, options were declared illegal by Barnard's Act of 1733. The Act was not effective and trading in options continued. The Act was repealed in 1860. During the financial crisis of 1931, they were again banned. Options trading resumed in 1958 and today London has the largest options market although options are also traded in France, Germany and Switzerland.

Options in U.S.A.

In the United States, securities options have a tainted past as there were a number of abuses. Their use was generally associated with pool activities and manipulations frequently involving insiders. From the 1920s to until 1973 securities options business was in the hands of a few small firms which eventually organized the Put and Call Brokers and Dealers Association. Their function was to facilitate option buyers and sellers (writers) by locating and becoming the opposite side of a transaction. Listed options on shares were introduced on the Chicago Board of Options Exchange (CBOE) in 1973. First call options were listed and later put options in 1977. In 1983 the first, index option began trading on CBOE. It was originally called CBOE 100 Index and was later renamed as S&P 100 Index or OEX (the ticker symbol). Options on futures contracts which were temporarily banned by Congress in 1978 were reintroduced in 1982. The first contracts were options on Treasury Bond Futures. In order to avoid price discrepancies an electronic link up designated as Option Inter-market Communication Linkage System was adopted.

New products and new exchanges to trade them on are coming into existence all over the world. The exchanges across the continents are linked. In 1984, the Singapore International Monetary Exchange (SIMEX) and the Chicago Mercentile Exchange (CME) formed a trading link over which investors could trade some contracts interchangeable on the two exchanges (called mutual offset). It was the first of several networks and systems that are leading to a globalized and increasingly automated world of 24 hours a day trading of securities. Globex, which electronically matches buy and sell orders entered from computer terminals in Chicago, New York, London and Paris was introduced on June 25, 1992.

Nature of Options Contract

A put gives the holder the right to sell usually 100 shares of stock at a fixed price for a fixed period. A call option conveys a similar right to buy. In order to obtain this privilege, the buyer (or long) pays a consideration to the seller or writer (short). The price per share at which the option may be exercised is called the exercise or striking price or simply the "strike". An options contract can be listed and traded like stocks in an options exchange. The Chicago Board of Trade created standardized exchange traded options with interchangeable features. All contracts of a specific kind on the same stock have identical expiration dates and striking prices leaving only the premium to be negotiated in an open auction market. Options became truly liquid vehicles. It became possible to trade puts and calls either to claim a profit or to cut a loss. Options are exercised in only 5 per cent of all options traded. Liquidity and visibility created by this market made possible adoption of several strategies. The key to the growth of the market was the ability to extract profits or cut losses through trading the contracts as opposed to exercise or awaiting expiration.

Call Option

A call option is a contract that gives its owner the right, but not the obligation, to buy a specified number of shares of equity stock at a specified price on or before a specified date.

An American call option can be exercised on or before the specified date. In the case of European options, the owner of the option can exercise his right only on the specified date.

The writer of the call option may or may not own the shares for which the call is written. If he owns the shares, it is a covered call; and of he does not, it is called a 'naked' call.

Assume that an investor purchases a 3 month call option on 100 shares at an exercise price of Rs.350 per share when the stock price is Rs.400. The option holder has the right to purchase 100 shares for Rs.350 each at any time over option life irrespective of actual market price.

This suggests that a call buyer expects the price of the underlying stock to rise above the exercise price. Minimum value of a call option has to be 50. Otherwise one can make a profit by buying it at Rs.350 and selling it at a market price of Rs.400. The longer the remaining life of the call option, the larger the option premium. The larger the exercise price the smaller the price of the option. The price of the call option increases as market value of stock increases. Finally, option price increases as the volatility of the stock increases.

Put Option

A put option on common stock allows the holder of the option to sell (put) a certain number of shares of the underlying stock at a prespecified price at a prespecified date. An American put option can be exercised on or before specified date whereas an European option can only be exercised on the specified date and not before it. If the price of the share rises above the specified price put option becomes worthless. A put option is of value as long as there is some chance that the stock price will move below the exercise price.

A put buyer expects the price of the underlying stock to fall below the exercise price. In contrast to call option, the minimum price for the put option is the difference between the exercise price and the price of the underlying stock.

Strike Price

The specified price is the strike price or exercise price. It is the price per share at which the option is exercisable. It is the price per share, the buyer of the call option must pay the writer for having written the call option or the price the writer must get from the buyer of the put option. It represents the amount per share a holder must pay in order to claim the shares. The strike price is selected by the options exchange. Generally strike prices are convenient numerical quantities above or below the currently prevailing market rates of the stock. If the current market rates go beyond the extremes of the available strike prices a new set of strike price series is introduced. In American markets strike prices are at intervals of $5 each.

Expiration Date

The specified date, on or before which an option in American market and on which an option in European market remains valid is called the expiration date. Beyond the expiration date the option contracts become void.

In the American markets, an option falls into one of the three cycles that determine its expiration date. Generally, options have an expiration period between three to nine months. The highest liquidity normally resides in those options which expire in the two upcoming months. Table 13.3 gives various cycles in which the options fall and the associated expiration months.

Table 13.3: Options Expiration Months

Each traded option falls into one of the following three sequential cycles. The table shows the available expiration months.

I. January Cycle

From Monday after the third Friday in	*Until the third Friday in*	*Available months*			
January	February	Feb	Mar	Apr	Jul
February	March	Mar	Apr	Jul	Oct
March	April	Apr	May	Jul	Oct
April	May	May	Jun	Jul	Oct
May	June	Jun	Jul	Oct	Jan
June	July	Jul	Aug	Oct	Jan
July	August	Aug	Sep	Oct	Jan
August	September	Sep	Oct	Jan	Apr
September	October	Oct	Nov	Jan	Apr
October	November	Nov	Dec	Jan	Apr
November	December	Dec	Jan	Apr	Jul
December	January	Jan	Feb	Apr	Jul

II. February Cycle

From Monday after the third Friday in	*Until the third Friday in*	*Available months*			
January	February	Feb	Mar	May	Aug
February	March	Mar	Apr	May	Aug
March	April	Apr	May	Aug	Nov
April	May	May	Jun	Aug	Nov
May	June	Jun	Jul	Aug	Nov
June	July	Jul	Aug	Nov	Feb
July	August	Aug	Sep	Nov	Feb
August	September	Sep	Oct	Nov	Feb
September	October	Oct	Nov	Feb	May
October	November	Nov	Dec	Feb	May
November	December	Dec	Jan	Feb	May
December	January	Jan	Feb	May	Aug

III. March Cycle

From Monday after the third Friday in	*Until the third Friday in*	*Available months*			
January	February	Feb	Mar	Jun	Sep
February	March	Mar	Apr	Jun	Sep
March	April	Apr	May	Jun	Sep
April	May	May	Jun	Sep	Dec
May	June	June	Jul	Sep	Dec
June	July	Jul	Aug	Sep	Dec
July	August	Aug	Sep	Dec	Mar
August	September	Sep	Oct	Dec	Mar
September	October	Oct	Nov	Dec	Mar
October	November	Nov	Dec	Mar	Jun
November	December	Dec	Jan	Mar	Jun
December	January	Jan	Feb	Mar	Jun

Option Premium

In the listed options market, the premiums are determined by open outcry between buyers and sellers in an auction on the exchange floor. Premium is influenced, first, by the relationship between the call's striking price and the price of the underlying shares. This is the intrinsic value of the option. When the stock's market price and the striking price are identical ("at the money"), the appreciation in the stock price is likely to be reflected in the option's price unless the call is close to expiration, (See Table, 13.4). When the call is in-the-money (striking price lower than the current market price of the stock) price changes of any kind are likely to be quickly transmitted to the premium because of arbitrage potential. The activities of the arbitrageurs, buying in cheap market and selling in the dear quickly closes the gaps by forcing premiums up and share prices down until an equilibrium is reached. 'Out-of-the-money' calls on the other hand, have no intrinsic value (the intrinsic value of a call is the amount the option is in-the-money) and represent a pure speculation on future price increases. Traders pay more for a call on a volatile growth stock than one of an old and established company. Secondly, potential for anticipated price changes is greater in a given four month duration than a 3 week one. Time value reflects the fact that the longer the option has to run until expiration, the greater the premium should be. Finally, volatility which is the propensity of the underlying security's price to fluctuate influences the option premium. The higher the volatility the higher the premium because there is again, a greater possibility that the option will move in-the-money Relative volatility and time are important factors in determining what premium a buyer should pay or a seller should accept. It is in the case of out-of-the money options that the market is highly speculative. They are also quite cheap reflecting the scant prospects for appreciation.

Table 13.4: In-the-Money, Out of the Money and At the Money

	CALL	*PUT*
In-the-money (An option with intrinsic value)	$S_t > k$	$S_t < k$
Out-of-the-money (An option with time value but no intrinsic value)	$S_t > k$	$S_t < k$
At-the-money	$S_t = k$	$S_t = k$

S_t = stock price at any time before expiration.

k = strike price.

Put and Call Valuation

The value of a call option on the expiration date is,

$$C = S - E \quad \text{for } S > E$$
$$= 0 \quad \text{for } S - E$$

where C = value of call

S = price of stock

E = exercise price.

The higher the stock price above the strike price, the higher the value of the call. When the stock price is below the strike price, the call price is zero. The down side risk of the call is limited to the price paid for the call.

The value of a put at expiration is,

$$P = E - S \quad \text{for } S < E$$
$$= 0 \quad \text{for } S - E$$

The value of a put is simply the difference between the price of the stock at expiration and the striking price. The lower the stock price is below the exercise price, the higher the value of the put. When the stock price is at or above the strike price, put has no value.

Option writer writes a call option on 100 shares of ACC at a strike price of Rs.2,500 and the expiration date of April 23, 1994. The writer charges a premium of Rs.20,000 on the option contract. Hence the premium per share works out to be Rs.200. The option writer would always want that the stock price does not go beyond Rs.2,700 in which case he makes a profit while the option buyer would want the stock price to go beyond Rs.2,700 in order for him to make any profit.

Profit-Loss Position of a Call Option

The profitability of an uncovered or naked call is presented in Figure 13.1. The call owner can never loose more than the option premium per share he has paid to the call writer even if the underlying share price goes down further. On the other hand, there is no limit to his gain if the share price goes beyond Rs.2,700. The naked call writer's position is exactly opposite of the call buyers position. He keeps the entire premium in case the stock price is less than Rs.2,500. As the price advances beyond Rs.2,500, the call writer's profit decreases and beyond Rs.2,700, he makes a loss.

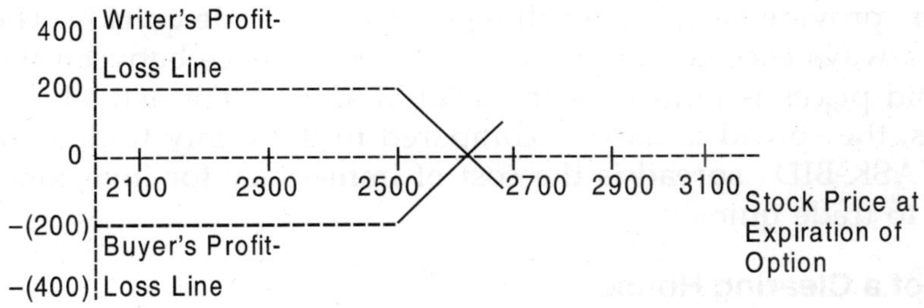

Figure 13.1 Profit-loss Position of Call Option

Profit-loss Position of Put Option

The profit-loss position of a put option with the same strike price, expiration date and option premium is presented in Figure 13.2.

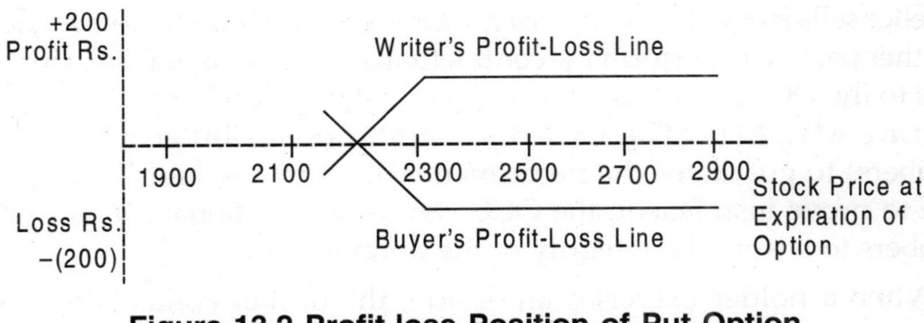

Figure 13.2 Profit-loss Position of Put Option

While the uncovered put writer keeps the entire premium as long as the share price is above Rs.2,500, the profit decreases till share price reaches Rs.2,300 and below this the put writer makes a loss.

The buyer of the put option, on the other hand would always want the price of the share to stay below Rs.2,300 in order to make a profit. At any price above Rs.2,500, the buyer losses the entire premium. If the price is between Rs.2,300 and Rs.2,500, the buyer looses less than the option premium and he can exercise his right to sell shares and cut his losses.

Market Makers

Each option exchange has one or more market makers who stand ready to trade by quoting a bid price and an asked price. Without market makers, an investor who wants to buy or sell any option would, have to wait for another investor to come along and offer to buy it. Market makers do their job by always offering to buy the option at the "bid" price when any investor wants to sell an option. On the other hand, by always offering an "ask" price for an option, they are able to provide options to the prospective buyer. Market makers provide liquidity for those wishing to trade quickly. The ask price always exceeds the bid price. The difference between the ask and bid prices is termed as the ask-bid spread. For actively traded shares, the spread is narrow compared to the thinly traded shares. The "ASK-BID" spread is the cost of immediacy for investors who want to trade quickly.

Role of a Clearing House

Options Clearing Corporation (OCC) is the regulatory body in the U.S.A. for the option contracts. It acts like a guarantor, standing guarantee for both the buyer and the seller. An option is created when a buyer and a seller agree on a price. Once the trade is made, OCC steps in and becomes a party to both sides of the trade. It is the intermediary in each transaction. In other words, the option buyer purchases the option from OCC, and the seller sells it to OCC. In this way, each investor does not worry whether the other party will perform the contractual obligation or not. Each investor looks to the OCC, which is an agency consisting of brokerage firms called Clearing Members. The OCC has capital (contributed by Clearing Members) to guarantee the performance of all trades, and if that capital were to prove insufficient, the OCC can draw additional funds from its members to ensure the integrity of the options markets.

When a holder exercises an option, the broker contacts the OCC. Prior to the opening of trading on the next business day, the OCC will randomly assign the exercise to a clearing member that has a customer who is short on that option. The clearing firm then either randomly assigns the exercise to one of its customers or else assigns it on a first-in-first-out basis. All brokerage firms are required to inform the customers regarding the method used.

The total number of option contracts outstanding at any given time is called the open interest. The open interest figure indicates the number of closing transactions that might be made before the option expires.

Covered Call Writing

Covered call writing is the simplest, most conservative and most widely used method of option writing. An investor holds the stock long at the same time sells (writes) a call on the stock. The use of a call puts a ceiling on the upside potential of the stock. The seller of the call in this instance is exposed to the downside movements of the stock but is not subject to the unlimited risk associated with selling the call outright where the risk position is similar to a short seller of the stock. Selling covered calls provides a partial hedge against a negative market sentiment. But selling of call options has an opportunity cost in terms of the opportunity foregone to capitalize on strong upward movements in the stock or the market in general. Risk is reduced along with return.

Protective Put Strategy

The strategy of an investor holding stock long and at the same time purchasing or put on the stock protects against downside fluctuations in stock. The long holder of the stock participates fully in the upward movements of the stock. While the return opportunity is unaltered the investor has limited the downside risk on the stock to the exercise price of the put. The loss would be limited to the cost of the put. There are alternative ways of purchasing protective puts for a portfolio. One is to buy directly a put on the portfolio. It will provide a downside protection but will naturally have a cost. An alternative way is to use trading rules to move assets in the portfolio thereby constructing an artificial or synthetic put. The synthetic put provides a downside protection and has a cost just as a conventional put.

Index Options

The most popular index option is one on S&P 100 Stock Index, OEX (Ticker symbol). The options on the index were not as successful as the futures contract on the same indicator. Index option provides a defense against systematic risk. The dollar value of all major index option contracts is arbitrarily set at 100 times the current index level. If the current OEX level were $327.95, the index is worth $32,795 and a full point move to 328.95 would represent a value change of $ 100/-. Contracts are traded in 1/8 point ticks or variations of $12.50. All index options are settled in cash. No securities are delivered.

Market options were originally traded on a standard cycle with 90-day intervals separating expiration months. Since 1985 index options are traded with expirations only in current month and two succeeding months. Striking prices are set at 5-point intervals with new ones added as the market moves up or down to the next level. If the index is currently trading at 327.95, striking prices would be available at 325 and 330.

The daily volume of OEX contracts in 1991 was 272,121.

The second most actively traded index option is the Standard and Poor's 500 index option (SPx). The daily average contract volume for this index in 1990 was 42,590.

Major Market Index (XMI) is the third most actively traded index option composed of 20 blue chip companies of which 17 are from Dow Jones Industrial. The correlation between the two is about 97 per cent. The trading volume is about 10 per cent of OEX.

OPTION VALUATION

Factors Affecting Option Values

The three prime factors that influence the value of an option are the expected variance in price or return of the underlying stock, the time remaining to expiration of the option contract and the level of interest rates. The greater the expected variance of price changes for a stock the higher should be the option value from that stock. Observation of the values of options over time confirms that options on higher-risk stocks persistently tend to have greater value than those in lower-risk stocks. The value of an option is primarily determined by the variance of the return. Time remaining to expiration of the option increases the variance of the distribution of returns or price changes. In effect the increased variance due to the lengthening of the time horizon gives added value to the option. Conversely, the reduction of the time to maturity reduces the value of option. Interest rates influence option values. Investors can obtain leverage in stock investing by borrowing or purchasing calls. Second creation of quasi equity security consisting of fixed income security such as treasury bill and a call would result in larger return at high interest rates. Higher interest rates result in increase in value of options while lower interest rates lead to lower value of options.

Black Scholes Pricing Model

The principle that options can completely eliminate market risk from a stock portfolio is the basis of Black-Scholes formula or model developed in 1973. An option pricing model is a mathematical formula that uses the factors determining option prices as inputs. The Black-Scholes model is a mathematical extension of binomial model which was not even discovered at that time. Early pricing models, however, supplied the intuition that an option can be priced by forming a riskless hedge portfolio consisting of stock and options. Black-Scholes applied stochastic calculus to derive the model. The formula can be used to measure both the value and risk of an option in relation to its underlying stock. In conjunction with capital asset pricing model, it can be used to construct optimal portfolios containing both options and other securities. The model assumes that the stock price follows one particular type of pricing process and the process must be unchanging over time.

It was noted earlier that an option price is determined by exercise price, time to expiration, risk free rate and parameters defining the volatility of the stock prices. The operation of hedging and hedging ratio are critical notions underlying Black-Scholes option valuation model. The model is based on the fact that it is possible *ceteris paribus,* to set up a perfectly hedged position consisting of long position, in an underlying stock and a short position in options on that stock or a long position in the option and a short position in the stock. Perfect hedge implies that over a stock price interval close to the current price any profit resulting from an instantaneous increase in the price of the stock would be offset by instantaneous loss on option position or vice versa. This implies that the relationship between the stock and the option value is effectively linear so that gains and losses are exactly offset.

The assumptions of Black-Scholes model are:

1. Capital markets are perfect. There are no transaction costs or taxes. There are no short-selling constraints and investors get full use of short-sale proceeds. All assets are infinitely divisible.
2. The stocks pay no dividends.

3. All investors can borrow and lend at the same risk free interest rate which is constant over the life of the option.
4. Markets are always open and trading is continuous.
5. Stock price follows a specific type of stochastic process called a diffusion process.

Under the above assumptions, the value of a call on non-dividend paying stock is:

$$C = SN(d_1) - Ke^{-rT} N(d_2)$$

where S = current price of the underlying stock.

K = strike price of the call option.

r = the risk free interest rate.

T = the time to expiration.

N(d) = the cumulative standard normal distribution function

$$D_1 = \frac{\ln(S/K)+[r+\sigma^2/2]T}{\sigma(T)^{1/2}} \quad \frac{\ln(S/K)+[r+\sigma^2/2]T}{\sigma(T)^{1/2}}$$

$$D_2 = d_1 - \sigma(T)^{1/2}$$

σ = the standard deviation of the underlying stocks returns.

ln(S/K) = the natural logarithm of S/K.

e^{-rT} = the exponential function of –rT. e^{-rT} is the present value factor when r is continuously compounded for T periods. Ke^{-rT} is the present value of K.

The Black Scholes Option Pricing Model (BSOPM) assumes that both r and σ are known and constant. It is usually best to employ an annual interest rate, r, in which case the time to expiration T, should be in years and *a* should be defined as the standard deviation of the stock's annual returns. It is also possible to define "r" as the monthly risk free interest rate. T as the number of months until expiration and σ should be defined as the standard deviation of the stocks monthly returns near the date the call expires for the value of r. It may be noted that the expected return on the stock does not appear in the formula. The value of an option is independent of the expected return. The volatility, or a, of the stock, however, is an important determinant of an options value, r is also, the only determinant of the value of the call that is not directly observable. The call value derived by the BSOPM is thus only as good as the σ used in the equation.

The volatility a is the standard deviation of the stocks annual return which is found by taking daily or weekly observations of the market prices (generally 15 to 30 observations are taken).

To illustrate use of Black-Scholes option pricing model, consider a stock currently selling at Rs.59, risk-free interest rate, 11.5% year; strike price Rs.60, time to expiration 3 months and *a* is 0.2. Given this information,

$$S = 59$$
$$K = 60$$
$$T = 3/12 = 0.25/\text{year}$$
$$r = 0.115/\text{year}$$
$$\sigma = 0.2/\text{year}$$

$$d_1 = \frac{\ln(S/K) - [r + \sigma^2/2]T}{\sigma(T)^{1/2}}$$

$$= \frac{\ln(0.98334) + 0.03375}{0.1} = 0.1694$$

$$d_2 = d_1 - \sigma(T)^{1/2}$$
$$= 0.1694 - 0.1 = 0.0694$$

Table 13.5 gives the cumulative probability of the standard normal distribution which may be used to find the probability that an observed value will be less than or equal to the value of interest.

$$N(d_1) = 0.5670$$
$$N(d_2) = 0.5275$$
$$Ke^{-rT} = 60e^{-(0.115)(0.25)} = 58.299$$
$$C = SN(d_1) = ke^{-rT}N(d_2) = 59 * 0.5670 - 58.299 * 0.5275$$
$$= 2.70$$

The call value, C of the option is Rs.2.70. As stated earlier, the, prices derived from Black-Scholes model depend upon accurate estimates for interest rate and a standard deviation. It is, however, a reasonable approach to pricing options. The model captures most of the important properties. However, some limitations with the practical application have to be noted. First the assumption of being able to set up a riskless hedge by rebalancing continuously and instantaneously is not realistic because the transaction costs impede continuous process and dissipate investment return. Further, price changes on occasions can be quite sizeable. Finally, the assumption of a risk-free rate is unrealistic.

OPTIONS TRADING IN INDIA

Need for Options

The Indian stock market although largely insulated from the international markets has been characterized by high price volatility. The upswing of 1000 points in the BSE sensitive index within a short span of two months followed by the "Securities scam" and the associated crash by 1200 points in 1991-92 clearly reflects the highly speculative tendencies in the Indian stock markets. Speculation has also spread to non specified shares wherein dealings are supposed to be settled on a cash basis every fortnight and also to the new equity issues before they are listed on the exchanges to the detriment of the uninformed investor. Stock markets need speculation since it is the driving force which builds up activity and ensures sustained interest of investors in the market. But speculation has to be controlled and regulated as excessive speculation leads to haphazard price movements unrelated to fundamentals.

Despite such high volatility in the market, Indian investors are still eager to invest in equity. The surge in investment in equity can be attributed to two factors: first, to the twin benefits of a variable yield and capital appreciation that equities offer; and, second to the lack of alternative attractive instruments for investment in the capital market. Although equity exposes the investors to tremendous market and price risks, still Indian investors find equity as the most viable and perhaps the most attractive form of investment. The risk exposure of market participants is further hightened by sentiment driving the Indian markets rather than the financial performance.

There is need to create a level playing field for operators who are capable and willing to take speculative positions in the market. The need for allowing some speculation in the securities market arises from the fact that a market based purely on investment will often be unable to clear, without price disturbance all the purchase and sale orders in a security as and when such orders arrive in the market. When the buy and the sale orders from genuine investors do not match in terms of volume at any time the presence of the speculator or market operator is useful for maintaining market continuity. But in the majority of the stock exchanges trading in differences takes place. If differences are paid on due time and transactions are completed and settled there would not be a problem. Where huge differences out of such adjusted transactions arise, payment difficulties are experienced, precipitating a crisis in the market leading to failure.

Table 13.5: Standard Normal Probability

$$d(x) = \hat{A}_{-x}^{x} \frac{1}{\sqrt{275}} \theta f^{2} 2dt$$

x	.00	.01	.02	.03	.04	.05	.06	.07	.08	.09
.0	.5000	.5040	.5080	.5120	.5160	.5199	.5239	.5279	.5319	.5359
.1	.5398	.5438	.5478	.5517	.5557	.5596	.5636	.5675	.5714	.5753
.2	.5793	.5832	.5871	.5910	.5948	.5987	.6026	.6064	.6103	.6141
.3	.6179	.6217	.6255	.6293	.6331	.6338	.6406	.6443	.6480	.6517
.4	.6554	.6591	.6628	.6664	.6700	.6736	.6772	.6808	.6844	.6879
.5	.6915	.6950	.6985	.7019	.7054	.7088	.7123	.7157	.7190	.7224
.6	.7257	.7291	.7324	.7357	.7389	.7422	.7454	.7486	.7517	.7549
.7	.7580	.7611	.7642	.7673	.7704	.7734	.7764	.7794	.7823	.7852
.8	.7881	.7910	.7939	.7967	.7995	.8023	.8051	.8078	.8106	.8133
.9	.8159	.8186	.8212	.8238	.8264	.8289	.8315	.8340	.8365	.8389
1.0	.8413	.8438	.8461	.8485	.8508	.8531	.8554	.8577	.8599	.8621
1.1	.8643	.8665	.8686	.8708	.8729	.8749	.8770	.8790	.8810	.8830
1.2	.8849	.8869	.8888	.8907	.8925	.8944	.8962	.8980	.8997	.9015
1.3	.9032	.9049	.9066	.9082	.9099	.9115	.9131	.9147	.9162	.9177
1.4	.9192	.9207	.9222	.9236	.9251	.9265	.9279	.9292	.9306	.9319
1.5	.9332	.9345	.9357	.9370	.9382	.9394	.9406	.9418	.9929	.9441
1.6	.9452	.9463	.9474	.9484	.9495	.9505	.9515	.9525	.9535	.9545
1.7	.9554	.9564	.9573	.9582	.9591	.9599	.9606	.9616	.9625	.9633
1.8	.9641	.9649	.9656	.9664	.9671	.9678	.9686	.9693	.9699	.9706
1.9	.9713	.9719	.9726	.9732	.9738	.9744	.9750	.9756	.9761	.9767
2.0	.9772	.9778	.9783	.9788	.9793	.9798	.9803	.9808	..9812	.9817
2.1	.9821	.9826	.9830	.9834	.9838	.9842	.9846	.9850	.9854	.9857
2.2	.9861	.9864	.9868	.9871	.9875	.9878	.9881	.9884	.9887	.9890
2.3	.9893	.9896	.9898	.9901	.9904	.9906	.9909	.9911	.9913	.9916
2.4	.9918	.9920	.9922	.9925	.9927	.9929	.9931	.9932	.9934	.9936
2.5	.9938	.9940	.9941	.9943	.9945	.9946	.9948	.9949	.9951	.9952
2.6	.9953	.9955	.9956	.9957	.9959	.9960	.9961	.9962	.9968	.9964
2.7	.9965	.9966	.9967	.9968	.9969	.9970	.9971	.9972	.9973	.9974
2.8	.9974	.9975	.9976	.9977	.9977	.9978	.9979	.9979	.9980	.9981
2.9	.9981	.9982	.9982	.9983	.9984	.9984	.9985	.9985	.9986	.9986
3.0	.9987	.9987	.9987	.9988	.9988	.9989	.9989	.9989	.9990	.9990
3.1	.9990	.9991	.9991	.9991	.9992	.9992	.9992	.9992	.9993	.9993
3.2	.9993	.9993	.9994	.9994	.9994	.9994	.9994	.9995	.9995	.9995
3.3	.9995	.9995	.9995	.9996	.9996	.9996	.9996	.9996	.9996	.9997
3.4	.9997	.9997	.9997	.9997	.9997	.9997	.9997	.9997	.9997	.9998

Contd....

x	1.282	1.645	1.960	2.326	2.576	3.090	3.291	3.891	4.417
(x)	.90	.95	.975	.99	.995	.999	.9995	.99995	.9999
2[1 – (x)]	20	10	5	2	1	.002	.001	.0001	.00001

How to use Table-.Illustration N(0.64) = 0.7389 N(-0.22) = 0.4129.

Source: Mood and Grybill *Introduction to the Theory of Statistics,* 3rd ed. New York, McGraw Hill Book Company, 1973).

There are several factors which contribute to excessive volatility in the stock markets. Overtrading by stock brokers on their account, insider trading, large scale manipulation of the market and shortage of adequate floating stock of good scrips are some of them. With good regulations, in place, listed option trading can definitely reduce the volatility. It was observed in CBOE, that options reduced price fluctuations.

An investment portfolio comprising mainly equity exposes the investor to tremendous market and price risks. The price risk for most part can be managed by holding a diversified portfolio and limiting the volume of investment in any one stock or industry. The other type of risk i.e. market risk or systematic risk is something more difficult to contend with. The difficulty primarily arises because the prices of stocks have an inherent tendency to move up or down together and consequently the market risk cannot be diversified away. The market offers no risk instrument that allows the investors to manage and minimize risk. Technically speaking, fund managers and very sophisticated investors may try to hedge market risk by offsetting long positions in one stock with short positions in others. Such action constitutes a risk hedge technique than a risk hedge instrument.

To meet the requirements of different kinds of investors the market has to be segmented so that small investors and big time players each have a distinct playing field. Shortening of settlement cycles to T+1 followed with the introduction of a derivative instrument like option has allowed the big market players as well as small investors to hedge against risk and reduce violent price fluctuations.

Effects of Options

The economic effect of options and futures trading relates to allocation of risk between investors who are willing to take risk and investors who are averse to risk. Options provide investors with the opportunity to hedge investment in the underlying shares and reduce the overall risk. The fact that it is possible to a certain extent to obtain protection against fluctuations in market prices is likely to increase the willingness of investors to commit capital in the securities market as a whole. At the same time, they provide opportunities to realize profits by reference to changes in the quoted price of individual securities.

Options on products or commodities were forbidden in USA for almost 40 years after options were regarded as the cause of the fall of the wheat price in 1936. Options have often been blamed for increasing price fluctuations in the underlying instrument. However, it is empirically established that the transferred risk has a price stabilizing effect.

Further a comparison of companies with options on their stock against companies which did not have options on their stock in USA, reveals that options reduce price fluctuations. Study of changes in the beta factor three years before and three years after the introduction of options (the beta factor is the company's price risk in relation to the general market price risk, with the market having a beta factor of 1 and risk free share a beta factor of 0), show that the beta factor fell for both groups, but most for the companies with options. Analysis of companies in Sweden shows the same result i.e., options increase the price stability of shares with options.

Effect on Share Trading

Several studies have been made of the general effect on share turnover of the launch of options in the USA. The studies found that share turnover increases in the shares of those companies in respect of which options have been launched.

A stock market is efficient if it is able, in rapid and accurate manner, to reflect new information through adjustments in share prices. Several studies have shown that shares with options adjust more quickly to new information. Option trading leads to a more efficient stock market.

Benefits to Investors

Most options buyers purchase puts and calls to increase their leverage when they expect a significant change in the share prices. As options purchased permit investors to control more shares than they could possibly control under any realistic set of stock margin requirements, especially in the USA, options can provide more return on the investors funds than any other method of investing in securities. The 100 per cent cash requirement applied to the purchase of puts and calls, and certain rules which prohibit individuals or groups acting in concert from buying more than a certain number of options, limit the individual's ability to leverage and pyramid investment. The investors who emphasize the importance of leverage on the upside in the case of calls, or on the downside in the case of puts, also focus on the importance of an option's ability to limit the investor's risk. Any buyer of a put or call knows the maximum loss possible at the time of purchase. This limited risk feature of options influences considerably institutional investors in the United States. In USA around 90 per cent investment is made in short-term debt instruments and rest 10 per cent in call and put options. Interest on the short-term debt will typically cover about one-third of any possible loss on the options. If the stock price advances sharply over the life of the options, the portfolio participates in this advance. On the other hand, downside risk is strictly limited to the amount of the option premium. This use of options will probably expand as institutional investors become more comfortable with options.

The purchase of options to construct a kind of synthetic convertible bond (the conversion feature provides an opportunity to share any appreciation in price of the underlying stock), actually match the risk reward requirements of an institutional investor far better than the more typical institutional strategy of covered writing. To the extent that an investor's goal is to limit portfolio risk exposure, the combination of short-term debt and a long option position has a maximum risk equal to the amount paid for the options. The covered writer's risk is reduced by the amount of the option premium received.

Further, options provide a pattern of returns that cannot be obtained with the stock. They permit writers to generate additional income on their portfolio. Another important property is that no subsequent out-of-product expenditures are ever required nor any funds ever received until the position is closed out.

Options provide unlimited flexibility in the risk management of a diversified portfolio. They can be used to accept or shed risk. Options help neutralize risk and obtain a higher return.

PREREQUISITES FOR INTRODUCTION OF OPTIONS TRADING

The listed options have a standardized price which is determined through a central auction market. Listed options also provide for interchangeability between options contracts and this facilitates the development of a secondary market in listed options. In this context, the role of an Option Clearing Corporation (OCC) such as the one in existence in U.S.A. is paramount.

The buyer and writer of options have a contract only with the regulatory body such as OCC which is the issuer of listed options. The option buyer relies on the clearing corporation to make good the contract. The writer's obligation is an obligation to the OCC, not to the buyer. His broker is one whom he happens to meet on the exchange floor. If a National Options Exchange is set up, the main OCC should be in Bombay with a wide network of branches.

The strike price of a listed option has always to end in Rs.5 or 10 unless a stock dividend or other capital change occurs after trading in the option begins. If TISCO is selling at Rs.121 a share at the time, options for a new expiration month are being listed for trading, the new TISCO option will have a strike price of Rs.120 per share. If the stock price closes above Rs.122.50 for two consecutive days, the exchange will add Rs.125 contracts for each expiration date beyond 60 days. Barring stock dividends, splits, and other capital changes, it will be impossible to buy or write a TISCO option on the exchange with a striking price between Rs.120 and Rs.125 per share.

In addition to standardization of strike prices, the exchanges will have standardized expiration dates. Options of the same stock have to fall in any of the following three cycles.

1. January/April/July/October
2. February/May/August/November
3. March/June/September/December

The longest maturity an option will have is nine months. The expiration date will be the Saturday after the third Friday in the month. This is the final time an option can be tendered to the Clearing Corporation. However, secondary market trading of the option would cease at 2.00 p.m. Indian Standard Time on the business day immediately preceding the expiration date. If a TISCO listed option is written on January 31, the last day it can be tendered to the OCC would be October 30.

Interchangeability of Options

Listed options provide for interchangeability between option contracts which facilitates the development of a secondary market in listed options. Interchangeability means that any listed option with a common expiration date and strike price is interchangeable with any similar listed option.

Publication of Prices

The prices at which listed option transactions actually take place have to be published daily. Published prices and known commission rates assure both buyer and writer of a fair market.

Scripless Clearing

One of the most important innovations pioneered by the option exchanges is the introduction of scrip-less clearing. Except in unusual cases where an option trader insists on evidence of the transaction in addition to a confirmation slip of a brokerage firm, the Options Clearing Corporation does not issue an option contract or certificate. This feature of listed option trading will reduce the amount of paper work and eliminates the physical movement of securities, in this case option contracts, between brokerage firms. OCC reduces the time required to clear a transaction and as the brokerage community gains additional experience with scrip-less trading, the cost of clearing a transaction will be very small. If scrip-less option trading is introduced, a very high option trading volume at low or minimum cost would result.

Equity Derivatives in India

Derivatives have gained popularity as instruments of risk management. In the three years after their introduction, they have registered a fivefold increase. Trading in equity derivatives in India began in June 2000 after the SEBI granted permission to the derivative segments of two stock exchanges, viz., NSE and BSE, and their clearing house/corporation to commence trading and settlement in approved derivative contracts. Various equity-based derivative products have been introduced in stages since June 2000. Initially, SEBI approved trading in index futures contracts based on two indices, viz., S&P CNX Nifty Index and BSE-Sensitive Index (SENSEX). The range of derivative products was extended further by commencement of trading in index options based on S&P CNX Nifty and SENSEX in June 2001, trading in options on individual securities in July 2001 and trading in futures on individual securities in November 2001. Stock options and stock futures are available on select securities. All contracts have a maximum of 3-month expiration cycle and are available with 1 month, 2 months and

3 months to expiry. Trading in equity derivatives at NSE was in the near month contract in March 2004. There has not been a broadening of trading away from the near month. All contracts expire on the last Thursday of the expiry month and a new contract is introduced on the next trading day following the expiry of the near month contract. The index options are European style (i.e., automatic exercise on the expiration day), while stock options are American style (i.e., automatic exercise on the expiration day and voluntary exercise prior to the expiration day). At any point of time, the exchanges provide contracts at different strike prices (i.e., in the money, near the money and out of the money) and option types (i.e., call and put) for each month. The 'strike price' is the price at which the buyer has a right to purchase or sell the underlying. Options trading faces considerable hurdles in terms of knowledge and awareness. As of March 2004 options accounted for only 11% of equity derivatives turnover and the remainder by futures.

Banks and primary dealers are permitted to undertake transactions in exchange traded interest rate derivatives in June 2003. Initially interest rate futures were introduced. Table 13.6 presents the structure of equity turnover market in 2003-04. Equity spot market was Rs.16 trillion and derivative market Rs.21.4 trillion. Total equity market of Rs.37 trillion constituted 130% of GDP. The equity market capitalization was 49% of GDP and the overall turnover ratio of equity market (spot + derivatives) was 265%. The equity derivatives turnover exceeded the equity spot market for the first time in August 2003. Index derivatives trading became active in 2003-04 accounting for 33% of equity derivatives trading. The biggest underlying on the NSE equity derivatives market by turnover were Nifty (Rs.6.01 trillion), TELCO (Rs.1.89 trillion), TISCO (Rs.1.68 trillion), Satyam Computer (Rs.1.24 trillion) and SBI (Rs.1.22 trillion).

Table 13.6: Equity Market Turnover (2003-04)

(Rs. Crores)

Equity derivatives (Total) of which:	21,42,521
Equity spot	16,02,152
Total equity turnover	37,44,673
Index derivatives	6,13,857
Equity options	2,70,367

The ratio of equity spot to index derivatives at NSE of 0.4 however greatly lags behind numerous markets where the index derivatives market ranges from 1.3 to 40.6 times larger than the equity spot market. When compared to Hong Kong NSE spot market is large but derivatives market is quite small.

Trading Framework

The trading framework for derivatives is similar to that for the cash market. The exchanges provide screen-based trading for derivative products on a national platform, which supports an anonymous order driven market. The SEBI has prescribed a two-tier membership structure to enable wider participation in the derivatives market. All trades have to be routed through a SEBI-registered trading member, who performs functions like order entry, order matching, etc. The other category of members, i.e., clearing members, clear and settle trades of all their trading members and undertake risk management. They can also enter and set limits to positions which a trading member can take. On the derivatives segment, a clearing member can also be a trading member; in this case, the member can clear and settle own proprietary trades and clients' trades as well as clear and settle for other trading members. The exchanges are also allowed to admit banks or custodians as professional clearing members. A new category of self-clearing members has also been created by SEBI, who clear and settle their own/clients' trades. The different types of members have to meet the eligibility norms, net worth and deposit requirements stipulated by the exchanges for each of these categories.

Clearing and Settlement

The clearing and settlement process integrates three activities – clearing, settlement and risk management. The clearing process involves arriving at open positions and obligations of clearing members, which are arrived at by aggregating the open positions of all the trading members. The trading members' open positions are in turn determined by aggregating his proprietary and clients' open positions.

All futures and options contracts are cash settled, i.e., through exchange of cash. All futures contracts for each member are marked-to-market (MTM) to the daily settlement price of the relevant futures contract at the end of each day. Daily MTM settlement of profits/

losses based on the closing price of the futures contract is done on T + 1 day. The final settlement is effected for expiring futures contracts and the process is similar to the daily MTM settlement. The final settlement price is the closing value of the index/underlying security on the expiry day. In case of index/ stock options, the buyer/seller of an option is obligated to pay/receive the premium towards the options purchased/sold by him. The premium payable amount and the premium receivable amount are netted to compute the net premium payable or receivable amount for each client for each option contract.

Risk Containment

A comprehensive risk containment mechanism has been designed for the derivatives segment. The risk containment mechanism for the derivatives segment essentially comprises the margining system and system of on-line position monitoring. The SEBI has stipulated a portfolio-based margining system, which takes an integrated view of overall risk in a portfolio of all futures and options contracts for each client. Initial margins (based on 99% Value at Risk) are applicable on gross basis at the level of trading/ clearing member and on net basis at the level of individual client and proprietary positions of trading/clearing member. In addition to initial margin, the calendar spread margin is charged. The exposure limits on gross open positions are determined on the basis of liquid net worth of members and the positions are monitored on real-time basis by the exchanges. A separate Settlement Guarantee Fund is required to be created out of the base capital of members for the derivative segments.

Turnover in the Equity Derivatives Market

Table 13.7 presents the turnover in the equity derivatives market-index futures and stock futures have registered a phenomenal growth on NSE. In 2003-04, index futures amounted to Rs.5,54,446 crores and stock futures Rs.13,05,939. At NSE the fivefold increase in turnover helped derivatives segment overtake the cash segment during 2003-04. This reflects growing knowledge in the market and a shift to more sophisticated trading strategies. Trading in index futures at BSE and stock futures at NSE accounted for a significant position of turnover in equity derivatives in 2004-05.

Table 13.7: Turnover in the Equity Derivatives Market (2001-02 – 2004-05)

(Rs. Crores)

The Stock Exchange, Mumbai (BSE)					*National Stock Exchange of India Ltd. (NSE)*				
Year	*Index Futures*	*Index Options*	*Stock Futures*	*Stock Options*	*Index Futures*	*Index Options*	*Stock Futures*	*Stock Options*	*Interest Rate Futures*
1	*2*	*3*	*4*	*5*	*6*	*7*	*8*	*9*	*10*
2001-02	1,276.30	78.30	451.60	115.51	21,482	3,766	51,516	25,166	—
2002-03	1,810.99	1.98	644.30	21.17	43,952	9,247	2,86,532	1,00,133	—
2003-04	6,571.52	0.03	5,171.05	331.61	5,54,446	52,816	13,05,939	2,17,207	202
2004-05	13,599.66	2,297.23	212.85	2.58	7,72,147	1,21,943	14,84,056	1,68,836	—

Source: RBI, *Annual Report* – 2003-04 and 2004-05.

The turnover under various segments registered increase at BSE but not on the scale witnessed at NSE and commands little market share. The dominant market product at BSE is the BSE SENSEX as an underlying for futures and options.

References

Bank for International Settlement, *Annual Reports* and *Quarterly Reviews.*

Chance, Dar M., *Options and Futures,* Second edition. The Dryden Press, Fort Worth, 1992.

Dubofsky, David A., *Options and Financial Futures: Valuation and Uses,* First edition, Singapore, McGraw Hill Inc., 1992, pp. 1-43, 177-217.

Feeney, Francis D, *A Guide to International Financial Derivatives,* Woodhead Faulkner, 1991. Government of India, *Economic Survey,* 2003-04 and 2004-05.

Gastineau, Gray A. *The Stock Options Manual,* First edition, New York: McGraw Hill, Inc. 1975, pp.1-31.

Hull, John, *Introduction to Futures and Options Markets,* Prentice Hall, NJ.

Hutchison, Robert C. and Just, Steven B. *Programming Using the C Language.* First edition, Singapore, McGraw Hill Inc. 1988, pp. 35-100.

Van Horne, James C. *Financial Management and Policy,* Eighth edition. New Delhi, Prentice Hall of India. 1991, pp. 80-120.

Bombay Stock Exchange Review, February 1993, pp. 43-73.

Kaldor, Nicholas, *Essays in Economic Stability and Growth.* Gerald Duckworth & Co. Ltd. 1961.

Mahajan, Vilas "Volatility of the Stock Market: India in Global Perspective", *Handbook of Articles from the Stock Exchange Review* (1989-1991). Jan. 1992, pp. 70-74.

"The Screen is the Future Master." *The Economist,* October 24, 1992, pp. 83-84.

"Peace Breaks out in Chicago's Bear Pits." *The Economist.* June 3, 1989, pp. 75-76.

"The Economic Significance of Options." *The Stock Exchange Review, Bombay Stock Exchange.* July 1991, pp. 37-39.

Report of the Committee on Derivatives, 1998.

Teweles, Richard J., Bradley, Edward S., and Tewles Ted M., *The Stock Market,* 6th Edition, John Wiley & Sons Inc., New York, 1992.

Gupta, Ramesh, "Derivatives Panel Report: 4 Queries." *Economic Times.* March 25, 1998.

Gupta, Ramesh, "Behaviour of Stock Index Futures", *Financial Express.*

Gupta, Ramesh, "Are the Domestic Markets Ready for Futures Trading." *Financial Express.*

Weiner, Neil S. *Stock Index Futures,* 1984, John Wiley & Sons.

14

REGULATION OF THE STOCK MARKETS

OBJECTIVE OF REGULATION

After the liberalization of the economy and opening the stock markets to foreign institutional investors the objective of the regulation of the stock markets is to ensure the growth of a normal market in a stable manner. It is common to consider a rise in share prices as good news and fall in prices as bad news. Share prices should in principle reflect underlying economic trends. A normal market may be defined as one in which most security prices register a modest growth and the average price earnings ratio is in low to mid teens. When bear market selling drives many market prices temporarily below their normal values the average price earnings ratios will go below the teens. In contrast in a bull market when most stocks will be temporarily overpriced the average price earnings ratios will be in high teens or twenties. While no sanctity need be attached to the numerical ratio, it might be noted that the average price earnings ratio for the past 25 years to 1990 on New York Stock Exchange was less than 14. The NYSE has since shown irrational exuberance taking the ratio to about 100. About $12 trillion had been added to American household wealth since 1994 largely because of gains in share prices. In our own country PE ratios (BSE SENSEX stocks) have been driven from a high at 52.6 in April 1992 to 32.5 in 1992-93, 35 in 1993-94 and 41.2 in 1994-95; and fell to 19.9 in 1995-96 and 15.3 in 1996-97. In 2004 (end March), it was 16.2 for BSE SENSEX and 20.7 for S&P CNX Nifty.

Stability is an essential prerequisite for vibrancy and vitality of the stock markets. Stability ensures fair and orderly price movements and builds up investor confidence. A major objective of regulation of stock exchanges is investor protection. Investor protection is a pre-requisite for the healthy and stable market. However a stable market should reflect not only demand but market values based on a good performance of the corporate sector in terms of earnings and cash flows against the backdrop of overall growth and prospects of the economy. During the period, (1989-90 to 1991-92), the sizeable flow of funds into the stock markets which reached enormous proportions in 1991-92 drove up prices, rather than any improvement in fundamentals. In just one year 1991-92, market capitalization of shares listed on BSE zoomed up by 327 per cent. Actually recession in industry was widespread (the index of industrial production fell by 0.14 per cent) and real GDP registered a very modest increase of 1.2 per cent in 1991-92. Excess demand in the stock markets resulted in pushing up price earning ratios to levels too high to attract funds for investment. The programmes conceived for investment by Foreign Institutional Investors (FIIs) announced in September, 1992 did not really take off because among other reasons PE ratios were too high (in 60's) as compared to other emerging markets. In 1996, the PE ratios in emerging markets were, Brazil 10.6, Thailand 11.97, Mexico 13.5, South Africa 15.0, Korea 19.4, Malaysia 28.6 and Taiwan 29.0. Even domestic investment would seek securities with stable and growing dividends with long term capital appreciation. The stock markets would benefit if we attract investors who do not behave like punters but as owners of companies; and similarly FIIs who are interested in steady income in the form of dividends and long term capital gains especially in view of the need to avoid sudden and whimsical flights of capital.

Central Listing Authority

A Central Listing Authority was constituted by SEBI on April 9, 2003. Central Listing Authority Regulations provided for a mandatory recommendation from CLA before listing in any stock exchange and appeal to SEBI and Securities Appellate Tribunal in case of refusal of issuance of letter of recommendation from CLA.

Self Regulation by Stock Exchanges and Supervision by SEBI

The objective of a stable market is sought to be achieved by two agencies at two levels. First, at the exchange level, the Board of Governors; and at the national level the Securities and Exchange Board of India (SEBI). The activities of the stock brokers are regulated by the

Board of Governors of the Stock Exchange. Stock exchanges are designed to be self regulatory. Actually, no stock exchange is granted recognition by the Government of India unless its Rules and Bye-laws are in conformity with such conditions as may be prescribed with a view to protecting the interests of investors. SEBI finalized in October 2003, the model bye-laws to be applicable to all the stock exchanges and asked them to amend their bye-laws accordingly. As a result stock markets have undergone major structural reforms. The Boards of various stock exchanges have been broad based so that they represent different interests and not just the interests of their members. At the national level, the Securities and Exchange Board of India exercises a supervisory role over the functioning of the capital market and the stock exchanges. The purpose and aims of SEBI are: Regulating the activities of stock exchanges and other securities market, registering and regulating the working among others of stock brokers, sub-broker and share transfer agents; banning insider trading in securities; and restricting the transactions pertaining to acquisition of shares and takeover of companies[38]. SEBFs role is to lay down a set of prudential norms and guidelines which would be aimed at investor protection and would be rigorously enforced while allowing for considerable autonomy and operational flexibility. In the case of stock exchanges, the overall external agency such as SEBI has to adopt a supervisory approach which is better on the details because it is less mechanical and more judgemental. The regulatory attitude is not suitable for a national level body. However, supervision of stock exchanges is not just a matter of setting the rules and getting them obeyed. There is clear need for overall supervision and monitoring of market activity in investors interest.

38. In this connection, the seven major purposes and objectives of the U.S. Securities and Exchange Commission (SEC) may be noted, (i) SEC ensures that public will receive adequate information about the securities traded in the various security markets, (this is achieved by the provision that securities sold to the public other than those issued by government, public utilities, sold to few institutional investors or issues below $ 300,000 in amount will receive adequate information), (ii) registration of exchanges to regulate their activities; (iii) requiring information about insider trading and the activities of the officers and directors in the securities of their company; (iv) registration of investment advisors to regulate their activities and to ensure that the market and participants operate in orderly fashion; (v) regulation of activities of brokers and dealers; (vi) regulation of credit that is involved in the market; and (vii) right of supervision over National Association of Securities Dealers (NASD) which is a self regulatory body of brokers and dealers.

Risk Management

A proper risk management system for the stock exchanges is a necessary precondition for the integrity and safety of the market. The main elements of risk management in stock exchanges in India comprise capital adequacy, exposure limits, margin requirements, counter-party guarantee in the surveillance system. Capital adequacy refers to the requirement on the part of the trading members of stock exchanges to provide base capital in specified assets in a prescribed proportion. Exposure norms, either in the form of scrip-specific trading limits or a ceiling on the cumulative outstanding position, are linked to capital. Furthermore, scrip-specific and broker-specific margins are collected from the members in order to reduce the risk associated with market fluctuations. While the margin system has limited the members' ability to take highly leveraged positions, the system of circuit filters (price bands) in which the trading in a scrip is halted once it crosses a band, acts as a direct measure to curb volatility. Circuit filters were first introduced in the US in the wake of a sharp fall in share prices. Counter-party guarantees in the form of a trade/settlement guarantee fund to honour the pay-in liabilities by a member act as a risk insurance system in the case of default. Besides, a surveillance system has been instituted in major stock exchanges to ensure efficient functioning of the market.

Minimum capital requirements have been stipulated at broker and sub-broker level. At present, gross exposure limits, stipulated at 15 times the base minimum capital and additional capital, and intra-day trading limits at $33^{1/3}$ times the base minimum capital and additional capital, are applicable. There are mainly three types of margins in operation, viz., a daily margin, mark-to-market margin and volatility margin in order to curb excess volatility and deter the build up of excessive outstanding positions. Members are required to pay the excess of the mark-to-market margin over the daily margin only if the former exceeds the latter. Price bands were revised from time to time to provide exit and flexibility in trading. There is a price band of 20 per cent (either side) for scrips which are neither included in the BSE SENSEX or S&P CNX Nifty, nor included in the list on which derivative products are allowed. To bring about a coordinated trading halt in all equity and equity derivative markets nation-wide, the SEBI prescribed with effect from July 2, 2001, an index-based market-wide circuit breaker system, at three stages of the index movement either way at 10 per cent, 15 per cent and 20 per cent. All the scrips attract a 99 per cent Value-at-Risk (VaR)-based margin. Stock exchanges have Settlement Guarantee Funds/Trade Guarantee Funds to face any exigencies that may arise. Major stock exchanges monitor the exposure and intra-day trading limits on a real time basis. A system of pre-set alerts has been introduced as part of the surveillance system. These risk containment measures have been able to enhance the safety of the market in times of extreme volatility, manage credit risk and ensure that settlements take place smoothly.

For safe and quick transfer of shares, all actively traded shares have been shifted to the dematerialized form, substantially reducing transaction costs and risks of bad delivery. Two depositories, viz., the National Securities Depositories Ltd. and the Central Depository Services Ltd. have established inter-connectivity between themselves and10 stock exchanges accounting for 99 per cent of the turnover have established connectivity with either of the two depositories.

SEBI released on February 23, 2004 comprehensive risk management framework for the cash segment of the market which contains the definition of acceptable liquid assets and the applicable haircuts, liquidity categorization of security, calculation of mark-to-market losses and computation and collection of VaR margins and other margins.

Protection of Investors

There are about 3500 active stock brokers who are members of the different stock exchanges and whose activities are subject to the Rules, Bye-laws and Regulations of stock exchanges.

Under the Rules, Bye-Laws and Regulations investors have certain rights which include consent of the client before a member enters into a contract with him as a principal, issue of contract whether as a principal or as agent after the contract is entered into, right of the client to close out an unfulfilled contract through any other member of the exchange, lodging of a complaint against any member who fails to implement the stock broking business with the stock exchange authorities who can take disciplinary action including suspension against the member if they are satisfied about the complaint and reference to arbitration.

A client or a member can refer any claim, difference or dispute with a member or a client, as the case may be for arbitration under the Rules, Bye-Laws and Regulations of the Stock Exchange. In 1996-97, at BSE in non members against members as against 231 cases filed, 326 (including backlog) were resolved/settled. Similarly as against 4,545 arbitration cases filed by members against other members, 4677 cases including backlog were resolved/settled. Complaints between member-brokers were primarily of matters relating to bad delivery, non-payment of sale proceeds, non-payment of securities purchased and non-settlement of accounts. In 1996-97 out of 21,133 complaints received from members against other members, 14,010 complaints were resolved. Complaints against bad delivery objection cases are being resolved within 21 days after setting up the Bad Delivery Cell.

Lack of transparency of transactions is a major shortcoming of the market. The investor does not know the actual date of the transaction. Investor should be informed the date and brokerage by noting them on the contract. The time of the transaction should also be mentioned as is the practice in other countries. Necessary guidelines were issued by SEBI in this regard. SEBI has also issued norms for regulating the transactions between the stock brokers and the clients. The norms make it compulsory for all brokers to keep their money and their clients money in two separate accounts. No payment for transactions in which the broker is taking a position as a principal is allowed from the clients account. It is mandatory for brokers to make payment to their clients or deliver the securities purchased within 48 hours of payout by the stock exchange. Purchase orders of clients can be executed only on payment of 20 per cent margin on the price of securities proposed to be purchased unless the client has equivalent credit with the broker. The norms also make it mandatory for a broker to issue the contract note to a "client within 24 hours of the execution of the contract. On the part of the client, full payment has to be made within two days of the execution of the contract having been issued for cash shares and seven days for specified scrips unless the client has already credit with broker.

As regards sale of securities, SEBI has prescribed that no client should be allowed to sell securities without paying a margin of 20 per cent on the price of securities proposed to be sold. Margin can be waived if securities to be sold are deposited with valid transfer document. In the case of sale also a broker has to issue a contract note to a client within 24 hours of the execution of the contract. Further, a client is required to deliver to the broker the securities sold with valid transfer document within 48 hours of the contract note having been issued.

Development of Stock Exchange as SROs

There are 23 stock exchanges recognized under Section 4 of the Securities Contracts (Regulations) Act, 1956. These exchanges were recognized/set up over a period of time to simulate the growth of the capital market by channelizing the savings of households and others. These exchanges are suitably empowered by Section 9 of SC(R) Act, 1956 to make laws for the conduct of business, regulation and control of contracts.

Inspection of Stock Exchanges

Stock exchanges facilitate transaction in securities and clearing and settlement of transactions. Indian stock exchanges have undergone several transformations during the past one year, in terms of management structure, functional details and effective regulation. SEBI annually inspects a sample of stock exchanges.

The objective of the inspections are to ensure that:

A. The exchange provides a fair, equitable and growing market to investors;

B. The exchange has complied with the conditions, if any, imposed on it at the time of renewal/grant of its recognition under Section 4 of the SC(R) Act, 1956;

C. The exchange's organization, systems and practices are in accordance with the Securities Contracts (Regulation) Act, 1956 and rules framed thereunder;

D. The exchange has implemented the directions, guidelines and instructions issued by the SEBI from time to time;

E. There are adequate control mechanisms and risk management systems.

During the year 2003-04, stock exchanges have been inspected and a thorough review of operations, organizational structure and administrative control of each exchange have been examined.

Indian stock markets have been buoyant during the year 2003-04 and indices registered significant growth. Because of this, special inspection of risk management of NSE, BSE, CSE, ASE and UPSE has been conducted. Follow-up inspections have also been conducted by procuring periodical compliance reports from the stock exchanges and conducting regular meetings with senior management of exchanges.

Follow-up of inspection reports was done by obtaining periodic compliance reports from stock exchanges and through meetings with the senior management of stock exchanges.

Promotion and Regulation of Self-Regulatory Organizations

SEBI, in its efforts to make regulation more effective and responsive to the fast changing market requirements has thought of promoting self-regulatory organizations in the Indian capital market. Several steps have been initiated towards this objective.

SEBI is contemplating the development of self-regulatory organizations (SRO) for market intermediaries. Stock exchanges are already acting on SROs and the SRO structure needs to be strengthened further. The objective for promoting intermediaries like stock exchanges as SRO is that since they have a better feed on the ground reality, they should take care of the micro aspects of regulations. The several inherent conditions of self-regulation are:

A. Self-regulation becomes the responsibility of the market and may result in greater acceptance of rules by the members of SRO;

B. It also provides market players with greater flexibility to respond to securities market;

C. It avoids duplication of responsibility: It is observed that over the years that if the regulatory body gets into micro regulation, it looses sight of the fundamentals, which in turn results in duplication of responsibilities; and

D. Besides, SROs are expected to have a better understanding of the ground realities.

However, for any organization/body like a stock exchange to function effectively as an SRO, it is necessary for it to enforce compliance of bye-laws, rules and regulations laid down by itself. Further, these SROs should be able to enforce and establish rules, which prevent manipulative trade practices and permit just and equitable principles of trade. Presently, such powers are conferred on the stock exchanges by Section 9 of the SC(R) Act, 1956, whereby they have to make bye-laws for the conduct of business, regulation and control of contracts.

Further, developing stock exchanges as self-regulatory organizations and enhancing their effective regulatory role, puts additional responsibility on SEBI to ensure that SROs are efficiently carrying out/ conducting their mandatory responsibilities.

Regulation of Trading

To ensure trading is conducted in an orderly and systematic manner and settlements take place in time without hitch, margins, limits on business, prohibition of further dealing, floor and ceiling prices, prohibition of speculative transactions, closing the market trading on account and circuit breakers are used.

Separation of Cash and Derivative Segments

Stock exchanges are required to separate the cash and derivative segments in terms of legal framework governing trading, clearing and settlement of the derivative segment, establishment of separate trade/settlement guarantee funds, separate membership and Governing Council/Clearing Council/Executive Committee.

Margins[39]

Margins are of three types, daily margins, carry over margins and ad hoc margin. Daily margins are collected in respect of every contract outstanding at the end of the day. They are normally payable in about 30 to 35 scrips out of a total of 89 scrips in the specified group. Rates of margin vary from about 10 per cent to 25 per cent in respect of 15 volatile scrips and 5 to 10 per cent with regard to others. In a rising market bears pay at about 50 per cent of the rates payable by bulls and the position is reversed in a falling market. The higher rates against bulls in a rising market and against bears in a falling market are recognized as a price corrective measure dissuading the bulls from purchases when the market is buoyant and the bears from sales when the market is depressed. Rates of margin are varied according to the requirements of the market situation.

Daily margins are payable on the gross position of a member. It is calculated on cumulative aggregate purchases and sales outstanding at the end of the day entered into by the member with other members in the market either on his own behalf or on behalf of his clients without setting off the purchases of the clients against the sale of another and vice versa. Margins are also payable on the transactions put through directly between clients of a member and his transactions with his clients as a principal. Daily margins are,

39. While the margin money is collected in stock exchanges in India to reduce liquidity and as cover against likely adverse movement of prices in USA margin refers to the bank credit against the collateral of securities. On the other hand, mark to the market is a formal notice used by the lender or borrower to make sure that the loan for short selling is secured at all time, by 100 per cent of the market value of the stock. If the stock price goes down, the broker representing the short seller sends a mark to the market to the lender's broker; it demands that cash be returned if the stock goes up, the lenders broker sends the notice for more cash to be deposited. Money should be paid immediately and there is no five day settlement rule.

however, not required to be paid for purchase and sales which result in actual delivery. Members are also given the facility of adjusting the margin for the business done in one security against the business done in any other security. On shortages in payment, penalty at the rate of 2 per cent of the margin amount is levied.

The second type of margin is the carry over margin payable by members on the aggregate of the net balance of purchases and of sales carried over from one settlement to another on account of each of their clients and on their own account as principals in all the specified shares, irrespective of the application of daily margins. While the minimum rate of carry over margin is 3 per cent of the making up price i.e., the price at which the transactions are carried over from one settlement to another, it is generally about 5 to 25 per cent. As in the case of daily margin, the rate of carry over margin is higher in respect of purchases in a rising market and in respect of sales in a falling market. The rationale behind carry over margin is to impound a part of the profit to correct prices. The rate of carry over margin is normally below daily margin rate. In the calculation of carry over margin, the daily margin already paid is adjusted.

The third type of margin is the ad hoc margin which is collected from individual members who overtrade. At BSE all members who have an outstanding position above Rs.3 crores are required to deposit ad hoc margins at the rate of 10 per cent of the business above Rs.3 crores as a matter of routine. In addition to ad hoc margins, further ad hoc margins are collected from members in case of precipitous rise or fall in the price of any scrip. Margins can be collected by members from their clients.

Mark-to-Market Margin

BSE had taken various regulatory measures during 1996-97 to improve the risk management system and to ensure the safety of the market: The computation of margin trades put in by members was computerized and mark-to-market on outstanding position of members was introduced in July 1996 in place of margin collected earlier on the basis of gross and net exposure. BSE prescribed an intra day trading limit (i.e., gross purchases + gross sales) of 33.33 times of the base minimum and additional capital deposited by the members. The monitoring of margin payments by members is done on a day-to-day basis. Restrictions were imposed on erring members.

Limits on Business

Limits on the outstanding business of a member are imposed with a view to preventing destabilization of the market because of the impact of large holdings on movement of prices. The limit is Rs.3 crores in the aggregate of all outstanding purchases and sales which can be carried forward and Rs.5 crores at any point of time.

During periods of bullish frenzy or bearish grip in the market, limits are also imposed on the total volume of business of a jobber, since jobbing could accentuate the trends in the market. Jobbing limits of Rs.50 lakhs per scrip and Rs.4 crores in aggregate were imposed on 3-2-1992.

Prohibition of Further Dealings

Since a large volume of outstanding business could prove to be a source of market instability, prohibition of further trading is often used to control trading. Normal trading is resumed only after the outstanding business gets reduced to a reasonable level. Further dealing in all 89 specified shares except for actual delivery were prohibited (3-2-92 and 5-3-92).

Floor and Ceiling Prices

Floor prices in the case of price declines and ceiling prices in the case of advances give time to the market for a pause and rehabilitation. The method is resorted for temporary periods to let the market to correct itself.

Short Sales and Long Purchases[40]

Speculative transactions which do not result in delivery popularly called short sales and long purchases lend breadth and liquidity to the market. Such transactions absorb large orders of purchase or sales without causing wide fluctuations in prices. The speculative transactions, however, aggravate the situation during a sustained period of boom or a prolonged bear phase. At such times prohibition on speculative transactions would stop the trends from accentuating further. In 1991-92, speculative deals were prohibited with transactions being restricted to delivery basis. Further limits were imposed on purchases even on delivery basis.

40. The device of marking to market may be used to ensure that the loan for short sale is secured at all times by 100 per cent of the market value of stock. In 'marking' money should be paid immediately and there would be no lag (5 days in USA) in settlement rule.

Trading on Account

Trading on account on the lines of trading on the London Stock Exchange was tried for some time on BSE. Trading on account permits free trading during a settlement period with all the transactions entered into during the period either resulting in delivery or being offset by opposite transactions. Trading on account does not permit carry forward of transactions from one settlement to another. Trading on account was operative from 22.10.1987 for a short period.

Circuit Breakers

Circuit breakers are applied for one or two hours to halt trading if the prices move by specified points from the previous days close. They reduce volatility of share prices and promote investor confidence. The BSE authorities applied circuit-breaker to suspend trading in the equity shares of Asian Paints Ltd., for one day on September 1, 1993, as the price increased by 12.9 per cent in the course of the day from Rs.310 to close at Rs.350 which is beyond the specified limit of 10 per cent.

Index Based Circuit Breakers (July 2, 2001)

An index based market wide circuit breaker system for scrips in rolling settlement mode which will apply at three stages of the index movement either way at 10%, 15% and 20% was implemented by SEBI effective July 2, 2001. The circuit breakers will bring about a coordinated trading halt in all equity and equity derivatives markets nation-wide. The market-wide circuit breakers would be triggered by movement of either the BSE SENSEX or the S&P CNX Nifty whichever is breached earlier. In addition individual scripwise price bands of 20% either way for all scrips in the compulsory rolling settlement except for the scrips on which derivative products are available. In the rest of the scrips that are not in compulsory rolling settlement, the existing price bands would continue to apply.

Circuit Filter Limits

BSE implemented new circuit filter limits (1996) on BOLT to curb price rigging. The price band within which a company's share price can move on a particular day is as low as 5 per cent in scrips which begin displaying symptoms of price rigging.

Closure of the Market

In extreme cases when the market is in totally demoralized condition, closure of the market is ordered to give a pause to the market and to correct itself.

EFFECTIVENESS OF THE REGULATORY MECHANISM

There is need for making the functioning of the stock market more efficient, transparent and responsive to the emerging needs of the system while at the same time ensuring adequate market liquidity. These challenges can be met successfully and the healthy growth of stock markets ensured if the shortcomings noticed in their working are set right. The deficiencies stem both from aspects of the functioning of the stock exchanges and the related issues of the adequacy and effectiveness of the regulatory framework.

While the exchange has several measures to regulate the market, their efficacy is a function of the effective reporting systems of members in regard to outstanding positions and trading volumes. Members' records carry inconsistencies in figures of sales and purchase and transaction prices are misrecorded. The result is the exchange does not have an accurate picture of the level of activity. The scam has revealed that the exchange authorities could not take prompt and effective corrective action when outside funds were fuelling intense speculative activity and share prices soared. In a large measure this was due to understatement or outright suppression of sales and purchases by members of the exchange. Obviously margins and limits on outstanding positions and trading volumes were imposed on understated volumes impairing the effectiveness of the measures. It is also widely held that the authorities of the exchange have not used their powers to regulate the market effectively against erring brokers because of the domination of the brokers on the boards of the exchanges[41].

Prohibition of Fraudulent and Unfair Trade Practices (October 25, 1995)

SEBI notified regulations prohibiting manipulation, misleading statements to induce sale or purchase of securities unfair practices relating to securities and laid down procedures for investigation into alleged contravention.

Rigging up of Prices

SEBI on December 21, 1995 announced a series of measures to control rigging up of prices and check other malpractices in the stock exchanges. These measures included penal margin on net undelivered portion at the end of settlement, special margin for buyers in case of rise in share prices, joint suspension of trading by stock exchanges in case of price stipulation.

41. This has been set right since by SEBI directive to increase the presence of outside directors on the Boards. In the case of BSE out of 17 directors only 8 would be from the brokers.

Stock Broker and Sub-broker Regulations

SEBI which is charged with the regulation and development of the securities market has issued Stock Brokers and Sub-brokers Regulations which prescribe the records and documents to be maintained and procedure for inspection of brokers. Inspection of stock exchanges and brokers is undertaken by SEBI.

Surveillance

I. Market Surveillance Mechanism

Market Surveillance plays a key role in ensuring safety and integrity of the market. It also ensures effectiveness and efficiency of the regulatory system. The separate market surveillance department has been strengthened to monitor market movements, identify price volatility, analyze its causes and take prompt action in close coordination with stock exchange and depositories. While the front line responsibility for market surveillance lies with the stock exchanges, SEBI keeps a constant oversight on the surveillance.

II. Integrated Surveillance System

SEBI commissioned a study under USAID assistance as part of Financial Institutions Reform & Expansion (FIRE) Project to design an appropriate structure for the proposed sophisticated surveillance model. It has been decided to have state of art technology-based system, capable of automatic alert generation in respect of price rigging, creation of artificial volumes, insider trading, etc. by accessing and analyzing variegated data from multiple sources.

III. Interim Surveillance Arrangement

Pending completion of the said sophisticated automated integrated surveillance mechanism, an interim enhanced surveillance mechanism has been put in place since late June 2003. As a coordinated surveillance platform provides a standing forum, for exchange of information/data, views and perceptions on market movement during the week, and to discuss emerging concerns or surveillance issues, if any, and to consider possible appropriate surveillance actions, called for.

Debt Market

National Stock Exchange's Wholesale Debt Market (WDM) had 3097 securities available for trading as on March 31, 2005. Total market capitalization of the securities available for trading on the WDM segment worked out Rs.14,61,734 crores as on March 31, 2005. The turnover was Rs.8,87,294 crores in 2004-05. Transactions in dated securities accounted for 95.7% of the total traded value in 2004-05.

Transactions in corporate debt securities accounted for only 20% of total traded volume in the WDM segment.

Secondary Market for Corporate Debt Securities (2003-04)

- With a view to providing greater transparency and protecting the interests of investors in debt securities, SEBI has prescribed new guidelines for regulating private placement of debt securities issued by the corporates.
- Full disclosure (initial and continuing) as per Companies Act 1956, SEBI (DIP) Guidelines 2000 and Listing Agreement are to be made by the companies.
- Credit rating of debt securities, appointment of debenture trustees, separate Listing Agreement, frequent furnishing of periodical reports to SEBI, etc., have been made mandatory to enhance the protection of investors in debt instruments.

Asset Backed Debentures

Finally, asset backed debentures. These are a new category of marketable securities that are collateralized by financial assets such as installment loan contracts. Asset backed financing involves a process called securitizing. Securitization is a disintermediating process in which credit from financial intermediaries is replaced by marketable debentures that can be issued at lower cost. Financial assets are pooled so that debentures can be sold to third parties to finance the pool. Repos are the oldest asset backed security in our country. In U.S.A. securitization has been undertaken for insured mortgages (Ginnie Mae 1970) mortgage backed bonds, student loans (Sallie Mae 1973), Trade Credit Receivable Backed Bonds (1982), Equipment Leasing Backed Bonds (1984), Certificates of Automobile Receivable Securities, (1985) and Small Business Administration Loans (1985). More recently credit receivables have been securitized. In the decade of 1980s financial asset backed securities have become a multi-billion dollar business growing faster than any other type of financing.

Securitization of DFI Portfolios

Securitization is a growing trend and can revolutionize capital markets in our country. Introduction on a seizable scale new debt instruments by securitization would enlarge the market and widen the range of debt instruments available for investment. It is empirically established that savings will grow with the increase in range of financial instruments for investment and markets. Issue of debentures with higher interest rates and credit rating is not enough to widen the debt market. It can in a large measure be achieved by the introduction of asset backed securities. In theory anything that has a cash flow can be securitized. The process can be initiated by securitization of the advances portfolio of national development finance institutions (DFIs) such as IDBI, IFCI, ICICI and SIDBI. Their total outstanding term loans are estimated at Rs.1,23,491 crores as at the end of March 1998. The quality of the securities would attract NRIs and foreign institutional investors. These securities may be released against foreign exchange payments. Since these securities amount to US $30 billion, they can be released at the rate of $6 billion per annum augmenting our resources. In the next five years, India can depend on its own resources and avoid recourse to any further borrowing abroad.

Securitization of the term loans of the four national DFI's involves credit enhancement by placing first the assets in trust with some third party such as a bank as collateral followed by provision of credit rating to remove the fear of default. Credit enhancement can be augmented further by a letter of credit and security bond from an international bank or syndicate of international banks. Over collateralizing the pool by say posting 125 per cent of the value of assets would also enhance strength of the securities. Since the pool of assets of the DFIs is highly diversified geographically, by debtor and collateral, risk of the pool is much lower than the individual assets/loans in the pool.

For the financial institutions and the economy as a whole liquidity is augmented. The amount realized from the sale of securities is likely to be much higher than the repayment by individual units. Further, as mentioned earlier, the economy gets the benefit of foreign exchange to modernize industry and help finance the infrastructure to help India become globally competitive.

Strengthening the Corporate Sector

The competitive strength of the Indian corporate sector especially manufactures in the context of globalization of the economy depends on productivity which is a function among others of the technology. Tax incentives play a vital role in renewal of technology. The budget for 1993-94 has initiated the process by reducing the import duty on specified capital goods for export thrust areas such as textiles, leather, marine products, gems and jewellery and the rates of import duty on project imports and on specified capital goods for the electronics industry. Introduction of investment allowance on a selective basis for these industries as well as units in any industry which are using obsolete technology has to be introduced. Renewal of technology can be given a boost by the grant of investment allowance. Actually, the units have to improve their bottom line to claim the allowance. Such a sea change in the fundamentals would improve cash flow, profitability and the prospects of the corporate sector. The prices of the securities of the corporate sector would then be backed by fundamentals than by sentiment as at present.

References

Bombay Stock Exchange, *Report and Accounts*, 1991-92 and 1996-97.

The Challenge of Global Money, *The Economist;* September 11-18, 1993.

Divecha, Arjun, Drack, Jaime and Stefek, Dan, "Emerging Markets: A Quantitative Perspective", *Journal of Portfolio Management*, 1992.

Brokers must Maintain Separate Accounts; SEBI. *Financial Express*, March 19, 1993.

The Economist, August 14, 1998.

Salaman Smith Barney, *A Guide to World Equity Markets*, 1998, Euromoney Publications.

Mayya M.R., *Regulation of Stock Markets and Investor Protection*, Seminar on Capital Markets, BSE, February 4, 1992.

Narsimham M., *Financial Sector Reform and the Capital Markets*, The Fourth Phiroze Jeejeebhoy Lecture, 1992.

Reserve Bank of India, *Annual Report*, 1992-93, 1996-97 and 1998-99.

Reserve Bank of India, *Report on Currency and Finance*, 1996-97, Vol. I & II and 1997-98 Vol. II.

SEBI, *Annual Report*.

GLOSSARY

All-or-None Order: An order that is not executed unless it can be filled in its entirety.

American Depository Receipt (ADR): A receipt that evidences shares of a company incorporated outside the United States. Transactions in ADR are made in lieu of transactions in the security itself, which is usually held by a trustee. The ADR is usually issued by a foreign branch of an American Bank.

The origin of Indian Global Depository Receipts (GDRs) is to be traced to ADRs. The GDRs are issued by foreign banks or investment trusts for trading especially in Luxembourg.

American Option: A put or call that can be exercised at any time prior to expiration. All listed options are of this type.

Amex: American Stock Exchange.

Arbitrage: The simultaneous or closely related purchase and sale of same or equivalent securities in an attempt to take advantage of price differences in the same or different markets. Arbitrage may or may not entail risk and involves options.

Asset-Backed Securities: Short or intermediate term securities collateralized by financial assets owned by the issuer. Examples are automobile loans and credit card receivables.

At-the-Money: The exercise price of an option and the price of its underlying security are equal.

Authorized Capital: The maximum amount of share capital authorized in the Memorandum or Articles of Association.

Back Office: The operations department of a brokerage firm dealing with non-sales functions.

Backwardation: Payment of money charges by a bear on the shares which he borrows to deliver against his sale. The backwardation charges usually become payable when there are several sellers who are not in a position to deliver shares to the buyers.

Badla Charges: Badla charges are the interest payable for carry-over of transactions from one settlement to the other for the value of the shares. Normally, badla charges are paid by buyers to sellers. They are also called contango or seeda badla. Undha badla or backwardation is payable by sellers to buyers because sellers are unable to tender delivery of documents.

Badliwala: An intermediary who provides the necessary finance for taking delivery of shares or lends the required shares for making delivery at the end of a clearing.

Bad Delivery: In sales of shares, a physical transfer of shares sold which does not conform to stock exchange rules. The defects in delivery must be corrected for the transfer to be completed.

Basis Point: One hundred basis points equals one percentage point.

Basis Risk: Difference between spot price of an asset and the futures price.

Bear: One who believes that market prices will fall. A bear market is a declining market.

Bear Spread: A combination of two or more positions, usually in options or future markets, that can be expected to be profitable when price levels fall.

Beta Coefficient: A volatility measure of the tendency of a share to move with the market. The beta of the market and of an average share would be one. Beta coefficients range between 0.5 and 1.5.

Bid: An offer of a price to buy or sell as in an auction. It also refers to the price one is willing to pay for a security.

Big Board: New York Stock Exchange.

Black Sholes: A valuation model for options based upon the price and volatility of underlying instrument, exercise price, interest rate and time to expiration.

Blue Sky Laws: State Security laws in the United States particularly as applied to new issues of securities. The State laws require registration of broker-dealers, representatives and investment advisors doing business in a State.

Book Value per Share: Is the amount obtained by subtracting total liabilities and preference shares from total assets (to get net worth) and then dividing the amount by the number of shares outstanding.

Bonus Shares: Shares issued by a company, by capitalization of free reserves, in a stated proportion to the shares held.

Boughtout Deal: A deal between the sponsor merchant banker and the issuer where the entire equity or related security is bought in full or in lots with the intention of off-loading it later in the market.

Bull: One who believes that market prices will rise. A bull market is a rising market.

Bull Spread: A combination of two or more positions, usually in options or futures markets, that can be expected to be profitable when price levels rise.

Call: 1. The option to buy a share at a specified price.

2. The requirement to pay the balance outstanding on a share allotted in the primary market.

Capital Asset Pricing Model: A pricing model that prices assets according to their market sensitivities (beta) against the average return of the market.

Capital Market: A financial market including equity and long term debt instruments.

Capitalization: Long term funds that are committed to a firm. Include all equity or net worth, preference shares and long term liabilities.

CBOE: Chicago Board Options Exchange.

Chaos Theory: The description of apparently random patterns such as coastlines, weather which appear self similar whatever the scale. This can apply to self contained systems dependent on initial conditions.

Chicago Board Options Exchange: Sponsored by Chicago Board of Trade dealing exclusively with listed options.

Churning: Excessive trading to benefit from the commission.

Circuit Breaker: A method employed to stop trading temporarily in the event of large price changes.

Common Stock: Equity shares are referred to as common stock in United States. As in India, they have last claim on residual assets and earnings of the corporation. Shares have voting rights of one vote per share. Common stockholders have the power to elect directors, authorize new stock issues and approve or disapprove major corporate changes.

Conversion: 1. A provision of a debenture which permits it to be converted into an ordinary share at the discretion of the holder. 2. An arbitrage technique wherein the trader simultaneously buys one hundred shares, sells one call option and buys a put creating a risk free hedge and a locked-in profit due to premium differences between the options.

Conversion Ratio: The number of shares into which one debenture is convertible.

Cornering: Large acquisition of shares by individuals to create a scarcity for delivery against the existing contracts.

Corporation: A business organization in the United States recognized as an artificial person with perpetual life and limited liability created under a State Charter, comparable to a public limited company formed under the Indian Companies Act of 1956.

Coupon Yield: The annual interest payable on debentures or government securities.

Covered Option: Option sold by an investor against shares in an account. A covered call is sold against a long position and a covered put against a short position.

Credit Rating: Measure the probability that a security issue will default. The Credit Rating Information Services of India Ltd. (CRISIL) rates debentures.

Cum-rights: including rights, especially in the case of rights issues by existing companies.

Cumulative: Usually applied to preference shares designated as cumulative preference shares. If a dividend is not paid in a year, it is carried forward and paid in the subsequent year, before payment of dividend on ordinary shares.

Current Yield: The annual interest payable on debenture divided by its market price.

Dealer: A securities firm or individual acting as a principal rather than as an agent.

Debentures: Debt securities issued by the company bearing a fixed rate of interest usually payable half yearly and principal amount on a particular date.

Demutualization: The conversion of a stock exchange from a mutual model where ownership management control and trading rights were combined to corporate service provider.

Depository Trust Company: A company owned by banks and broker-dealers for the safe-keeping and clearing of securities including options.

Dilution: A reduction in the actual or potential value of a share that can result from issuing more of the same security while the firm's total assets and total earnings remains unchanged.

Dow Jones Averages: Dow Jones publishing company issues market indicators to signify changes in industrial transportation, utility and composite group of stock.

Down Tick: A transaction at a price below the last price. Ticks are normally one-eighth point of a US Dollar in the United States and Re. 0.25 in India.

Earnings Per Share (EPS): Earnings refer to income of a company after depreciation and taxes. EPS is total earnings divided by number of equity shares outstanding.

Efficient Market: A market in which prices of securities immediately reflect all available information.

Exercise Price: Price at which an option is exercisable.

Face Value: Value as appears on the face of the share. Same as Nominal or Par value of share or debenture.

Fourth Market: Purchase and sales made directly between institutions which involve no brokers or dealers.

Future Value: Future value = (Present Value) (1.0 + interest rate).

GTC (Good-till-Cancelled): An order to buy or sell a securities position that is good until it is filled or cancelled by the customer.

Hedge: Protecting a long position in one asset while being short in another in order to reduce overall risk.

Hypothecation: The pledging of securities as collateral.

Indenture: Formal agreement between the issuer of debenture or bond and its buyers.

Index: A measure based upon comparison with a base year which is normally designated as one hundred.

Index Option: A cash-settled listed option based on an index or average.

Insider: One who is restricted from trading in a company's shares because he has access to price sensitive information. Insiders include Officers, Directors, Auditors, and large shareholders.

Instinet: Institutional Networks Corporation: An automated stock exchange used by institutions to trade securities automatically.

Interest Rate Swap: Agreement between two issuers to exchange coupon payments.

Interest Rate Risk: Variability of return to investors caused by changes in market rates of interest.

Inter-Market Trading System: An electronic network linking the floors of NYSE or Amex with the floors of Regional Exchanges trading the same shares in an effort to provide access to the most favourable prices.

In-the-money: An option with intrinsic value.

Investment Company: A company organized primarily to invest in the securities of other companies which could be either closed-end or open-end. Shares of closed-end investment companies are traded on the exchanges whereas shares of open-end companies are bought and sold by the investment company itself. Open-end investment companies and mutual funds are synonymous.

Jobber: A member of the stock exchange who is allowed to deal in securities only with a member-broker or with other jobbers but not with public.

Junk Bonds: Corporate bonds of low credit rating, below BBB of Standard and Poors or Baa of Moodys.

Kerb Trading: Unauthorized trading in securities outside official hours.

LBO: Leveraged Buy-Out. Purchase of a firm's stock primarily with borrowed funds. Buyers are often the firm's management.

Leverage: The use of borrowed funds to increase total return on invested capital.

Leveraged Buy-Out: A strategy used to acquire a publicly held corporation by offering to exchange the shares for an amount of cash or debt greater than the market value of the shares. The company is then converted to private ownership. The buyers are usually the management of the company and the funds are typically generated through the issuance of low-rated debt backed by shareholders equity.

LIBOR (London Interbank Offer Rate): Relatively short term fluctuating borrowing rate among London banks. LIBOR is a benchmark for pricing Eurodollar loans.

Limit Order: An order for which buyers specify the highest price that can be paid or for which a seller specifies the lowest price that can be accepted.

Liquidity: Quality of an asset of being readily convertible to cash without suffering a decrease in price in order to effect a hasty sale.

Listed Securities: Shares, debentures listed on a stock exchange for trading after complying with stock exchange listing requirements.

Long Position: Buying and holding an asset in hopes of profiting from its cash dividends, interest, price increases or other benefits.

Margin: The funds required to be deposited by one purchasing securities in the U.S.A.

Margin Account: A brokerage account which enables a client in U.S.A. to borrow against eligible securities purchased in or deposited into the account.

Mark to the Market: As a broker who has advanced money to another for shares borrowed in a customer's short sale. To request a return of part of the money if the shares' market value declines. The reverse will take place if the market value increases.

Market Maker: A dealer in securities that makes firm bids and offers for his own inventory account.

Market Order: An order that is to be filled immediately at the best possible price.

Marking to the Market: The name of procedure in which margin traders either must pay additional maintenance margin money or can withdraw cash proceeds at the end of every trading day when the market price of their asset moves either against them or for them, respectively.

NASD (National Association of Security Dealers (USA)): An association of brokers and dealers in USA created under the Maloney Act of 1938. Regulates over-the-counter dealers in corporate securities, investment banking and mutual funds.

NASDAQ (National Association of Security Dealers Automatic Quotations): A system for providing a network of competing brokers and dealers electronically with current price quotations to enable them to operate, in effect, as a stock market without a trading floor.

National Index: BSE National Index is compiled with 100 shares including 30 covered in the SENSEX and 70 selected on an All India basis (1983-84 = 100).

Nikkei 225: Average of 225 Japanese shares traded on the Tokyo Stock Exchange.

Option: The right to buy or sell a security at an agreed price during a specified period or on a specified date.

Option Writer: The seller of an option who guarantees performance by a deposit of cash, securities or both.

Options Clearing Corporation (USA): Owned by domestic options exchanges and issuer of all listed options.

Out-of-the-money: An option with time value but no intrinsic value. The current market price of the underlying stock is below the striking price of a call or above that of a put.

Over-the-Counter market: Stock exchange formed by financial institutions and subsidiaries of nationalized banks to facilitate companies who cannot meet the listing requirements. OTC is a floorless exchange.

Pari Passu: Equal in all respects. Two securities are said to rank pari passu when there is no difference between them whatsoever as to any rights between them.

Plus Tick: A transaction of a listed share at a price above the last price.

Price Earnings Ratio (PER): The current market price of a share divided by its earnings per share for the previous twelve months.

Primary Market: The market for new issue of shares. No fixed location or exchange. The proceeds of the sale of securities in a primary market are received by the issuer.

Private Placement: Direct sale of securities between an issuer and an investor, usually a financial institution. Merchant Bankers active in the capital markets usually organize and negotiate the financing of a private placement for a fee.

Price to Book Value and Dividend Yield Ratios: Price to book value ratio expresses the market price of a share in relation to book value and is published on a day-to-day basis by Bombay Stock Exchange. It represents the market valuation of every rupee of equity of companies and the extent to which the market value is protected by the shareholders equity, whereas yield percentage shows the return on investment at current market prices. It is calculated as a percentage of the total equity dividends paid by the group of companies to their total market capitalization at the point of time.

Profit Taking: Active selling of a share which has risen in price. As sellers realize their profits, the price gets depressed in the process.

Program Trading: Computer-driven arbitrage between shares that make up various stock indexes and futures or options on those indexes in the U.S.A.

Prospectus: An official statutory document issued by companies offering securities to the public for subscription; must contain a full disclosure of the companies status and prospects.

Random Walk: A system in which the next change in value is purely random, except may be for a systematic trend, not influenced by direction of previous change.

Record Date: The date on which security holders must be registered in the books of the company to receive the dividends or other rights pertaining to the shares.

Red Herring or Preliminary Prospectus Issued in USA: An early edition of the prospectus intended to inform interested parties about an unregistered new issue. Not to be used as a selling device. Does not indicate price, offering date and other such information.

Repo: Repo is a purchase agreement. A short term loan between dealer and customer, collateralized by debt securities. The seller (borrower) agrees to buy back the securities at a higher price, at an agreed cost. The period, in practice, ranges from a fortnight to one year. The interest is market determined and built into the repo transaction. Repo transaction is undertaken between commercial banks, financial institutions, stock brokers and Discount and Finance House of India (DFHI).

Reverse Repo: A repurchase agreement by the lender rather than the borrower in order to acquire securities that have been sold short.

Scam: Scam refers to the large diversion of bank funds to purchase of shares in the market. The origin of funds is to be traced to the use of fictitious Bank Receipts and SGL notes (receipts issued by RBI evidencing ownership of securities) in the repo transactions of commercial banks and permitted the proceeds to be credited to brokers' accounts rather than the banks in whose names they were issued.

SEAQ: Stock Exchange Automated Quotations. The London equivalent of NASDAQ.

SEBI: Securities and Exchange Board of India.

SEC: Securities and Exchange Commission, USA. Established in 1934 to regulate issuance and trading of securities and securities markets.

Secondary Market: Market where shares are traded after being issued.

Securities and Exchange Board of India (SEBI): Constituted under the Securities and Exchange Board of India Act, 1992. It is the duty of SEBI to protect the investors in securities and to promote the development of, and to regulate the securities market.

Securities Contract (Regulation) Act, 1956: Provides for recognition of stock exchanges; approval of rules of the exchange relating to the powers of management of the governing body and its constitution, admission of members and regulation and control of contracts in securities. The Act empowers the government to make or amend *Suo moto* the rules and bye laws of the exchange. The Act also empowers the government to make inquiries into the affairs of exchanges and its members, to suspend business and withdraw recognition given to an exchange.

Securities Industry Automation Corporation: Organization jointly owned by NYSE and Amex to provide data processing, clearing, communications and other services.

Securities Investor Protection Corporation: Protects customers to stated maximums against losses of cash or securities suffered because of a brokers' bankruptcy.

Security: An investment contract in which money is invested. The investment is in an expectation of profit. Examples of securities are shares, debentures and options.

SENSEX: Sensitive Index of Equity Prices of 30 companies from both specified and non-specified groups issued by the Bombay Stock Exchange on the basis of market activity on the days BSE is open. (1978-89 = 100).

Settlement Date: Date on which securities sold must be delivered or the date on which securities bought must be paid for.

Shelf Registration: Under Securities Exchange Commission Rule 415 (USA). A form of registration whereby established issuers are allowed to pre-register securities and await favourable market conditions before offering.

Short: Sale of a security which is settled by the delivery of borrowed securities rather than by delivery of securities owned by the seller. Sometimes the seller may not own securities at all.

Sinking Fund: A means of amortizing a debenture issue by means of regular annual payments.

Specialist: An exchange member operating as a dealer or a broker, whose function is to act to maintain a fair and orderly market in securities assigned to him and also to hold limit or stop orders for other brokers. Executing such orders when possible in return for part of the commission.

Spread: The difference between the price bid by dealer and the price which he asks.

Stabilization: Support of the market price of new security issues in USA by the underwriting group in order to help sell the issue. It amounts to legal manipulation.

S&P 500: Standard and poors' index of 500 companies is a value weighed average of stock prices of the largest 500 American corporations.

Stock Holding Corporation of India: Set up in 1988 to introduce a book entry system for the transfer of shares.

Stock Index Futures: Agreement to buy or sell a specified amount of an underlying stock Index traded on a regulated exchange for a specified price for settlement at a specified time.

Straddle: A combination of option of one put and one call with identical exercise prices and expiration dates. The put and call are exercisable and can be traded individually.

Super Dot: Designated Order Turnaround. An electronic system devised by NYSE to allow odd lot orders and round lot orders of up to 30,099 shares to be transmitted from brokerage firms directly to posts on the exchange floors.

Tarvainiwala: A jobber or specialist who deals in shares located at the same trading post. A professional two-way operator trading in and out of the market for a small difference in price, serving as a functional figure in creating a continuous market for shares vesting them with liquidity and marketability.

Third Market: Trading in securities listed on an exchange by non-member firms over-the-counter.

Tombstone (US expression): Published advertisement listing the underwriters of a securities issue.

Trading Post: A numbered location on an exchange floor where shares of specified companies were earlier traded.

Underwriting: An individual/institution guaranteeing procurement of subscription in part or in full of a securities issue made to the public.

Volatility: The degree of fluctuation over a given period in a stock based upon the standard deviation in the price.

Warrant: A share purchase right that gives its holder the right to purchase a specific number of shares at a specific price within a specified period or in perpetuity. It is normally attached to debt instruments or preference shares. If attached by a coupon to another instrument, it is non-negotiable. If issued alone it is negotiable.

Wash Sale: A sale or purchase of shares at the same time by the same party to create an illusion of great activity in the share with the object of increasing the price. It is an illegal act.

Writer: A person who sells a call or put and thereby assumes the obligation to buy or sell a share at the exercise price upon demand by the Options Clearing Corporation (USA) if the position is not offset before the expiration date.

Zero Coupon Bond: A bond which pays no current interest. Such a bond sells at a deep discount from its redemption price. The deep discount bond of IDBI of Rs.1 lakh with a maturity of 25 years was sold for Rs.5000/-.

INDEX

Index